NOSSA ANI
NUESTRA AMERICA

Purdue Studies in Romance Literatures

PSRL volume 52

NOSSA AND *NUESTRA AMÉRICA*

Inter-American Dialogues

Robert Patrick Newcomb

Purdue University Press
West Lafayette, Indiana

∞ The paper used in this book meets the minimum requirements of American National Standard for Information Sciences—Permanence of Paper for Printed Library Materials, ANSI Z39.48-1992.

Printed in the United States of America
Design by Anita Noble

Library of Congress Cataloging-in-Publication Data

Newcomb, Robert Patrick.
    Nossa and Nuestra América : inter-American dialogues / by Robert Patrick Newcomb.
        p.   cm. — (Purdue studies in Romance literatures ; v. 52)
    Includes bibliographical references and index.
    ISBN 978-1-55753-603-7 (pbk. : alk. paper) — ISBN 978-1-61249-151-6 (epdf) — ISBN 978-1-61249-150-9 (epub) 1. Brazilian literature—History and criticism. 2. Spanish American literature—History and criticism. 3. Comparative literature—Brazilian and Spanish American. 4. Comparative literature—Spanish American and Brazilian. 5. Nationalism and literature—Brazil. 6. Latin America—Civilization. I. Title.
    PQ9514.N49 2012
    860.098—dc23   2011023378

Contents

Contents

Acknowledgments and Note on Translations

This book would not have been completed without the collaboration and support of a number of individuals and institutions. I would like to first thank my colleagues in the Department of Spanish and Portuguese at the University of California-Davis, my mentors from the Department of Portuguese and Brazilian Studies at Brown University, and the editorial board of Purdue Studies in Romance Literatures.

Special recognition is due to the following individuals: Onésimo T. Almeida, Leopoldo M. Bernucci, Alfredo Bosi, Sérgio Campos Matos, Lúcia Helena Costigan, Earl Fitz, Richard A. Gordon, James Green, Pedro Meira Monteiro, Victor K. Mendes, and Terry, Koggy, and Michael Newcomb, Marimar Patrón Vázquez, Pedro Pereira, Geoffrey Shullenberger, Luiz F. Valente, Nelson H. Vieira, Lisa Voigt, and Kelley Weiss. Additional thanks are due to the graduate students who participated in my *Luso-Hispanic Encounters* and *Sueños utópicos y pesadillas distópicas* seminars, my graduate peers from Brown, and too many staff professionals and research librarians to mention. This project benefited from the institutional support of the Andrew W. Mellon Foundation, the David Rockefeller Center for Latin American Studies (Harvard), the Council for European Studies (Columbia), and the Luso-American Development Foundation. Publication of this book was made possible by the financial support of the Office of the Dean of the Division of Humanities, Arts and Cultural Studies of the College of Letters and Science, Universitiy of California–Davis.

I take full responsibility for any factual, translation, or transcription errors contained in this volume. Quotations from the works under study appear in the original Spanish or Portuguese, while quotations of critics appear in translation. Translations from the Portuguese and of Spanish critics are mine except where otherwise noted. Longer translations of quotations from the two primary Portuguese authors appear in an appendix at the back of the book, keyed by number.

An abbreviated version of Chapter 2 appears under the same title in *Hispania* 93.3 (2010): 368–79. A condensed Spanish-language version of Chapter 4 will appear in the forthcoming volume *Nuevas aproximaciones a Alfonso Reyes,* ed. Ignacio M. Sánchez Prado and Amelia Barili (Monterrey: Universidad Autónoma de Nuevo León). I am grateful to the editors of those works for permission to use the material here.

Introduction

This Our Disunion

De todas las literaturas sudamericanas, ninguna es
tan poco conocida entre nosotros como la del Brasil
[. . .] Sin ser un caso común, á veces un nombre
dotado de mayor resonancia, rompe la indiferencia
reinante y vence la incomunicación intelectual que
separa las secciones de nuestro continente. Sólo
por una rara excepción, una obra nacida bajo una
estrella propicia, adquiere entre nosotros carta de
ciudadanía.

>   —Martín García Mérou
>   *El Brasil intelectual* (1900)

Pouco nos interessam, a nós brasileiros, os assuntos
americano-espanhóis. Nossos olhares, nossos
pensamentos, nossos gostos embicam quase sempre
para o Velho Mundo [. . .] Os mais dados às longas
itinerações preferem quase sempre, ao sentir a
majestade imponente dos Andes ou a magnificência
mirífica da selva amazônica, o gozar da civilidade
serena das ruas londrinas ou da apatia risonha de
Paris. [1]

>   —Sérgio Buarque de Holanda
>   "Santos Chocano" (1920)

In a 1993 call-to-arms for comparative Luso-Hispanic studies,
evocatively titled "Down with Tordesillas!," the critic Jorge
Schwartz observes the "problem of integrating" Brazil into a
coherent idea of Latin America and calls for a "critical reflection that is capable, when considering Latin America, of duly
including Brazil" (186–87). Schwartz's call should, of course,

1

be extended to address the traditional lack of attention paid by Brazilian writers and scholars to their literature's ties to Spanish America, and to that of Spanish Americans vis-à-vis Brazilian literature. Further, the scope of Schwartz's analysis may be expanded beyond Latin America, to include other contexts (peninsular, transatlantic, etc.) in which Luso-Hispanic relations are staged. Schwartz presents comparative Luso-Hispanic studies, which we may succinctly define as an academic approach that calls for sustained comparative analysis of literary and cultural actors, artifacts, and discourses originating in Spanish- and Portuguese-speaking areas, as an emergent phenomenon. He exhorts his readers to join the "new generation" of critics, "dedicated [. . .] to the elimination of the line of Tordesillas" (195). Here the boundary established by papal fiat in 1494, dividing the known world into Spanish and Portuguese spheres of influence, and which defined the ostensible border between Spanish and Portuguese America, stands in for a long period of literary and cultural non-communication between the Spanish- and Portuguese-speaking spheres, during which substantive cross-border dialogue has been the exception rather than the rule, and misunderstandings and differences of opinion over matters geopolitical, economic, and intellectual have been all too common.

This long history of Luso-Hispanic "disconsonance," as David William Foster has termed it,[1] inevitably puzzles those readers outside Latin American and peninsular intellectual circles, as well as those academics working in disciplines other than Luso-Brazilian and Hispanic studies: surely the linguistic proximity of Portuguese and Spanish, along with centuries of intertwined history dating back to the Roman occupation of Iberia, or *Hispania*, would account for a greater degree of mutual influence? While the notion of a Luso-Hispanic relationship characterized by vibrant linguistic and thematic cross-fertilization may be appropriate for medieval and early modern Iberia, in which *Galego-português* (linguistic ancestor to modern Portuguese) was a prestige language for lyric poetry across the peninsula, and during which men of letters such as Luís de Camões (c. 1524/25–1580), author of the Portuguese national epic *Os Lusíadas* (The Lusiads, 1572), wrote in both Portuguese *and* Castilian, this became less and less the case as Portugal and Spain developed as distinct national polities with competing imperial agendas. This tendency toward intellectual and cultural disengagement became especially pronounced following a sixty-year period of Iberian dynastic union (1580–1640) under the Spanish Habsburgs, a time frequently remembered in Portugal as one of occupation.[2] As the two peninsular kingdoms moved away from the center of European imperial power and in the seventeenth and eighteenth centuries slid toward political and economic marginality, the vibrant Luso-Hispanic literary and intellectual dialogue of earlier times definitively gave way in favor of a shared gaze toward the new centers of global influence—that portion of western and central Europe *além Pireneus* ("beyond the Pyrenees"), and the Anglo-American world of the North Atlantic. This was such that by the nineteenth century, Latin American and peninsular intellectuals would invariably learn French long before they became conversant in another Iberian language, leading to numerous instances in which young Spanish- or Portuguese-speaking writers discovered the work of peers from across the Luso-Hispanic frontier via French critics and translators—a tragicomic phenomenon lamented by Spanish writer-philosopher Miguel de Unamuno (1864–1936), himself a tireless champion of Luso-Hispanic dialogue.[3]

While old habits may die hard, there is evidence that this long pattern of Luso-Hispanic disengagement, eloquently characterized in 1989 by Brazilian architect Oscar Niemeyer as *essa nossa desunião* ("this our disunion"), is beginning to change.[4] If the critic Antonio Candido may claim that "each of our countries still [looks] more to Europe or to the United States than to its neighbor" (*Recortes* 131), recent decades have seen a growing number of voices in Latin America, North America, and Europe call for a corrective to the "disconsonance" that has traditionally impeded dialogue between Portuguese- and Spanish-speaking writers, and between academics working in Luso-Brazilian and Hispanic studies. One may cite relatively recent contributions by scholars like Schwartz, Foster, Earl Fitz, Eduardo Lourenço, and Silviano Santiago, as well as the publication of Luso-Hispanic-themed essay collections and dedicated issues of scholarly journals, the foundation of the Memorial da América Latina in São Paulo (Latin American Memorial, 1989) and the Centro de Estudos Ibéricos in Guarda,

Portugal (Center for Iberian Studies, 2001), and the authoring of a number of full-length comparative studies of Brazilian and Spanish American writers and texts.[5] I do not believe that this uptick in interest can be attributed to a single cause, but would rather cite a set of contributing factors, including institutional and economic integration (i.e., MERCOSUR/L in South America and European Union membership for Portugal and Spain),[6] advances in communications technology, the much-invoked force of globalization, and the efforts of specific Latin American and peninsular intellectuals—many of whom shared the experience of exile during the 1960s and 1970s—to advance the cause of dialogue.[7]

This emergent Luso-Hispanic comparativism charts the mutable, often fraught history of Luso-Hispanic literary and cultural relations, and at its best goes beyond simple encouragement of "the more rigorous forms of comparative literary analysis" (Foster 977), or the delineation of genealogies of past Luso-Hispanists (such lists might include Antero de Quental, Oliveira Martins, Juan Valera, Manuel Bandeira, João Cabral de Melo Neto, Natália Correia, and José Saramago, among others). While these are necessary and useful actions, comparative Luso-Hispanic studies should, in my view, ultimately concern itself with questioning the deeper ontological value of categories such as *Latin America, Ibero-America,* and *Iberia*—which, as much as they have been invoked to foster group identity and express fellow-feeling across national borders, have also been used to reinforce binary, polarizing distinctions, as between *nuestra América* and the "other" North America (to cite José Martí's famous distinction), and perhaps less noticeably, between Spanish America and Brazil. The reflexive, historicizing orientation of the comparative Luso-Hispanic project allows it, as with other broadly anti-essentialist critical discourses, to challenge received notions of national and supranational identity—an operation that has broad implications at the level of disciplinary organization, first in Latin America and Iberia, where Portuguese and Spanish are taught as "national" languages and literatures, and second, outside of the Luso-Hispanic world, as in the United States academy, where these languages are frequently joined at the hip in nominally bilingual departments of "Spanish and Portuguese."

It is in the hope of contributing to this emergent Luso-Hispanic comparativism that I have written *Nossa and Nuestra América: Inter-American Dialogues*. This volume examines how Brazilian and Spanish American public intellectuals writing in the late nineteenth and early twentieth centuries used the essay to propose transnational and continental identities for Latin America that would transcend national boundaries and achieve broader geopolitical and cultural syntheses. *Nossa and Nuestra América* centers on four essay-writing public intellectuals, two Brazilian, two Spanish American. These are Uruguayan critic José Enrique Rodó (1871–1917), Brazilian writer-diplomat Joaquim Nabuco (1849–1910), Mexican humanist Alfonso Reyes (1889–1959), and Brazilian historian and critic Sérgio Buarque de Holanda (1902–1982). This book engages a long-standing, contentious discussion on "the idea and the name" of Latin America (Arturo Ardao's term), and looks specifically to Brazil's evolving and often conflicted relationship with Spanish America to illuminate the challenges associated with identity projects such as those clustered around the term *América Latina*. In demarcating a series of dialogues and disjunctions between four of Latin America's most important public intellectuals and national exegetes, this book demonstrates how Brazil has continually occupied a *necessarily problematic* position in the Americas, with Brazil consistently challenging the coherence of the continentalist rhetoric that has typified a good part of Spanish American nationalist-exegetic discourse, from Simón Bolívar's "Carta de Jamaica" (1815) forward, as well as the viability of the category of "Latin America" itself. In "connecting the dots" between four exemplary figures in Latin American literary and intellectual life, *Nossa and Nuestra América* makes the case for *sustained comparative analysis* of Brazilian and Spanish American literature, history, and culture, and for the broader Luso-Hispanic comparativism outlined above.

Before proceeding to the first chapter, clarification is due regarding the book's title, as well as my choice to focus specifically on Rodó, Nabuco, Reyes, and Buarque. *Nossa and Nuestra América* deliberately references Martí's notion of "our America," juxtaposing the Spanish original (*nuestra América*) with its less resonant Portuguese form (*nossa*

América). In doing so, I aim to suggest, on the one hand, the limitations of Spanish American–origin continentalist projects and paradigms for Brazil, and on the other, the lingering resonance in Latin America of continentalist discourses grounded in a sense of *nosotros* or *nós* ("we/us"). As for my decision to focus on Rodó, Nabuco, Reyes, and Buarque to the exclusion of other Spanish American and Brazilian essayists: my choice of writers was made with an eye toward balancing the essayist's *depth* of engagement with Luso-Hispanic relations against his canonical *prominence* and *centrality*. My goal, ultimately, has been to offer a study that looks in detail at a set of writers who have something of substance to tell us about Brazil's place in Latin America (even if this aspect of their work has been downplayed by critics), and who have exerted a sufficiently strong influence in their respective literary and intellectual traditions to make their thoughts on Luso-Hispanic relations of vital interest for a broad range of readers. While I could have structured *Nossa and Nuestra América* around any number of alternate Latin American essayists, many of whom feature in the long list of writers referenced secondarily in this volume (these include Rubén Darío, Gilberto Freyre, José Martí, José Vasconcelos, José Veríssimo, and numerous others), the decision to focus on Rodó, Nabuco, Reyes, and Buarque was also a function of my sustained, specific curiosity regarding these four writers, each a deeply engaging, contradictory, and important thinker in his own way. While the legitimacy of this last factor as a criterion for selection is perhaps debatable, it has nonetheless guided this project, and I hope to transmit at least some of my enthusiasm for these writers to those who read this book.

Chapter One

Counterposing *Nossa* and *Nuestra América*

Es una idea grandiosa pretender formar de todo el
Mundo Nuevo una sola nación con un sólo vínculo
que ligue sus partes entre sí y con el todo.
> —Simón Bolívar
> "Carta de Jamaica" (1815)

As aves, que aqui gorjeiam, / Não gorjeiam como lá.
> —Gonçalves Dias
> "Canção do exílio" (*Song of Exile*, 1843)

Pueblos americanos, / Si jamás olvidáis que sois
hermanos, / Y a la patria común, madre querida
[. . .] [2]
> —Andrés Bello
> "El hombre, el caballo y el toro" (published 1861)

In the introduction that opens this book, I contextualized
my interest in Brazil's position in Latin America within an
emerging—albeit still minority—scholarly trend toward comparative Luso-Hispanic approaches. In this chapter I will explain how this broad interest finds focus in the context of this
book. I will introduce my analytical model for evaluating how
Spanish American and Brazilian public intellectuals have used
the essay to consider questions of national and continental
identity—an inquiry that in turn leads writers like José Enrique
Rodó, Joaquim Nabuco, Alfonso Reyes, and Sérgio Buarque
de Holanda to consider the role of Brazil in the intellectual
construction of Latin America. While this book covers the late
nineteenth and early twentieth centuries, a series of decades in
which Latin American elites attempted to adapt national and

continental identities to the challenges of uneven economic modernization and the consolidation of US hemispheric hegemony, the problem of Brazil's place in Latin America predates this period, and continues to be relevant today. Consequently, I will argue in this book for the broader applicability of my analytical model.

Comparative paradigms are an enduring feature of Spanish American and Brazilian discourses on the nation, as well as of the Hispanist, Latin Americanist, and Luso-Brazilianist scholarship that attempts to engage and contextualize these discourses. Indeed, as various scholars have noted, many of Latin America's most successful analytical paradigms, such as Rodó's *arielismo* and José Martí's *nuestra-americanismo*, are the products of comparative studies between an apparently unified "Latin America" and some other geo-cultural region (i.e., Europe or Anglo-America) identified as a more or less unified center of global power, influence, and "universal" culture. Building on the idea that internationalism is somehow "innate" to Latin America and its representative writers and thinkers— a notion put forth by Rodó, Oswald de Andrade, Jorge Luis Borges, Reyes, and others[1]—we might be tempted to attribute a fundamentally comparative vocation to Latin Americanism as a discipline. Leaving aside the essentialism that underpins this argument, we must nonetheless observe that comparative work on Latin America has occurred unevenly: comparative Brazilian–Spanish American analyses, for instance, have remained grossly underdeveloped relative to comparative US–Latin American and European–Latin American studies. Sustained comparisons between Brazil and Spanish America at the levels of culture and ideas, on the order of Sérgio Buarque de Holanda's typological distinction between the Luso-Brazilian *semeador* ("sower") and Spanish American *ladrilhador* ("harvester, cultivator") from his interpretive essay *Raízes do Brasil* (Roots of Brazil, 1936), have been rare in Brazilian thought and virtually non-existent in Spanish America. The minority of Spanish American intellectuals who have taken a substantive interest in Brazil, as well as those relatively few Brazilian intellectuals who have dedicated themselves to studying Spanish America, have lamented a general lack of mutual awareness across the Luso-Hispanic frontier, particularly in terms of dialogue on literature, culture, and ideas. Martín García Mérou, the Argentine critic whose *El Brasil intelectual* (1900) is one of the first (if not *the* first) book-length studies on Brazilian literature by a Spanish American writer, introduces his volume by observing that, "[o]f all the South American literatures, Brazil's is the least known to us," with "us" referring both to García Mérou's home country of Argentina and to Spanish America generally. "In the same way" that the work of Argentine authors tends not to circulate outside Argentina, García Mérou asks, "how many of our young writers are familiar with the work of Rui Barbosa, Joaquim Nabuco or José Carlos Rodrigues, with the novels of José de Alencar or Machado de Assis, or with the critical essays of Sílvio Romero, José Veríssimo, Carlos de Laët, or Araripe Júnior?" (1–2). Decades later, Sílvio Júlio, a Brazilian writer and academic whose voluminous production includes several critical texts on Spanish American themes, including *Estudos Hispano-Americanos* (Spanish American Studies, 1924) and *Cérebro e Coração de Bolívar* (Head and Heart of Bolívar, 1931), noted in 1954, with apparent frustration and a good amount of self-congratulation that, "I was—if we exclude three or four insignificant predecessors, and one truly respectable one: Oliveira Lima—the pioneer of *bolivarianismo* or *americanismo* in Brazil" (7). Remarking on his particular affinity for the Uruguayan writer-critic José Enrique Rodó, Júlio comments: "I recall perfectly my titanic, indescribable effort between 1912 and 1930 to convince Brazilian intellectuals to, at the least, read [. . .] *Ariel*! [. . .] What idiotic smiles, what insolent disinterest I had to endure!" (9; author's emphasis).

In attempting to explain this lack of significant Luso-Hispanic dialogue, the distinguished Brazilian critic Antonio Candido proposes in his essay "Os Brasileiros e a Nossa América" (Brazilian and Our America) that Brazilian–Spanish American intellectual relations should be understood in terms of an "accentuated asymmetry," in the sense that Brazil "has been more concerned with the Hispanic [American] bloc than the latter is with Brazil," though Candido notes that this relationship is subsumed by a greater geopolitical and cultural asymmetry—that between Latin America and the European/ North American center. This renders intellectual traffic between Brazil and Spanish America relatively minimal, though

Candido still believes it to be skewed in favor of greater Brazilian interest (*Recortes* 130–31). Rather than focusing on the varying levels of mutual interest to be seen among Brazilian and Spanish American writers, as does Candido, I would instead place the emphasis on the *guiding assumptions* that underlie these Brazilian–Spanish American comparisons, along with the purposes to which essayists and public intellectuals from Brazil and Spanish America apply these characterizations. Though in passing, we should acknowledge Candido's accuracy in presenting Brazilian–Spanish American comparisons as almost always subordinate to overarching preoccupations with Latin America's relationship to Europe and/or the United States. Where Brazilian writers have attempted to characterize Spanish American history, culture, or identity in relation to Brazil, as in the cases of Vianna Moog, Manoel Bomfim, and Gilberto Freyre, these Luso-Hispanic comparisons have almost always served as secondary features of more sustained comparisons with the US–European center, and have frequently been limited to cursory discussions of Brazil and Spanish America's shared Iberian "roots"—a practice that remits to the attempts of nineteenth-century Portuguese and Spanish exegetes to establish the bases for a shared Iberian "genius."[2]

One of my aims in this book is to promote comparative Brazilian–Spanish American approaches and Luso-Hispanic studies generally by showing how the question of Brazil's role in the intellectual construction of Latin America can help illuminate a broader, crucially important problem—the discrepancy between the received idea that "Latin America" represents an internally coherent, stable concept, and the reality of the idea's numerous inconsistencies and tensions, both internal and external. To this end, in this chapter I will: (1) offer a brief discussion of the term "Latin America," focusing on its history and the ends to which it has been applied; (2) explain why Brazil is *necessarily problematic* with regard to the idea of Latin America; (3) illustrate how Spanish American and Brazilian intellectuals have responded to this problem in essays that address themes of national and broader regional identity, and; (4) analyze writings by Simón Bolívar and José Bonifácio, foundational figures in Spanish American and Brazilian nationalist discourse, in relation to this model.

I. "Latin America": A Brief History of a Controversial Idea

Scholarly consensus has it that the term "Latin America" was coined by Michel Chevalier (1806–79), a French intellectual, politician, economist, and diplomat who was in the United States between 1833 and 1835. Chevalier followed the lead of fellow French traveler Alexis de Tocqueville (1805–59), whose impressions of the antebellum-era US were collected in *Democracy in America* (1835–40), by publishing his own impressions in his *Letters on North America* (1836). While the main body of Chevalier's text is concerned with the former thirteen colonies, he uses his introduction to contextualize the New World within global civilization's apparent forward march, which he describes in terms of a series of geographically oriented exchanges between East and West, and North and South.

Chevalier's analysis is broadly reflective of Romantic-era ideas of shared racial or civilizational character or "genius," which were given particular attention in early nineteenth-century Germany. There, thinkers like Prussian historian Leopold von Ranke (1795–1886) and philosopher G.W.F. Hegel (1770–1831) organized notions of *Volksgeist* into broad dialectical oppositions between the so-called Latin and Anglo-Saxon/Teutonic peoples at the levels of race, history, and character. In his *History of the Latin and Teutonic Nations* (1824), a young Ranke set out to prove the overriding "unity of our nations in idea, in action, and in development," even as he maintains a distinction between the core protagonists of European history as either "Latin" (France, Spain, Portugal, and Italy) or "Teutonic" (Germany, England, and Scandinavia). Ranke additionally describes broad migratory exchanges of peoples and ideas between a Latin South and a Teutonic North. For his part, Hegel famously remarked in his *Lectures on the Philosophy of History* (published 1837) that, "America is the land of the future," though the full implications of his oft-cited statement cannot be fully appreciated unless it is quoted in its entirety: "America is [. . .] the land of the future, where, in the ages that lie before us, the burden of the World's History shall reveal itself—*perhaps in a contest between North and South America*" (86; my emphasis). Like Ranke—and as we shall see, Chevalier—Hegel believed that North and South America embodied opposing

11

principles, which the colonizers inherited from their European forbearers (Hegel remarked in his lectures that, "what takes place in America, is but an emanation of Europe"). These differences manifested themselves principally in the modes of settlement practiced in the North and South (predatory conquest in South America, productive colonization in North America), and in religion, with the North Americans' industrious Protestantism contrasting to the South's Catholicism, under which Hegel alleges that "only force and voluntary subservience are the principles of action" (82, 84).

Chevalier carried forward Hegel and Ranke's dialectical vision of European history, and followed the former in describing the North/South and East/West historical exchanges as transferring westward to the Americas with the European "discovery" of the New World. Chevalier writes in the prologue to his *Letters on North America* that, "[t]hat form of civilization which has prevailed among the peoples of Europe has moved in its march over the globe from east to west. From its cradles in old Asia and upper Egypt, it advanced, by successive stages, to the shores of the Atlantic, along which it spread itself from the southern extremity of Spain to the northern point of the British Isles and the Scandinavian peninsula" (*Society* 1). Once civilization has moved from East to West and established itself in Europe (presumably via the Greeks and Romans), Chevalier describes the North/South—or Teutonic/Latin—exchange as the operative dynamic at work in shaping history. While Chevalier backdates Ranke's analysis to classical antiquity, he moves away from Ranke's insistence on the "unity in diversity" of the Latin and Teutonic civilizations. Chevalier instead places the emphasis on the contribution of race to the formation of distinct "Latin" and "Teutonic" characters, and points out fundamental differences between the two groups. Though he presents both the Northern European, proto-Germanic peoples *and* Southern Greco-Roman civilization as central to progress, he invests North and South with different historical functions and represents them as divergent civilizational types, possessed of different strengths and weaknesses:

> By turns each of these forces, one from the North, one from the South, whose combined action constitutes the motive power that carries mankind forward, has been overborne by

the other. Thence it is that our civilization, instead of advancing in a straight line from east to west, has swerved in its march, from north to south, or south to north, taking a winding course, and gathering up at each turn purer drops from the blood of Shem [representing the South] or Japhet [the North]. There has been, however, this difference between the North and the South; the South has most often acted on the North by sending it the germs of civilization, without overrunning it with a new race, while the North has awakened the slumbering civilization of the South by pouring into its enervated population swarms of hardy barbarians. (*Society* 2)

Following Chevalier's argument, this interaction gives rise to "two families" of European civilization, the Latins in the South and the Teutons or Anglo-Saxons in the North. With Europe's early modern maritime expansion across the Atlantic, these civilizations come to reproduce themselves in the New World along the same North/South axis: "South America, like southern Europe, is Catholic and Latin. North America belongs to the Protestant and Anglo-Saxon population" (*Society* 6). Though Chevalier's analysis is similar in structure to Ranke and Hegel, Chevalier inverts Hegel's championing of Anglo-Teutonic North America, moves away from Ranke's ecumenical position, and reveals his own partisan identification with the "Latin" camp and his specific loyalty to France. Writing in the wake of Spain's loss of much of its American colonial empire in the early decades of the nineteenth century, Chevalier presents France as the most vigorous of the Latin nations, in contrast to "the sleepy Spaniards of Mexico and the Philippines," and as the natural "head of the Latin group," and "the depository of the destinies of all the Latin nations of both continents [. . .] It belongs to her to rouse them from the lethargy into which they are plunged on both continents, to raise them to the level of other nations, to enable them again to take a stand in the world." The logic of Chevalier's argument, inflected with a great deal of ethnic nationalism, allows him to argue for an active French presence in the Americas: "[T]o me France seems called upon to exercise a benevolent and wholesome care over the people of South America, who are not yet fit to take care of themselves" (4, 8–9). This paternalistic idea would manifest itself in the foreign policy of Emperor Napoleon III during the 1861–63 French-led punitive expedition to Mexico and subsequent

French-sponsored imperial government under Austrian prince Maximilian (1864–67).³ As Napoleon III's economic advisor, Chevalier supported France's Mexican adventure in a series of articles published in the *Revue des Deux Mondes* and collected in *Le Mexique ancien et moderne* (1864). Indeed, one could argue that Chevalier laid the intellectual groundwork for the invasion in the prologue to his *Letters.*

Despite the initial interventionist connotations of Chevalier's idea of *Amérique latine*, Spanish American polemicists, among them the Colombian José María Torres Caicedo (1830–89), and the Chilean Francisco Bilbao (1823–65), quickly appropriated the term and applied it to projects that were quite distinct from—if not directly opposed to—Chevalier and Napoleon III's imperial agenda for the Americas. Given this terminological "repackaging," as well as the ubiquity today of "Latin America" as a more or less neutral descriptive term for the portion of the Western Hemisphere lying south of the Rio Grande or Bravo, it seems pertinent to ask whether "Latin America" as a category is irredeemably tied to a narrative of French ethno-imperial domination, especially given that alternative designations—Bolívar's *América meridional*, Martí's *nuestra América*, and so on—are likewise tied to their own political projects.

As various scholars have noted, *América Latina* or *Latinoamérica* is only one of the many designations that have been used to refer to that part of the hemisphere made up (mostly) of Spain and Portugal's former American colonies, and which stretches from the US-Mexico border to Tierra del Fuego. Among the many terms that have been applied to the region (in part or in whole) are the Aztec *Anáhuac*, the Incan *Tawantinsuyu*, and the Tupi-Guarani *Pindorama*,⁴ along with *las Índias* (derived from Columbus's misidentification of the New World), *Colombia* (championed by Francisco de Miranda, among others), *América meridional* (Bolívar's preferred term), and *nuestra América* (Carlos O. Bunge, José Martí). As Arturo Ardao notes in his valuable study, *Génesis de la idea y el nombre de América Latina* (1980), "Latin America" is a "terminological creation"—as are its rival designations—corresponding to competing historical readings and ideological projects (8–9). "Latin America," therefore, should not be viewed as a perfect descriptor for the region it represents, but rather as a historical and ideological creation with a particular intellectual genealogy, a term that has as much capacity to exclude as it does to include, an artificial designation without ontological value, whose effective "reality" exists to the extent that it is popularly accepted as referring to, and perhaps embodying, the essence or spirit of a specific region. As Walter Mignolo wryly observes in his volume *The Idea of Latin America* (2005), "[b]efore 1492, the Americas were not on anybody's map, [. . .] the Incas and the Aztecs did not live in America or, even less, Latin America" (2). In other words, "America" and "Latin America," while they may refer to actually existing landmasses, are not *a priori* features of the American landscape, but geographical and historical *inventions*—an eminently sensible idea pioneered by Edmundo O'Gorman in his appropriately titled study *La invención de América* (1958). Given that this book will engage in extensive discussion of contested definitions and divergent understandings of "Latin America" and of Brazil's role in the articulation of this concept, I should make my position clear: I will not argue for one or another definition of Latin America as reflecting the region's essential "reality"—indeed, I do not believe any single term capable of wholly expressing Latin America's "essence." Rather, I will attempt in the coming chapters to describe the *confluences* and *disjunctions* between certain essayists' understandings of Latin America as a concept, and of Brazil's specific role in alternately reinforcing and challenging this concept.

Moving from geo-cultural designations to the academy, we might define "Latin Americanism" as a discourse that concerns itself with Latin America at the conceptual level and with its variegated cultural production, and thereby *implicitly affirms* the coherence of "Latin America" as an idea. This notion has both revisionist and revolutionary applications: for O'Gorman, Ardao, and others (including Alfonso Reyes, Gilberto Freyre, and Ángel Rama), "America" and the names applied to its composite geographic, linguistic, ethnic, and political "sub-Americas" (Ardao's term) are central to the way the inhabitants of the Americas view themselves cartographically, with the internal diversity implied by the "sub-Americas" ultimately serving to reinforce the coherence of the broader concepts of *América, América Latina,* and *Hispanoamérica.*[5] While "America" and its component parts may, then, admit multiple and simultaneous

15

meanings, the reformist position would argue that this potential for multiplicity is a dynamic feature of the American condition rather than a problematic contradiction, with regional and nomenclatural diversity ultimately resolving itself in geo-cultural and terminological unity. As Rama notes in his influential study *Transculturación narrativa en América Latina* (1982):

> The unity of Latin America has been and continues to be a project [. . .] recognized by international consensus. It is grounded in persuasive arguments and enjoys real and powerful unifying forces. The majority of these are located in the past, having deeply shaped the lives of its peoples: they run from a common history to a common language and similar modes of behavior [. . .] From this unity, which is real to the extent that it is a project [*real enquanto proyecto*], real in terms of the bases that ground it, bursts forth [*se despliega*] an interior diversity that is the more precise definition of the continent. Unity and diversity has been the formula preferred [for Latin America] by analysts in a variety of disciplines. (57)

And as Ardao writes, no doubt unconsciously echoing Ranke's "unity in diversity" formula for Latin and Teutonic Europe, "America is a unity, but also a plurality. America exists, but so do Americas, that are no more and no less than distinct parts of the whole expressed by the term in the singular" (*Génesis* 18). For Ardao—and one suspects, for numerous Spanish American continentalists—the troubling political implications of Chevalier's original articulation of *Amérique latine* are redeemed by the Spanish American nationalists who repurposed and deployed the term as *América Latina*, in order to promote regional solidarity in the face of mid to late nineteenth-century US expansionism in Central America and the Caribbean, and who recast Bolívar's call for a united *América meridional* in the racialized language of the time. Bilbao, responding in his *Iniciativa de la América* (1856) to the perceived threat of the "domination of Yankee individualism," argues for the creation of a confederation of South American republics in defense of the *raza latinoamericana*, on the following grounds:

> Our origin is the same and we live divided from one another. One and the same is our beautiful language and we do not speak to each other. We have the same beginning and, iso-

lated from one another, we march toward the same end. We
suffer the same illness and we do not combine forces to ward
it off. We have the same goal and we turn our backs to one
another to achieve it, we have the same obligation and we do
not bind together in order to meet it. (365, 371)

Torres Caicedo proceeds along similar lines in his *Unión
Latino-Americana* (1865), arguing that "[t]hose American
countries that have the same origin, common interests, identical
traditions, the same institutions, the same language, the same
religion and common aspirations, are called upon to unite, because union is the most irresistible and most fruitful of affirma-
tions" (22). He appeals to the idea of a common Latin heritage
in reassuring his readers that Europe, and particularly France,
will respect a Latin American confederation: "Who can doubt
that the first nation of the Latin race—France—will be the first
to labor in the same spirit of justice?" (92).

Various peninsular and Ibero-American intellectuals over
the years have, of course, objected to the term "Latin America,"
for a variety of reasons and from a variety of ideological stand-
points. Aurelio M. Espinosa, writing in the US journal *Hispania*
in 1918, called for Hispanists to "use always the old, traditional
and correct terms, *Spanish America, Spanish American,*" instead
of "Latin America," a supposedly "new, improper, unjust, unsci-
entific term" that he considered vague and deceptive (142–43).
As might be expected, Brazil proves a thorny issue for Espinosa
in arguing for the terminological accuracy and convenience of
"Spanish" over "Latin" America. He is forced to qualify his
argument for the region's linguistic (and therefore cultural)
unity, writing that "[t]he language of all Spanish America,
excluding Brazil, is *Spanish,* good *Castilian Spanish*" (141;
author's emphasis). Later, and after referencing Rodó's very
questionable 1910 interpretation in his article "Iberoamérica"
of a statement by the Portuguese writer Almeida Garrett that
"we [Portuguese] are Spanish, and all of us who inhabit the
[Iberian] peninsula should proudly consider ourselves Spanish" as grounds for Brazil to be considered a Spanish American
country,[6] Espinosa admits that "a few there are who [. . .] feel
the necessity of differentiating between the Spanish American
republics that speak Spanish and those that speak Portuguese."
He proposes the semantically awkward solution of "using the

term *Hispanic American* in the general sense, to include Brazil, and the term *Spanish American* either for the whole [Brazil included] or for the Spanish-speaking countries exclusively." In any case, Espinosa cautions against the comparatively more elegant, but to his mind misleading solution of terming Brazil a "Latin American" nation, and of "us[ing] terminologies that are wholly false" (143; author's emphasis).

The Brazilian *modernista* writer and critic Mário de Andrade approaches the problem from a much different angle in a 1928 newspaper piece, the first of a three-part series on "Argentine Modernist Literature" published in the *Diário Nacional*. Andrade declares that he is "horrified" by "all this about 'Latin America'" (qtd. in Antelo 165). His negative reaction may be accounted for by his perennial skepticism toward nationalism in general, and by his sense of Brazil's regional uniqueness and difference from its neighbors. Andrade explains that he rejects patriotism in all but the most local sense, considers being born in Brazil a "fatality," and is wary of the abstract international "fraternity" of the kind espoused by Pan-Americanists such as Joaquim Nabuco, the Brazilian writer-diplomat discussed in this book's third chapter (165, 170). As such, Andrade "consider[s] odious any enlargement of the concept of the homeland [*pátria*] that does not embrace all of humanity." Moreover, he inveighs against the idea of a "continental psychological or ethnic unity," and adds that "[e]ven if for argument's sake we accept that the historical and economic conditions facing the countries of a given continent are exactly the same, this is not sufficient to create a continental social idea [*conceito social continental*] because these are neither permanent nor intrinsic conditions" (165). In other words, shared history or economic challenges do not, for Andrade, translate to Latin American fraternal ties, which would for Andrade have to be based on racial and civilizational commonalities he views as non-existent. Andrade fixes on the case of Brazil to drive home his contention that Pan-Americanists' calls for continental solidarity, which he terms "false little infatuations," are based on a misguided assumption of continental sameness: "[S]ocially, in its corner of South America, Brazil is a stranger and a giant. Different races, different pasts, different ways of speaking—these are reasons for undeniable difference!" (166).

Despite Espinosa and Andrade's differing objections and clearly distinct intellectual orientations, side-by-side analysis of their positions is useful in that they both implicitly deny *a priori* ontological claims made on behalf of "Latin America" as a category, and point to the term's historicity as key in explaining its rise to prominence as well as its imprecisions—among these its tendency to fold Brazil into a narrative of shared language, colonial past, and republican political revolt that is grounded in a specifically Spanish American history that, as we shall see, has frequently been claimed for "Latin America" as a whole. On this point, scholars like Ardao, Sergio Guerra Vilaboy and Alejo Maldonado Gallardo acknowledge that the term was initially applied by Spanish American nationalists like Bilbao and Torres Caicedo to Spanish America *only*, as an expression of the Spanish American nations' shared "Latin-ness," and in binary opposition to the "Anglo" US. This leaves Brazil, Haiti, indigenous and Afro-Latin communities, and various Caribbean islands outside this binary and in a state of conceptual limbo.[7] For these scholars, whose arguments rest on the assumption of a shared Latin American identity or consciousness of the kind advocated by Rodó, Reyes, and more recently, by Mexican philosopher Leopoldo Zea, this does not seem problematic.[8] Their position effectively posits that liminal groups or territories (like Brazil) will eventually adopt the term "Latin America" as a salutary form of resistance to Yankee imperialism, and will thereby gain access to the collective Latin American sense of belonging, its sense of "we" or "us."[9] César Fernández Moreno succinctly presents the position he shares with Ardao, Rama, Guerra, and Maldonado in the following question and answer: "What is Latin America? The only sure thing we know of, for now, is that it is ours" (18).

For others, including post-colonial critic Walter Mignolo, the frustrating contradiction between the reality of America's "invention" by European explorers and cartographers and the persistent belief in its essential "American-ness," along with the ideological implications and exclusionary tendencies manifested in the term "Latin America," necessitate a more radical effort to "uncouple the name of the subcontinent from the cartographic image we all have of it" in order to "unravel the geopolitics of knowledge from the perspective of coloniality, the untold and unrecognized historical counterpart of modernity" (*Idea* x–xi). For the author of *The Idea of Latin America* (2005), *América Latina*, in contrast to the "dissenting" example of Martí's apparently more radical *nuestra América* paradigm, represents a "consenting" project of the "Creole-Mestizo/a elites" that is irredeemably implicated in the silencing of indigenous, Afro-Latin, and other subaltern voices. Mignolo's schematic opposition—which, incidentally, understates the "ideality" of Martí's thinking on the Americas—would see Spanish American essayistic discourse divided between an *América Latina*-identified tradition, politically conservative to reformist, wedded to philosophical idealism (as with Rodó's *arielismo*), and whose projects for continental unity are grounded in claims of shared linguistic, historical, and racial heritage, and a *nuestra América*-identified camp, politically radical and Marxian/materialist in orientation, and whose own projects for regional integration are grounded in a collective experience of deprivation and oppression, and are tied to the region's place in the global economic system. Mignolo, favoring this second group, advocates substituting "Latin America" for an unnamed alternative identified by a varied group of post–Cold War, post–9/11 political actors effectively working in concert, though he is unable to propose an alternate term nor does he explain the interest of his broad cross-section of advocacy groups in the renaming project (*Idea* 45, 59). Regardless of these unresolved details, Mignolo is correct to point out that the idea of "Latin America" is shot through with contradictions against which the strength of an alleged, shared Latin American "consciousness" may prove insufficient. In the following section, I will explore the idea that Brazil constitutes one such problematizing agent, and that Brazil is in fact *necessarily problematic* with regard to the idea of Latin America.

II. The Problem: Brazil as
Necessarily Problematic

One of the structuring assumptions of this book is that within the Latin American essayistic tradition, Brazil retains a unique status with regard to the idea of Latin America, as both a *necessary* and *problematic* participant in the region. Brazilian intellectuals and US-based Luso-Brazilianist scholars invoke the notion of Brazil's alleged singularity or uniqueness with some frequency, and in ways that sometimes strike me as insufficiently rigorous, at times appearing to uncritically celebrate Brazilian "difference" in reified form, and to the detriment of affirming possible cross-border commonalities.[10] As such, I will attempt here to clearly define what I mean by Brazil's unique, *necessarily problematic* position with regard to "Latin America" as a concept.

First, regarding Brazil as *problematic*: Brazil is certainly not alone as a site for contesting Latin America's geographical, cultural, linguistic, and historical coherence. Despite the received opinion that Latin America represents a series of more or less interchangeable Spanish-speaking nations—an idea that has been perpetuated in reductive form by those outside observers who scorn Latin America as a collection of "banana republics," and that has been more sympathetically developed by successive generations of Latin American essayists and other exegetes invested in the affirmation of a Latin American *magna patria*, as Rodó had it—"the term *Latin America* remains notoriously imprecise," as César Fernández Moreno notes (5; author's emphasis). Indeed, Brazilian writer Manoel Bomfim used this imprecision in the preface to his 1929 study *O Brasil na América* (Brazil in America) to question the basis for "Latin Americans" using "Latin America" as an identifying term at all, proposing that only foreigners and "all those who do not know us" use it:

> We others [*nós outros*]—Argentines, Peruvians, Brazilians, Chileans . . . all of whom are called *Latin Americans,* never think in terms of *Latin America* [. . .] We only consider the various peoples that pundits claim constitute the Latin-ness of America. The same occurs with any foreigner who has made his life here with us: he will speak of—Venezuela, Paraguay, Mexico, Nicaragua . . . but he will never feel the need to concentrate his energy on this concept—*Latin America*. In contrast, all those who do not know us, if they like to spin theories, and speak in terms of social, historical and political phenomena, do not fail to emphatically repeat puerile preconceptions about that unreal unity—Latin America. (31; author's emphasis)

On this point Bomfim is in the minority among Latin American (though perhaps not Brazilian) essayists, as attested by the vast

21

bibliography of essayistic texts dealing with the supposedly "unreal unity" of Latin America including, ironically enough, Bomfim's earlier study *A América Latina: Males de Origem* (Latin America: Originary Ills, 1905). Bomfim's *volte face* from Latin Americanist to skeptic of Latin American unity is somewhat of a mystery, though it may reflect a similar, albeit more successful analytical shift on the part of one of Bomfim's primary sources, the Portuguese historian J.P. de Oliveira Martins, author of an 1879 history of Portugal that was widely read among the Luso-Brazilian literati, as well as a *História da Civilização Ibérica* (History of Iberian Civilization, 1879). Oliveira Martins's readership extended to the Spanish-speaking world and his ideas were championed by Spanish intellectuals like Marcelino Menéndez y Pelayo, Juan Valera, and Miguel de Unamuno. Regardless, Bomfim's critique in *O Brasil na América* speaks to a long-standing recognition that the idea of Latin America, fundamentally coherent or not, suffers from at least some degree of imprecision.

Haiti represents a particularly important liminal case with regard to the idea of Latin America. As Mignolo observes, "[t]he unthinkable aberration of Haiti has always been discreetly absent from [Latin American] geography because Haiti took its own route and was the first 'deviant' example. 'Haiti' is an idea that is neither Latin nor Anglo [. . .] In spite of the strong presence of Spanish colonialism in Haiti, Haiti is still peripheral, if not absent, from the 'idea of Latin' America" (*Idea* 111–12). Yet Haiti exhibits a number of shared features with its neighbors, in terms of the legacy of slavery, its colonial-era plantation-based economy, its successful early nineteenth-century republican revolution (the second in the hemisphere, predating Bolívar), and its profound present-day development challenges, exacerbated by Haiti's devastating 2010 earthquake. Brazilian musicians Caetano Veloso and Gilberto Gil summed up Haiti's complex relationship with regard to Latin America in a 1993 composition: "O Haiti é aqui / O Haiti não é aqui" ("This is Haiti / This is not Haiti," or "Haiti is here / Haiti is not here"). Brazil joins Caribbean nation-states and territories, as well as indigenous and Afro-Latin communities throughout the hemisphere, as problematic with regard to the idea of Latin America.[11] Where Brazil differentiates itself—and this is a key point—is that unlike Haiti or Belize, say, Brazil's geographic centrality and size, as well as its historical and increasingly apparent political influence, economic power, and level of global visibility, render it a *necessary* as well as *problematic* component of viable definitions of Latin America, whether these definitions are advanced by Latin American essayists, US-based Latin Americanist scholars, or by anyone else.[12]

The necessity of Brazil's participation in Latin America, whether understood geographically, politico-economically, culturally, or even at the level of terminology, becomes immediately apparent by looking at Brazil's place on a map of the Western Hemisphere. Brazil, having escaped the fate of so many of its Spanish American neighbors and retained its territorial integrity and political unity following independence in 1822, occupies a vast space at the center of the South American continent, its coast facing the same Atlantic Ocean from which the Iberian maritime explorers and colonizers, as well as innumerable enslaved Africans, first arrived. Brazil's broader geography, as much as the specific topographical features of Rio de Janeiro, may have inspired Rodó in his 1916 piece "Cielo y agua" to describe Guanabara Bay (and by extension, all of Brazil) as the "gateway to America," a "triumphal arch" through which "the Latin genius" passed in its "sublime adventure" of exploration and settlement (*Obras* 1245). Brazil is larger than the continental United States, borders every nation in South America with the exception of Chile and Ecuador, and has Latin America's largest population (and the world's fifth largest), representing a full 50 percent of the South American total. Brazil's territorial size and centrality are reinforced by its status as a regional political and economic power, both historically and especially in the last decade, as Brazil has emerged as the region's most dynamic and diversified economy, and has pursued a foreign policy that places it between staunch US allies such as Colombia, and the bloc of left-oriented populist governments led by Hugo Chávez's Venezuela. Rio de Janeiro's selection in October 2009 to host the Olympic Games in 2016 was widely and in my view correctly interpreted as recognition of Brazil's regional preeminence and its rising global profile. In short, a "Latin America" conceived in cartographic or geopolitical terms appears much less imposing—and arguably nonviable—without Brazil.

If, following Mignolo, all nation-states are subject to the *omphalos* syndrome (the belief that one's society occupies a place of divinely appointed geographical centrality—i.e., China as the "Middle Kingdom"), Brazil's location presents a unique problem for Spanish American thinkers and political actors who, from Bolívar forward, have been interested in affirming *América meridional, Hispanoamérica,* or *América Latina* as a community of nations defined by a shared history, language, and culture: how to occupy the (Brazilian) center of a region in the name of a hispanocentric continental identity or "supranationality."[13] In describing the Spanish American and Brazilian sides of my analytical model in the following paragraphs, I will argue that Spanish American intellectuals, in writing continentally themed essays, have by and large adopted the strategy of rhetorically *projecting* a Spanish American identity onto Brazil and of attempting thereby to incorporate Brazil into their calls for a fraternal, pan-Latin American unity. Across the border, their Brazilian counterparts have generally taken a very different approach, looking inward and developing a solidly *national* interpretive tradition, affirming Brazil's national singularity, and making limited, non-fraternal and strategic overtures to Spanish America. At the risk of gross oversimplification, it might be said that from the Brazilian perspective, shared participation in MERCOSUR/L does not make for the assertion or acknowledgement of family ties.

III. One Side of the Coin:
Spanish American Identity Projection

Having summarized the genesis of the term "Latin America," its diffusion among Spanish American and Brazilian writers and critics, and the specific problems posed by the potential inclusion of Brazil within Latin America as a geo-cultural category, I now turn to a related issue: how Spanish American critics, specifically those interested in applying the idea of *América Latina* to projects aimed at unifying the Spanish American republics in political, economic, and cultural-intellectual terms, have responded to the question of Brazil. This in turn requires consideration of how Spanish American writers and political actors have articulated a sense of shared regional identity premised on the interaction of national and "supranational" or continental loyalties, the latter strongly connected to terms like *América meridional, magna patria, nuestra América*, and of course, *América Latina* or *Latinoamérica*. Here it is helpful to draw on Benedict Anderson and Anthony Smith, whose seminal contributions to the study of nationalism provide a good deal of our theoretical vocabulary for discussions on the topic. I will look first to one of Anderson's observations from the "Creole Pioneers" chapter of his widely read *Imagined Communities* (1983). In discussing the role of North and South American political figures and intellectuals as early formulators of modern nationalism, Anderson refers to the "well-known doubleness" or the two-tiered quality of "early Spanish-American nationalism," arguing that the "cramped pilgrimage" of the typical *criollo* bureaucrat circulating among the Spanish American colonies (but never reaching Madrid), along with the gradual development of a Spanish American regional press, created a sense of solidarity that made the struggles of the citizens of say, Mexico City relevant to peers in Lima, Buenos Aires, or Havana. The two-tiered structure Anderson sketches in the chapter ties one's national identification as a Mexican, Argentine, or Cuban (what I term Spanish American *discrete nationalism*) to a broader identification with a supranational entity commonly designated as "Latin America," which might be identified as Spanish American *broader nationalism* or *supranationalism* (57, 61–63).[14]

Accompanying Smith's argument that "'Pan' nationalisms" on the order of Spanish American continentalist discourse may "underpin the national state by linking it to a wider category of 'protected' states and strengthening its cultural profile and historic identity through opposition to culturally different neighbors and enemies," we may note that the aforementioned *discrete* and *broader* Spanish American nationalisms, far from competing, appear to co-exist and even work to reinforce one another. This two-tiered sense of national identity would allow individuals to select the more appropriate designation—national (i.e., Mexican, Argentine, Cuban, etc.) or broader (*hispanoamericano* or *latinoamericano*)—depending on circumstances.[15] Simón Bolívar, the Venezuelan-born South American independence leader and an important early exponent of this two-tiered Spanish American nationalism, does just this in his 1815 "Carta de Jamaica," alternately referring to Venezuela (then set to join Gran Colombia) and to the whole of *América meridional* as *mi patria* (my country/homeland), depending on the level of specificity he requires.[16] Indeed, the many Spanish American thinkers and political figures who have from the beginning of the nineteenth century invested themselves in the project of strengthening ties between the component parts of the Latin American *magna patria* have generally presented these discrete and broader nationalisms as mutually reinforcing, as we have seen for Francisco Bilbao and José María Torres Caicedo, and as we shall see shortly for Bolívar. By way of analogy, as Edouard Glissant argues for the Caribbean, "[o]ne is not Martinican because of wanting to be Caribbean. Rather, one is really Caribbean because of wanting to become Martinican" (224).

While Anderson, along with Smith and Ardao, provides us with a robust conceptual framework for theorizing Spanish American nationalism, by focusing on specific phenomena like colonial-era bureaucratic circulation and the rise of print capitalism, he fails to describe what I consider the root cause of this unique form of nationalism. In my view, we need to look at colonialism more broadly, and in particular its interactions with Spanish America's unique geo-historical structure[17] as a series of contiguous territories that during the colonial period were governed from the same metropolis and according to a common set of norms and laws. Beginning in the first years of the nineteenth century, these territories developed into a group of contiguous nation-states whose civic cultures and institutions derived (at least in terms of European colonial influence) from a common Spanish point of origin. Most of these nations, excepting Uruguay, Puerto Rico, the Dominican Republic, and Cuba, won their independence as part of a common early nineteenth-century republican independence struggle from Spain in which combatants and propagandists operated far beyond their home cities or regions.[18] As evidence for this "supranational" reading of Spanish American history, we might recall the several nineteenth-century schemes for Spanish American political union (Gran Colombia, 1819–30; República Federal de Centroamérica, 1823–40; Confederación Perú-Boliviana, 1836–39) and policy coordination (various regional conferences and group treaty signings, use of shared diplomats, and so on).[19] I cannot find evidence that Brazil, governed as a constitutional monarchy from 1822 to 1889, participated in any of these initiatives prior to its adoption of the Republic, with the exception of one or two invitations to a regional congress. As will be referred to in Chapter 3, Brazilian participation in Pan-American diplomatic efforts would have to wait for the early years of the twentieth century and the diplomacy of the Baron of Rio Branco and Joaquim Nabuco, who even then encountered skeptical responses from countrymen like Eduardo Prado and Euclides da Cunha, intellectuals who viewed the earlier monarchical regime's lack of attention to Americanism as evidence of a healthy independence of national identity. I will touch on Prado and da Cunha, two of Brazil's more prominent "hispano-skeptics," later in this chapter.

Returning to our main argument, it seems logical that in penning essays on questions of national and broader regional identity, Spanish American intellectuals would draw on historical, linguistic, and cultural ties between the nation-states that grew out of Spanish colonialism, particularly at those moments when more local loyalties appeared inadequate to counter outside threats. This is the case of José Martí's highly influential, impressionistic and even rhapsodic essay "Nuestra América" (1891), in which the author calls for those living from the "Bravo a Magallanes" to reject the narrow-minded localism of the *aldeano* ("villager") and to begin learning about each other as a precondition for success in an imminent struggle against the United States—a rising power that in the preceding decades had, to Martí's mind, shown its annexationist and interventionist designs in Mexico and the Caribbean (37, 44). With their nation apparently unable to access these historical, cultural, and linguistic ties, Brazilian intellectuals have tended to ground their own, more limited calls for continental unity in pragmatic, as opposed to identity-based arguments, as is the case for Nabuco, and for the critic José Veríssimo (1857–16) in the pan-American themed articles he wrote for the journal *O Imparcial* during the early 1910s.[20]

To recap my argument thus far, I have contended that Brazil represents a necessary component of any viable definition of Latin America, and that Spanish American essay-writing intellectuals, in taking up the challenge of defining "Latin America"

as a category, particularly in order to advance projects for supranational policy coordination, resistance to foreign powers
(such as the United States), and intellectual-cultural reform,
have from the nineteenth century forward tended to defend
a two-tiered nationalism premised on mutually reinforcing
discrete and broader loyalties and identifications. At this point
we will move away from the notion of Brazil as *necessary*, to
consider Brazil as *problematic* with regard to the idea of Latin
America. If my assumption is correct that Spanish American
essayists are compelled to include Brazil in their paradigms for
a Latin American *magna patria*, then it follows that they face
the challenge of incorporating an element that can easily be defined as heterogeneous, assuming the case for Latin American
unity is made in broadly culturalist terms. Brazil is, after all, a
nation whose colonial origin and language are *not* Castilian,
which did *not* participate in an early nineteenth-century republican revolution, whose customs and religious practices have
been interpreted by some as distinct, and whose intellectuals
have on the whole defined their country as lying outside the
magna patria, as we shall see in the following pages. Upon the
prototypical Spanish American writer's attempt to rhetorically
incorporate Brazil into the *magna patria*, the country's evident
dissimilarity from its neighbors immediately threatens to dis-
rupt the mutually reinforcing, two-tiered character of Spanish
American nationalism, by compelling the Spanish American
writer and reader to identify with a nation (Brazil) whose experience is in many ways distinct, whose history defies Spanish
America's shared republican and revolutionary political roots,
and whose opinion leaders during the late nineteenth and early
twentieth centuries did not on the whole embrace the idea of
a shared Latin American identity. In facing the challenge of
Brazil, I argue that Spanish American thinkers have tended
to adopt a strategy of *identity projection*[21]: that is, in their essayistic arguments for Latin American unity, they rhetorically
project a Spanish American identity onto Brazil, drawing freely
on Brazilian examples in rounding out their arguments (as Brazil geographically rounds out the South American continent),
while relying on a conceptual framework that collapses the
distinction between *Latinoamérica* and *Hispanoamérica*.[22]
Willfully or unconsciously ignoring signs of Brazilian difference, these essay-writing intellectuals "resolve" the problem

of Brazilian non-conformity by representing Brazil (sometimes explicitly, more often by implication) as if it were a Spanish American nation.

This sort of identity projection abounds in Spanish American essayistic and critical writing, and numerous examples concerning Brazil can be found dating from the early nineteenth century to the present. For a relatively recent case, one need look no further than Ángel Rama's *La ciudad letrada* (1984). In the opening sentences of Rama's enduringly influential, posthumous study on the topographical and discursive configuration of power in colonial Latin America, the author characterizes the development of the Latin American city in these terms: "From the remodeling of Tenochtitlan following its destruction by Hernán Cortés in 1521, to the inauguration in 1960 of the most fabulous dream of a city of which Americans have been capable, Lucio Costa and Oscar Niemeyer's Brasilia, the Latin American city has basically been a product of the mind [*un parto de la inteligencia*]" (1). Rama's use of the term *inteligencia* implies a rationalized attitude toward urban organization on the part of the Spanish (and presumably Portuguese) colonizers, to which the city represented "the dream of an order," or the concrete expression of the rigid social hierarchy that these colonizers were attempting to impose on the New World (11). As Rama explains, the Iberian colonizers' attraction to rational, pre-planned, even utopian spaces, aside from constituting a response to the organizational deficiencies of late medieval/early modern European cities, was a function of "Baroque culture, which utterly penetrated social life and had its culminating expression in the Spanish monarchy" (14). Rama's "ordered city" model may successfully describe inland, colonial-era cities like Mexico City or Puebla (Mexico), where a four-sided *zócalo* or *plaza mayor* is ringed by the sites of religious, civil, and military authority (i.e., the cathedral, government headquarters, and barracks), with streets emanating outward in a grid pattern. However, just as Rama's foucauldian description of the Ibero-American intellectual who lived and worked in these cities as a *letrado* is not entirely adequate to describe Brazilian writers and intellectuals (as it additionally fails to describe many colonial-era Spanish American *letrados* on the periphery of the empire), Rama's application of a rationalized urbanizing agenda to the Portuguese in Brazil, as well as his implication that Portugal participates in a historical trajectory providentially culminating in Baroque-era Spain, is misplaced. To the contrary, Luso-Brazilian historiography has long downplayed the importance of the Iberian dynastic union (1580–1640), in which a Spanish Habsburg sat on the Portuguese throne, and has retrospectively defined this period as one of Spanish occupation and oppression of Portugal, redeemed by the "Restoration" of Portuguese independence under the Bragança dynasty. As a Luso-Brazilian metropolis, Brasilia is the pre-planned exception rather than the urban rule, and there exists a long tradition in Brazilian (and Luso-Brazilianist) intellectual production of exalting the seemingly chaotic twists and turns of cities like Rio de Janeiro. Brazilian writer Lima Barreto says as much for Rio in his novel *Vida e Morte de M.J. Gonzaga de Sá* (Life and Death of M.J. Gonzaga de Sá, 1919). As the title character eloquently puts it:

> Rio de Janeiro was not built according to the theory of perpendicular and oblique angles. She suffered, *as have all spontaneous cities,* the influx of the environment in which she was built and the social vicissitudes through which she has passed [. . .] If she does not have the regularity of a surveyor's strict geometry, she is regular in terms of the hills that distinguish her [from other cities] and make her what she is. (578; my emphasis)

Sérgio Buarque de Holanda would take up this point in his interpretive essay *Raízes do Brasil* (1936), to be discussed at length in Chapter 5. Buarque cites urban differences between Brazil and Spanish America as evidence for the explanatory authority of his archetypal opposition between the Brazilian *semeador* ("sower") and the Spanish American *ladrilhador* ("harvester, cultivator") as key to understanding more profound differences between Brazil and Spanish American society. Buarque observes that in Spanish American cities, "As ruas não se deixam modelar pela sinuosidade e pelas asperezas do solo; [os colonizadores espanhóis] impõem-lhes antes o acento voluntário da linha reta" (96; "the streets do not allow themselves to be shaped by the soil's shapes and limitations; [the Spanish colonizers] instead impose[d] on them the willful mark of the straight line"). According to Buarque, the opposite is true for

Brazil: "A cidade que os portugueses construíram na América não é produto mental, não chega a contradizer o quadro da natureza, e sua silhueta se enlaça na linha da paisagem" (110; "The city that the Portuguese built in America is not a mental product, it does not contradict nature's design, and its silhouette winds around the landscape's contours").

Could Rama have been unaware of the "spontaneity" so often ascribed to the typical Brazilian city, and powerfully displayed in the dramatic topography of Rio de Janeiro, or of the prominence in Brazilian thought of the idea of the naturally ordered city? This is unlikely, given Rama's depth of engagement with Brazil (he collaborated with both Antonio Candido and Darcy Ribeiro), as well as his frequent references in his work to Brazilian history, letters, and culture.[23] Rather than a case of ignorance, I would argue that Rama, in citing Brasilia as a "representative" example of Brazilian and broader Latin American urban organization, projects a Spanish American identity—whether consciously or unconsciously—onto Brazil in the interest of successfully extending his *ciudad ordenada/ ciudad letrada* paradigm to the whole of Latin America. Without Brazil and the long list of valuable examples it provides, Rama's continentally framed argument fails to extend to a territory that, by any definition of *omphalos*, lies at the center of Latin America. Indeed, in his earlier work *Transculturación narrativa de América Latina* (1982) Rama's treatment of Brazil as liminal with regard to the category of "Latin America" resembles in certain respects the treatment the country would receive in *La ciudad letrada*. In *Transculturación narrativa*, which as a volume of Spanish American literary criticism is notable for the extent to which it relies on Brazilian literary examples, Rama commits a semantic slippage that we will see is quite common in Spanish American essayistic and critical writing: he refers to Brazil alternately as a component part of *Hispanoamérica*, and as exterior to it, depending on whether his argument in that instance calls for inclusion of Brazil or for a broad distinction between Brazil and Spanish America.[24] One suspects that, as much as Rama's presentation in *Transculturación narrativa* and *La ciudad letrada* of Brazil as liminal to "Latin" or "Spanish" America is a function of an actually existing ambiguity concerning Brazil's relationship to this category, it is also responsive to a constitutive tension in Spanish American essayistic and critical discourse—between the imperative to *extend* the scope of the argument for unity to a "full" or sufficiently large geographical space, which would necessitate Brazil's inclusion, and a strategy of *grounding* regional unity in factors such as shared history, culture, and language, which might signal Brazilian exclusion.

IV. The Other Side of the Coin: Brazilian Exceptionalism

Moving across the Luso-Hispanic frontier and to the other side of my analytical model, Brazilian intellectuals, at least in the nineteenth and early twentieth centuries, have on the whole been less apt to identify (or imagine) historical and cultural ties between Brazil and Spanish America, and have tended to characterize their nation's continental participation in more limited, pragmatic terms and in response to a desire to maximize Brazil's political and economic standing in the region, rather than in the fraternal language (*nuestros hermanos*, etc.) so often seen on the Spanish American side.[25] A good anecdotal illustration of this difference can be found in the telegrams exchanged between José Enrique Rodó and the Baron of Rio Branco, then Brazil's foreign policy chief, in November 1909, in regards to an impending border treaty between Uruguay and Brazil. Where Rodó writes to Rio Branco of an agreement that "has worked to further strengthen the old friendships of these two fraternal peoples [*estos pueblos hermanos*]," Rio Branco's response is free of this fraternal language, and is framed in terms of the fulfillment of Brazil's national interests. He judges that the agreement will "contribute to further consolidate the friendship between Uruguay and Brazil, as *we Brazilians* so greatly desire" (qtd. in Etcheverry 7n6; my emphasis).

Critics have pointed to a variety of political, psychological, and historical causal factors in seeking to account for the inward-looking—as opposed to supranational or continentally directed—orientation of Brazilian nationalist and exegetic discourse. As mentioned earlier, monarchists from the generation of José Bonifácio de Andrada e Silva, as well as that of Joaquim Nabuco, Eduardo Prado, and Euclides da Cunha, cited Brazil's regionally unique institutions and practices (constitutional monarchy, prolonged slavery, etc.) as differentiating factors—and at times as proof of their nation's superiority over its neighbors. Early to mid-twentieth century intellectuals like Buarque and Gilberto Freyre, in the context of anthropological and historical interpretations of Brazilian society and culture, presented the allegedly unique, quintessentially "Brazilian" traits of flexibility, racial tolerance, and a consensus-oriented political culture as accounting for a uniquely Brazilian developmental path and worldview. These characterizations of the collective Brazilian *Volksgeist* endure in the popular imagination (as they do analogously in any number of countries), and more surprisingly, in academic discourse—this despite the broad anti-essentialist turn that has characterized academia in recent decades. In a March 14, 2007 address at Brown University, entitled "Brazil: A Latin American Nation?," Fernando Henrique Cardoso, President of Brazil from 1995 to 2003 and a trained sociologist, cited a number of factors, including Brazil's Portuguese-origin pragmatism, along with its language, history, and size (Cardoso contended that as a large nation, Brazil is essentially inward-looking), as accounting for Brazil's long-standing insistence on following its own path in terms of foreign policy, national self-conceptualization, and intellectual reflection. While in the last few years the Brazilian political and economic establishments may have undertaken an unprecedented campaign of outward-looking regional institution and relationship-building (under Cardoso's successor, Luiz Inácio Lula da Silva), Cardoso cautioned that in the main, Brazilians do not seek to identify themselves entirely with their neighbors, but rather look more selectively for those "parts" of the Latin American experience with which they might realistically identify. Cardoso's rhetoric is notably more cautious than that of Michelle Bachelet, President of Chile from 2006 to 2010, who invoked a fraternal language with deep roots in Spanish American intellectual history in a 2006 guest essay for *The Economist*, in which she argued for the importance of a strong Latin American alliance:

> From the past we have learned that there is strength to be found in unity. That is why integration is so vital for a region composed entirely of small and middle-sized powers. From the present we have learned that dreams are important, but pragmatism is no vice if it is aimed at helping people live

healthier and happier lives. This may seem like a triviality, but it is not. Our founders, the *libertadores*, shared these sentiments, knowing that there would be no freedom without democracy, and no democracy without unity. As we approach the bicentenary of many of our republics, including my own, we are mindful and hopeful of that unachieved, but achievable, Latin American dream. (42; author's emphasis)

A Brazilian exegetic tradition that is focused on national singularity and that remains skeptical (and sometimes openly hostile) toward approximation to Spanish America found expression early in the monarchical period, in institutions like the Instituto Histórico e Geográfico Brasileiro (Brazilian Historical and Geographic Institute, established 1838) (Burns 8). The IHGB, whose membership included early Brazilian historian Francisco Adolfo de Varnhagen, advanced an interpretive paradigm for Brazilian history that presented the monarchy as the guarantor of Brazil's territorial integrity, political unity, and economic and social stability—in contrast to the disorder and periodic threats represented, in the minds of many, by the tumultuous Spanish American republics of the mid-nineteenth century. German naturalist Karl F.P. von Martius expressed precisely this position at the close of his thesis *Como se Deve Escrever a História do Brasil* (How the History of Brazil Should Be Written, 1843), his successful entry to an IHGB competition on the same topic. As Antonio Candido notes, the idea of Brazil's national distinctness from Spanish America was key to the Empire's self-legitimizing historical vision: "The tradition handed down from Independence had the monarchical regime justifying itself before Brazilian liberal public opinion by guaranteeing unity, [and] preventing the fracturing and turbulence that marked the destiny of Spanish America, which was seen as a collecting basin of agitators and caudillos, with the former French colony of Haiti providing the extreme, feared example of a slave uprising that should be avoided at all costs" ("Os Brasileiros e a Nossa América," in *Recortes* 132). This inward-looking tendency, focused on the affirmation of Brazil's difference from its neighbors, left a strong imprint in late nineteenth- and early twentieth-century Brazilian essay-writers and *intérpretes* ("interpreters") such as Nabuco, Manuel de Oliveira Lima, da Cunha, Bomfim, Freyre, and Buarque. The broad corpus of Brazilian "interpretive" essays and studies, anthologized by Nova Aguilar in the three-volume *Intérpretes do Brasil* (Interpreters of Brazil, 2000), stands in stark contrast to the more expansive, continentally themed Spanish American essayistic tradition exemplified by Torres Caicedo's *Unión latino-americana,* Martí's "Nuestra América," Rodó's *Ariel,* and José Vasconcelos's *La raza cósmica* (1925), among many other texts.[26]

As with Spanish America, I find it helpful to view Brazilian writing on the nation as fundamentally an expression of *nationalism*, understood in the terms staked out by Anderson, Smith, and Ardao. In comparison to Spanish American discourse on the nation (think Bolívar, Martí, Rodó, etc.), national-exegetic discourse in Brazil tends to operate quite differently. Here the nation has been predominantly affirmed not by establishing Brazil's regional ties to a *magna patria*, but rather through the defense of its *difference* from Portugal, the European center, the United States, and Spanish America. This "search for the 'Brazilian specificity,'" as historian Emília Viotti da Costa terms it (172), can strike the uninitiated as a somewhat circular process, operating according to a logic by which certain features of Brazilian life (use of Portuguese, Brazil's imperial history—and more popularly, Carnaval, global soccer dominance, Amazonian wildlife, and *capoeira*), are elevated to the status of unique national characteristics, and then classified as quintessentially Brazilian precisely because of their uniqueness. As Mário de Andrade and Roberto Schwarz have both noted, fixation on national distinctiveness can have a stultifying effect on intellectual discussion no matter the national context, making for less-than-stimulating literary and cultural debates (who is the more "Brazilian" writer, José de Alencar or Machado de Assis? Is the protagonist of Manuel Antonio de Almeida's comic novel *Memórias de um Sargento de Milícias* (Memories of a Militia Sergeant, 1854–55) a *pícaro* in the Spanish mold, or an authentically Brazilian *malandro*?), and reducing textual analysis to the assessment of a novel, essay, play, author, or character's potential for national allegory.[27] As Andrade ironically observed in 1928, alluding to a literary nationalism he viewed as superficial and outmoded, "[h]ere in Brazil, we're still very consciously Brazilian and in this sense we haven't progressed much from the days of [nineteenth-century Romantic novelist] José de

Alencar" ("Literatura Modernista Argentina—I," qtd. in Antelo 167). And as Schwarz warns in his celebrated article "Nacional por Subtração," the critical operation of "nationalism by subtraction" (that is, the attempt to locate a nation's "authentic" cultural core by mentally subtracting so-called foreign elements), partakes of a misguided belief in "purity of customs," as Andrade put it. Moreover, Schwarz notes that it is based on a false assumption that an "authentic" Brazilian culture can be located by removing all foreign influences, and it ignores both Brazil's historical location on the periphery of global capitalism and the fact that Brazil participates in a world defined by ever-increasing cultural and material exchange. Adapting Schwarz's argument to Spanish America, we may identify a Spanish American "nationalism by accretion," which departs from the equally flawed supposition that Latin America represents an internally consistent and stable entity in which all of the region's (Spanish-speaking) inhabitants can participate equally, and through which they can more fully realize their own nationhood (33, 39).[28]

Where the idea of national exceptionalism as expressed in Brazilian essayistic writing becomes particularly interesting for me is when it is presented comparatively, as a *counterpoint* to the identity projection found in so many Spanish American essays—that is, when Spanish American identity projection and Brazilian exceptionalism are counterposed, and considered as two parts of the same process, two responses to the same problem of defining the nation's relationship to the broader region or continent, and by extension, of negotiating this broader region's relationship to the world at large. Together, these actions illustrate how Brazil and Spanish America's distinct profiles (Brazil as the only former Portuguese colony in Latin America, paradoxically occupying the region's geographic, economic, and political center; Spanish America as a series of contiguous nations formed from the same colonial history and largely participating in the same independence struggle) lead to distinct forms of nationalist discourse. As Luís Cláudio Villafañe G. Santos notes, the idea of Brazil's singularity within America dates at least from the early nineteenth century, and as a discourse cultivated by the emergent Brazilian intelligentsia, can be seen as a partial reaction to contemporary events in Spanish America:

> The broad idea of America presupposed a difference between this New World and its former metropolises, a distinction grounded in the notion that American republicanism had broken with the Europe of the monarchs. Brazil's singularity began manifesting itself at this point, with the construction of an identity that, in a certain way, reaffirmed the (internal) power relations of the colonial era [. . .] the Empire conceived of itself [*inventava-se*] as a bastion of civilization ("European," naturally) surrounded by anarchic republics, as an Empire that, while remote and tropical, was fundamentally civilized, and, therefore, "European." (25)

In addition to steering imperial-era Brazilian foreign policy away from inter-American initiatives, the idea of Brazil's fundamental distinctness from Europe, North America, and its "anarchic" Spanish American neighbors profoundly influenced the nation's intellectual development. The Brazilian intelligentsia's remarkable and long-standing commitment to national interpretation, which has manifested itself in eloquent form from Ambrósio Fernandes Brandão's *Diálogos das Grandezas do Brasil* (Dialogues on the Great Things of Brazil, 1618) to the *Intérpretes do Brasil* anthology project (2000), is not, however, without its ugly reverse side. This can be seen in unflattering characterizations of Spanish Americans by Brazilian writers and critics that bear striking resemblance to the characteristic features of the Spanish *leyenda negra*, or "Black Legend," in which the Spanish (and by extension, Spanish Americans) were described by foreign, and principally French, English, and German commentators beginning in the sixteenth century as, among other things, "indolent, jealous, fanatical, disdainful of what is foreign, ignorant and [. . .] slave[s] to the priests" (Juderías 190). Indeed, numerous Brazilian writers and thinkers during the nineteenth and early twentieth centuries described Spanish Americans as tending almost pathologically toward excess, obsession, violence, cruelty, and insanity, and the Spanish American republics as marked by rigid social hierarchies, the obsessive search for wealth, bloody civil conflict, mad religious fanatics, and despotic *caudillos*. In the following paragraphs I will attempt a brief survey of some of these descriptions, focusing specifically on Eduardo Prado, Euclides da Cunha, Manoel Bomfim, Clodomiro Vianna Moog, and Gilberto Freyre.

37

Eduardo Prado, a monarchist who edited the *Comércio de São Paulo* newspaper, lays out his vision of post-imperial Brazil's place in America in *A Ilusão Americana* (The American Illusion), a polemical text suppressed by the Brazilian republican government upon its publication in 1893. Here Prado rejects both the ideas of Latin American solidarity and of closer Brazilian ties to the United States, which his erstwhile monarchist colleague Joaquim Nabuco would soon begin advocating under the banner of Pan-Americanism. Prado fixes on "Spanish [American] eruptions" of revolutionary violence, judges elections in Spanish America to be "synonymous with civil war," and in sum, describes "[t]he confused and horrible history of all these [Ibero-American] nations [as] a river of blood, a continual extermination" (8, 10, 56). Prado grounds his case for maintaining imperial-era traditions of continental non-participation and close European ties in an argument for Brazilian national identity as regionally unique. He writes that Brazil

> [f]aces the rising sun, with its urban centers easily accessible to Europe, and is closer to the European continent than the majority of American nations. Separated from them by its origin and language, neither the physical nor the moral Brazil forms a system with those nations [. . .] [T]he deep roots and eternal pillars of the Brazilian bedrock are Brazil's alone. (10)[29]

In a series of articles written in the early 1900s and in response to a border dispute between Brazil and Peru in the region of the Alto Purús and Alto Juruá (in the present-day Brazilian state of Acre), Brazilian writer and journalist Euclides da Cunha, author of *Os Sertões* (Rebellion in the Backlands, 1902), a classic account of the 1896–97 Canudos rebellion, echoes Prado's unfavorable characterizations of Spanish America and Spanish Americans, as well as Prado's rejection of continental engagement as a foreign policy priority for republican Brazil. In "Solidariedade Sul-Americana" (South American Solidarity), one of the pieces collected in the volume *Contrastes e Confrontos* (Contrasts and Confrontations, 1907), da Cunha posits that "[t]he Republic freed us from the isolating listlessness [*remanso*] of the Empire and threw us into a dangerous South American solidarity. We fell into the foreigner's

not-always-lucid field of vision, which he incessantly fixes on
the peoples, and the *governments* or 'governments' (ironically
emphasized or written in quotes) of South America" (134; author's emphasis and quotes). For da Cunha, South American
solidarity implies *violence*, particularly violence brought about
by caudillos, whom he describes as perpetuating "the turbulent
restlessness, the fixation on glory and the desire for combat that
led to the downfall of Spain in the seventeenth century" (35).
With Peru serving as a test case, da Cunha, in an argument reminiscent of the *civilización/barbarie* distinction favored by Spanish American exegetes such as Argentina's Domingo Faustino
Sarmiento, divides Spanish America between two civilizational
models or tendencies, much as he contrasts Brazil's "modern,"
urban southeast and its "backward" northeastern interior in *Os
Sertões*. The first of these models is identified with peaceful
production (personified by the Incas) and the other with destruction (symbolized by the "military brutality of Spain," which da
Cunha credits with leading to the downfall of Incan civilization)
(114).[30] The foreign observer, da Cunha argues, compounds
the problem of South America's deep internal divisions by
spuriously contrasting cases of South American "success" with
those of "failure," creating a false impression of continental
uniformity. While the foreigner may lump Argentina and Brazil
together as "successes," this does not mean that any real bond
exists between the two nations. He concludes "Solidariedade
Sul-Americana" in this way: "If this South American solidarity
is admittedly a very beautiful and absolutely impossible ideal,
and has the sole effect of tying us to the traditional disorders
of two or three irredeemable peoples, and of making it impossible for us to meet the demanding standards of true progress,
then let us discard it [. . .] Let us move forward—*in our old
and splendid isolation*—toward the future; and, conscious of
our strength, toward conflict [with Peru] and the defense of the
Amazon" (138; my emphasis). As Candido explains, alluding
to the multi-polar Brazilian foreign policy favored by the Baron
of Rio Branco, then Brazil's Foreign Minister, da Cunha "was
skeptical of the tendency of his time, which was toward the
reinforcement of links with the nations of the [Latin American]
subcontinent, despite the constant strife and the risk of being
yoked by North American imperialism" (*Recortes* 135–36).

Importantly, hostility toward Spanish America and opposition to closer continental ties are not prerequisites for this sort of caricatured, ultimately uncharitable representation of Spanish Americans by Brazilian intellectuals. The critic José Veríssimo (1857–1916), an ardent defender of inter-American reciprocity who consistently championed Spanish American literature and culture to his Brazilian audience and attempted to convince his readers of the importance of events taking place in the Spanish American republics, referred in a 1913 article on the Mexican Revolution, "O Caso do México" (The Mexican Case) to "the Spanish Americans' insubordinate, undisciplined spirit, prone to revolt" even as he commented on a North American journalist's apparently misguided belief in a "mysterious and more or less mystical *Latin American character*" (*América Latina* 127, 130–31; author's emphasis).[31] In another article, "A Regeneração da América Latina" (The Regeneration of Latin America), Veríssimo describes Spanish America (in which Spanish, the "language of warriors," is spoken) as fundamentally uncivilized, even as he defends his lack of personal prejudice. He writes:

> I have an intimate feeling for Latin American fraternity; never once, since I was a boy, have I shared in my people's prejudice against the Spanish peoples of America, [which was] inherited from the Portuguese and fostered by our battles in the River Plate [region]. I love them all, and I am disgusted by hostility toward any one of them; but I cannot convince myself of the idea that they might rise so quickly above the economic, social, and moral misery in which they, with very rare exception, live. My intellect [. . .] refuses [. . .] to see them differently than they are, even in a distant future. And if the so-called biological laws of natural selection are true, and are as inflexible as astronomical or physical laws— which I permit myself to doubt, incidentally—these peoples will not have an independent future [*um futuro próprio*]. (19–20)[32]

Manoel Bomfim's long historical essay *O Brasil na América* (1929), in which the author pivots from the pan-Latin American approach of his earlier study *A América Latina: Males de Origem* (1905) and explores the bases of an exclusively Brazilian identity by "look[ing] to the remote history of a Brazil in formation, when its virtues appeared," may be cited as providing a less sympathetic example of an essentializing assessment of Spanish Americans, which Bomfim couples with skepticism toward the idea of a shared Latin American character (28). Shortly after terming the idea of Latin America an "unreal unity" in his study's first chapter, Bomfim describes the Spanish (and by extension, Spanish American) character as "impetuous and imposing," marked by the "vice of resounding intransigence," and an "exaggerated personal zeal," and characterizes the *caudillo* as "the exaggerated expression of Spanish independence, of the self-centered egotism to be found in the barbarity of a colonization that was simultaneously controlled and unhinged" (46, 70, 75, 365). He then defines the prototypical Portuguese as a "Spaniard who control[s] and contains himself" (365). These characterizations are notable, since Bomfim had previously attacked notions of racial determinism (which might account for the pervasive *independentismo* of the Spanish and Spanish Americans) in *A América Latina*, in which he likewise defends a Latin America-wide analytical frame he would later reject in *O Brasil na América*.[33] In his later volume, Bomfim goes as far as to declare that "[i]n the formation of traditions that come to define nationalities, everything comes down to *historical* differentiations," though this does not stop him from making solidly essentialist characterizations of Spanish Americans in that text (39; my emphasis).[34]

Clodomiro Vianna Moog and Gilberto Freyre, who feature alongside Sérgio Buarque de Holanda among the most prominent of Brazil's early to mid-twentieth century national exegetes, likewise fall prey to essentialism in their descriptions of Spanish America and Spanish Americans. In introducing his study *Bandeirantes e Pioneiros* (*Bandeirantes* and Pioneers, 1955), which is structured as a comparison of Brazil and the United States, Vianna Moog (1906–88), a lawyer, journalist, and literary intellectual, denounces both racialist and materialist interpretations of history in favor of an eclectic though generally culturalist position, arguing that "there [. . .] are no superior or inferior races, only ethnic types with diverse inclinations, cultures, and tendencies, rendered equally capable of success or failure by the sort of culture that predominates at the time they are called to fulfill their destiny" (46).[35] For Vianna Moog, historical materialism likewise errs in excluding "that new, unpredictable and uncontrolled element known as *life*" from its lists of behavioral causes and effects (72; author's emphasis). Vianna Moog's stated opposition to methological dogmatism seems intuitively reasonable, though the real test of his approach occurs when different peoples are exposed to similar material conditions, as were the Spanish and Portuguese colonizers in South America. Where the reader might expect a nuanced comparative analysis of the ways in which the "inclinations" of the Portuguese and Spanish interacted with the land and resources (not to mention indigenous peoples) they encountered in America, Vianna Moog reverts to a pathological language, describing the Spanish colonizers in terms reminiscent of the *leyenda negra*, characterizing their pursuit of precious metals as a "delusional dream of quick riches." For good measure, he then ties this "delusional dream" of easy mineral wealth to *caudillismo,* which he cites as the assumed "congenital ill of the Spanish American republics," and as one of the causes of Spanish America's eventual fragmentation (186).

Rather than contrast Brazil and Spanish America *a la* Buarque and Vianna Moog, Pernambuco-born sociologist and cultural anthropologist Gilberto Freyre (1900–87), tends in his reflections on colonial Latin America to describe the Portuguese and Brazilians as manifesting the highest expression of traits he also observes in the Spanish and Spanish Americans. In other words, when Freyre makes Luso-Hispanic comparisons he appears more interested in differences of *degree* rather than of *kind*, with Luso-Brazilians consistently emerging as more fully developed or more adequately endowed than their Spanish American counterparts. For instance, in celebrating the alleged "flexibility" of the prototypical Portuguese colonizer in his highly influential and controversial study *Casa-grande e Senzala* (The Masters and the Slaves, 1933), Freyre describes the Portuguese as "[a] Spaniard without the warrior's fire or the dramatic orthodoxy of the conqueror of Mexico and Peru" (*Intérpretes* 2: 315). And in the volume *O Luso e o Trópico* (The Lusitanian and the Tropical, 1961), Freyre judges that "[t]he merit seems to fall to the Portuguese along with the Spaniard and, or *perhaps more than* the Spaniard, of being the European who in a pioneering sense brought to Europe from the tropics the greatest number of values and techniques, which proved themselves capable of changing the life, economy, and culture of Europe by tropicalizing them" (98; my emphasis). Freyre specifically identifies this privileged "tropicalizing" role with Brazil in the preface to his collection *O Brasileiro entre os Outros Hispanos* (The Brazilian among the Other Hispanics, 1975), and deftly adapts the notion of Brazilian national *singularidade* within Latin America to his argument for the prototypical Luso-Brazilian as somehow "more" or "greater" than the average Spanish American: "[One may] affirm that this nation—the Brazilian—is doubly Hispanic: the only one to be characterized by a *singularity* that reinforces, rather than compromises, its condition as the direct inheritor of Spanish values just as it inherits Portuguese values. It is then not an intruder in the Hispanic community [of nations]—which includes Portugal just as much as Spain—but rather the *most complete expression* of what, in this community, is a culture that is *simultaneously one and plural*, when considered in terms of its sociological characteristics" (xlix–l; my emphasis).

At this point I would like to shift focus, moving from what has essentially been an introductory discussion—in which I have considered the genesis of two distinct forms of nationalist discourse in Latin America, one practiced in Spanish America and the other in Brazil—to the heart of the book, which is composed of a series of in-depth authorial profiles. In order to give proper grounding to these individual analyses of Latin American "interpreters" operating in the late nineteenth and early twentieth centuries, I will conclude this chapter with a comparative discussion of two important forerunners to the writers featured in chapters 2 through 5 of this book: these are Simón Bolívar, the Spanish American independence leader, and José Bonifácio, who played a similarly crucial role in working toward Brazilian independence. Their writings and political involvement in the early decades of the nineteenth century were key in establishing the dominant modes through which Spanish American and Brazilian nationalism—and supranationalism—would come to be expressed in writing. It is not an exaggeration to state that without Bolívar, texts like Rodó's *Ariel* and Reyes's *Última Tule* would be impossible, as would Nabuco's *Balmaceda* and Buarque's *Raízes do Brasil* without Bonifácio. Let us turn first to Bolívar, then to Bonifácio.

V. Simón Bolívar: Brazil at the
Margins of "Meridional America"

Examples of rhetorical identity projection onto Brazil by Spanish American essayists and public intellectuals are of course not limited to the late nineteenth or early to mid-twentieth century—indeed, this strategy for dealing with Brazil's Latin American location dates at least from the first years of Spanish American independence, as we may confirm in the writing of one of the founders of Spanish American continentalist discourse, Simón Bolívar. During and after the independence struggle he helped to lead, Bolívar (1783–1830) aggressively defended his project of creating a federation of independent Spanish American states in his correspondence, speeches, and other writings. While Bolívar envisaged his federated *América meridional* as effectively limited to the Spanish American republics, he leaves ample room in his writings on the subject for this space to extend to the whole of the New World, or at least that portion of the Western Hemisphere south of the United States. In this section I will discuss the tension that can be perceived between these two presumably divergent understandings of "meridional America," and I will argue that Bolívar's extension (on paper) of the term to encompass much of the New World *including Brazil* is a function of the two-tiered Spanish American nationalism I have described in this chapter, and which Bolívar played a key early role in formulating. In my analysis of Bolívar's writings, I hope to show that *El Libertador* took the at-first-glance contradictory step of defining "meridional America" as both exclusively Spanish American *and* as a broader, even hemispheric entity (which would include Brazil), for the same reason as have so many later Spanish American intellectuals: to promote a definition of Latin America that would allow Bolívar to identify both with Venezuela (his discrete nationality) and with broader entities such as Gran Colombia and ultimately the whole of *América meridional.*

In the 1815 "Carta de Jamaica," which Bolívar wrote from exile in the English colony of Jamaica, he describes the state of Spanish America's ongoing revolt, and reflects somewhat skeptically on the region's chances for adopting republican government. As in many other texts, Bolívar identifies both Venezuela (or extending outward somewhat, Gran Colombia) and the whole of Spanish America as his homeland, or *mi patria* ("Jamaica" 169, 171).[36] As was stated earlier, Bolívar's goal was to liberate the former Spanish colonies from Madrid and to transform them into a federation.[37] This goal was grounded in an understanding of *América meridional* as united on a number of levels—historically, ideologically, linguistically, culturally, racially, and so on. In addition to drawing on liberal democratic theory, Bolívar grounded his argument in an emerging Romantic-era discourse of the people and the nation as bonded by way of a common character or "genius," which in political terms finds logical expression in the nation-state. Referring to Spanish America, Bolívar argues the following: "Because it has a common origin, a common language, similar customs, and one religion, we might conclude that it should be possible for a single government to oversee a federation of the different states eventually to emerge" (*Writings* 27–28). Incorporating the idea of providential miscegenation into his argument, Bolívar contends that "we, who preserve only the barest vestige of what we were formerly, and who are moreover neither Indians nor Europeans, but a race halfway between [*especie media*] the legitimate owners of the land and the Spanish usurpers—find ourselves forced to defend these rights against the natives while maintaining our position in the land against the intrusion of the invaders"[38] (*Writings* 18; *Proclamas* 174–75).

As historical scholarship and his own words indicate, Bolívar was concerned with liberating the former Spanish colonies *only*, and did not envision the young Haitian and North American republics as anything more than allies bonded to "Meridional America" by a common democratic commitment. As Bolívar explained in a May 30, 1825 letter to fellow independence leader Francisco de Paula Santander: "The Americans from the North and those from Haiti, simply because they are foreigners, are too heterogeneous in character to fit in. Therefore, I will never agree to invite them to take part in our American system" (*Writings* 167).[39] Bolívar was even more wary of Brazil (the center of the Portuguese Empire between 1808 and 1821 and an independent monarchy from 1822), repeatedly referring to the Brazilians as "Portuguese"—a designation that may reveal a bit of ethno-linguistic prejudice on Bolívar's part, but more likely reflects his view that the Brazilian people were not yet

"Americans" because they had not yet defined themselves as such through the transformative experience of a republican revolution.[40] As Gerhard Masur observes, Bolívar "had many reasons for looking upon Brazil with aversion" (522). We will explore two such reasons. First, despite his occasional authoritarian gestures, Bolívar was a convinced republican, and he could therefore not tolerate Brazil's government, which from 1822 was presided over by a Portuguese-born prince. Bolívar incorrectly believed that D. Pedro I's constitutional monarchy was doomed to fail, as had abortive attempts at monarchy in Mexico and Haiti. In a toast Bolívar offered in Lima in 1823, "to the Liberty of America," he declared: "A Toast [. . .] because the peoples of America [*los pueblos americanos*] will never again consent to build a throne in any part of their territory. Just as Napoleon was buried in the immensity of the ocean and the new emperor [Agustín de] Iturbide was cast off the throne of Mexico, let the usurpers of the rights of the American people fall, so that not one of them remains triumphant in the whole of the vast extension of the New World" (*Proclamas* 243). Further, Bolívar wrote the following in a January 6, 1825 letter to Santander: "The death of Iturbide is the third chapter in the history of the American princes, with Desalines, Christophe, and he suffering the same fate. The emperor of Brazil may follow them, and supporters should take note" (*Cartas* 4: 244)[41]

Second and perhaps more importantly, Bolívar was concerned that imperial Brazil posed a military threat to the newly independent Spanish American states, particularly if Brazil allied itself with the European monarchies of the Holy Alliance—Russia, Prussia, and Austria. As Bolívar wrote to Tomás de Heres on August 6, 1825, "[t]his emperor of Brazil is young and legitimate, and he may be secretly controlled by the Holy Alliance, and make war on us [. . .] as the heir to all the rights lost by the Bourbons" (*Cartas* 5: 62). Bolívar's fears were stoked by moves in 1825 by a Brazilian army officer in Mato Grosso to annex the Chiquitos region of Bolivia (to which Bolívar logically took offense, as Bolivia had recently been named for him), and by Brazil's concurrent campaign to reestablish its authority over the Banda Oriental, the territory that would become Uruguay, long disputed between the Luso-Brazilians and Spanish Americans.

Bolívar's correspondence reveals his concern that these Brazilian moves reflected the opening gambit of a Holy Alliance-sponsored campaign against the Spanish American republics. While Bolívar's fears were exaggerated, there is evidence that for a time he entertained the plan of invading Brazil and dethroning D. Pedro I, which would have suited both Bolivian and Argentine interests. Ultimately, Bolívar authorized a limited, Peruvian-led campaign to recover Chiquitos, fearing the implications of a wider confrontation with Brazil and its potential European allies. According to Ron L. Seckinger, only "seasonal rains" prevented the Peruvian troops from attacking, which gave the Brazilians time to withdraw to Mato Grosso, and possibly averted a major conflict between Brazil and the Spanish American republics (27). Meanwhile, Great Britain, whose economic interest called for stability between Spanish America and Brazil, negotiated the settlement between Argentina and Brazil that created the independent republic of Uruguay in 1828. Nonetheless, Bolívar's saber-rattling 1825 declaration to Argentina's plenipotentiary ministers (who had petitioned him to support Argentina in its effort to assert control over the Banda Oriental) is revealing of his feelings toward Brazil, D. Pedro I, and the Chiquitos and Banda Oriental affairs:

> In truth, we have an incontestable right to be surprised that an American prince, recently independent from Europe, who has been involved in our noble insurrection, and who has raised his throne not on shaky ground, but on the indestructible bases of the sovereignty of the people and of the law: this prince, who seemed destined to be a friend to his neighboring republics, still occupies a province and a city that do not belong to him, and in this way controls one of our most noble nations. Elsewhere, his troops recently invaded our province of Chiquitos, assaulting it and insulting us with barbarous threats, and when our arms took them by surprise and sent them running, they took our property and our *citizens* with them! And yet these infamous violators of the people's rights have not been punished; our peoples have been humiliated and our Glory offended; yet we give thanks for these events, which have added new knots to the ties that bind us together, so that we will reclaim our rights just as we first affirmed them. (*Cartas* 5: 123; author's emphasis)

Thus far, Bolívar's vision of a federated *América meridional* is consistent with the borders of Spanish America, and does not seem to entail any significant identity projection onto Brazil—though his implication of Brazilian involvement in the Spanish American independence struggle in his 1825 declaration is interesting in this regard. Though on second look, we may begin to uncover broad identity projection on Bolívar's part from the opening lines of the 1815 "Carta de Jamaica." Here Bolívar introduces his homeland, which he reports as suffering under Spanish oppression, as "an immense, varied, and mysterious land as [vast as all of] the New World"—this despite the fact that large swathes of the hemisphere were colonies of other European powers—including Jamaica, where Bolívar was residing in exile at the time (*Writings* 12). He repeats this characterization in more graphic terms in a speech given the same year, declaring that "all of America is dyed with American blood," though historically speaking this was far from the case in 1815 (*Proclamas* 107). Returning to the "Carta," Bolívar describes how "America fights with [. . .] defiance," again, despite the fact that much of the hemisphere in 1815 was then not in revolt (this includes parts of the crumbling Spanish American empire, as well as Brazil, and again, the Anglophone Caribbean), or in the case of the United States and Haiti, had already completed successful independence wars (*Writings* 13–14). Perhaps Bolívar's most glaring example of identity projection comes later in the letter, when he speculates on the prospects for forming a single Spanish American government. Note that instead of speaking in terms of "Meridional America" or the plurality of the former Spanish colonies, Bolívar writes of "the idea of merging *the entire New World* [*todo el Mundo Nuevo*] into a single nation with a single unifying principle to provide coherence to the parts and to the whole" (*Writings* 27; "Jamaica" 172; my emphasis).

If we know that Bolívar's continental vision did not, at the concrete level, extend to Brazil, Haiti, or the United States, then why would he use language that implies just the opposite? Far from constituting an example of linguistic carelessness, or proof of ethnocentric ignorance of the non-Spanish-speaking portions of the New World, I would argue that Bolívar's *rhetorical* enlargement of Spanish America through the use of phrases like "all of America" and "the entire New World" is designed to defend a double or two-tiered sense of Spanish American nationalism that lies at the heart of his political and military program. Bolívar implies in the 1815 "Carta" that it is by identifying with the whole of "America" that he may empathize with the sufferings of Argentines, Mexicans, Peruvians, and other non-Venezuelans, and through which he is spurred to fight in their defense. This fellow-feeling is apparent in an 1818 message to the "inhabitants of the River Plate," in which Bolívar speaks in the name of the Venezuelan people as "your brothers" (*Proclamas* 159). Bolívar's continental identification is made plausible by his presumption that Venezuelans and Argentines share a common parentage, history, language, and customs, and as I argued previously, that they are bonded by a common revolutionary commitment and territorial contiguity. In his 1822 "Delirium on Chimborazo," an exercise in self-mythologization written in impressionist terms and not to be taken literally, Bolívar personifies his united "Meridional America" in the "God of Colombia" who Bolívar describes as living at the summit of the Chimborazo volcano in Ecuador, where He resolves to share his wisdom with the general (*Writings* 135–36). If Bolívar were to acknowledge the non-participation of certain sectors of the Americas—particularly Portuguese-speaking, obstinately monarchical Brazil—his argument for Spanish American unity under a confederated government would lose one of its principal supports: its extension, at least on the rhetorical level, to encompass "all of the New World."

VI. José Bonifácio: Armed Spaniards, Young Republics, and the "Tempered Monarchy"

Just as Simón Bolívar's writings provide us with an early example of the projective quality of Spanish American nationalist/supranationalist discourse, with Bolívar putting Brazil in the curious position of being rhetorically included in *América meridional* even as he pursued a policy toward Brazil that oscillated between non-engagement and open hostility, José Bonifácio de Andrada e Silva (1763–1838), a key figure in Brazil's achievement of independence in 1822, serves to illustrate the early development of a Brazilian discourse of selective approximation to Spanish America and of national *singularidade* ("singularity"), a term perennially used by commentators such as Gilberto Freyre, as in his speech "A Propósito de José Bonifácio" (Regarding José Bonifácio, 1972). Despite Bonifácio and Bolívar's shared status as national independence heroes—Brazil's "Patriarch of Independence" and *El Libertador*, respectively—the two men followed distinct career trajectories and exhibited significant ideological divergences and what would appear to be personality differences as well: in his 1972 speech Freyre describes Bonifácio and Bolívar in Cervantine terms, and with his characteristically erudite brand of fearless typecasting, judges Bonifácio to have more successfully blended Sancho Panza's pragmatism and Don Quixote's idealism than his Venezuelan counterpart ("José Bonifácio" 10–12). Differences aside, Bolívar and Bonifácio were both preoccupied with the rhetorical and practical challenges posed by their neighbors—imperial Brazil in the case of Bolívar and republican Spanish America in the case of Bonifácio. While Bonifácio gives comparatively less attention to Spanish America in his essayistic and poetic writing than does Bolívar to Brazil, what Bonifácio has to say about the Spanish American republics is nonetheless significant, in part as an illustration of the pragmatism, privileging of consensus, and solidly national focus that would become hallmarks of nineteenth-century Brazilian political thinking. Moreover, Bonifácio's writing serves as early evidence for the Brazilian intelligentsia's limited interest in Spanish America relative to Europe, and later, relative to the United States.

Bonifácio's views differ from Bolívar's in several crucial respects. First, scholars seem to agree that the "patriarch" of Brazilian independence was committed to Brazil remaining within the Portuguese Empire throughout his time as a student and bureaucrat in Europe, and through his 1819–22 period of service in Brazil as Prince Pedro's counselor.[42] However, as the Portuguese prince's desire to remain in Brazil as regent became untenable in the face of calls from the *Cortes* in Lisbon for him to return to Europe, Bonifácio adjusted his position to favor Brazilian independence as a constitutional monarchy presided over by Pedro, his close ally and friend.[43] Second, Bonifácio was a convinced monarchist, a view to which Bolívar (unlike José de San Martín and Agustín de Iturbide) fundamentally did not subscribe, despite his autocratic tendencies and stated doubts about Spanish America's fitness for republican government. As Emília Viotti da Costa explains, Bonifácio defended constitutional monarchy as the best means for Brazil to achieve liberty and gradual reform while preserving national unity and social order. Bonifácio's 1791 visit to revolutionary France, during which he witnessed the "excesses of the revolution," was key in forming his monarchist preferences. Here Bonifácio's experience mirrors that of English conservative Edmund Burke, author of the well-known *Reflections on the Revolution in France* (1790), as well as those of likeminded rightists, anti-revolutionary centrists, and moderate liberals. Moreover, Bonifácio prefigures fellow Brazilian monarchist Joaquim Nabuco's exposure to French politics in 1873–74, an episode that will be discussed in Chapter 3. As Viotti da Costa has it, "[i]n the simplest terms, José Bonifácio would be a liberal, but never a democrat" (30).[44] The liberal-monarchist orientation of Bonifácio's thinking becomes clear upon examining his writings: in one of his many epigrams, Bonifácio writes that "one must be very prudent in making reforms: one must understand the true state of the times, what they will allow to be reformed and what should remain of the old. Nothing should be done by leaps and bounds, but gradually, as in nature" (*Projetos* 175).

Third and finally, Bonifácio is remembered as a pragmatist who prioritized national unity over doctrinal purity, an early exemplar of a tendency in Brazilian politics that, whether actually existing or idealized, has been captured in terms like *conciliação* ("conciliation") and the positivist motto "order and progress" (featured on the Brazilian flag as *Ordem e Progresso*). It is interesting as well to note that fanaticism (*fanatismo*) features as one of Bonifácio's conceptual bugbears, specifically in his poetry.[45] One Bonifácio scholar, Raul de Andrada e Silva, contends that it was "an understandable opportunism [. . .] in the positive sense of the word," and not ideology, that steered Bonifácio toward constitutional monarchy. Bonifácio believed that "constitutional monarchy, with a solid and well-respected central authority, was the most effective means of consolidating [Brazil's] independence, reconciling it with liberalism while also maintaining the territorial and political unity of the immense country" (Viana Filho, *José*

Bonifácio 53). Importantly, Bonifácio's pragmatism was also informed by his view of Spanish America:

> What truly defines José Bonifácio's position within the independence campaign was that he wanted [independence] above all else, but without compromising national unity. With a statesman's broad vision, he understood that this would be difficult to achieve without the monarchy, or more precisely, without the figure of D. Pedro. He had reason to think this way, since the example of Spanish America, which was drowning in terrible internal conflicts, was nearby. (Viana Filho, *José Bonifácio* 38)

Of the relatively little Bonifácio has to say about Spanish America in his writings, what he does say reflects a view of the Spanish American states as an unstable, republican counterpoint to Brazil's orderly constitutional monarchy—a vision that seems grounded at least minimally in a *leyenda negra*-informed worldview we can see expressed in his poem "A Criação" (Creation), which describes the greed, fanaticism (here capitalized for good measure), arrogance, and violence of the Spanish *conquistadores*:

> Desembarcam ousados homens-monstruos;
> E após o estandarte correm, voam,
> Que Fanatismo, que cobiça alçaram.
> Imbeles povos, Índios inocentes!
> Do armado Espanhol provam as iras.
> Que Deus fizera um Mundo crêem os Tigres
> Para ser prêsa sua. Em tôda parte
> Americano sangue, inda fumando,
> A terra ensopa, e amolenta as patas
> Dos soberbos ginetes Andaluses.
> (*José Bonifácio* 60) [3]

Moving from poetry to political theory, Bonifácio's defense of constitutional monarchy is likewise informed by what he views as the largely negative example of Spanish America. On the positive side, the Spanish Americans, in their decision to adopt the Republic, embody the liberty to which Brazilians, as fellow Americans, aspire: "Brazil wants to be free; and has the example of all the young States that surround it" (*Projetos* 202). However, as Spanish America's difficulties in reconciling republican government to local conditions during the early years of independence illustrate, liberty would not be achieved in Brazil through the Republic—at least in Bonifácio's opinion. He explains: "The constitutional empire was the most analogous to [Brazil's] customs; and with the freedom this promised and guaranteed everyone was content, such that it was unnecessary to make bitter sacrifices in the name of the republican ideal, which the experience of [Brazil's] neighbors showed to be anarchic and violent" (203). As with the chaos of failed republicanism, Bonifácio believed that liberty likewise becomes compromised on the other extreme of the political spectrum, in a despotic monarchy. Bonifácio makes this argument in his ferocious critique of D. Pedro I's 1823 decision to dissolve the legislature, which he considers, "more than a crime [. . .] a grave error." Reasoning that imperial tyranny compromises the long-term stability of a constitutional monarchy, a model of government he considered particularly difficult to maintain in a continental climate marked by the newly minted Spanish American republics' hostility toward Brazil, Bonifácio writes that "[i]t should be kept in mind that [Brazil] is surrounded by new republican States that believe, with all the vigor of youth, that America should expel royalty. They believe that they are right in fearing the strength of an empire being born, with Pedro at its head" (217). Or put another way, "[i]f monarchies everywhere must surround themselves with splendor, and win hearts by their liberality and magnificence, this is even more the case in Brazil, surrounded [as it is] by republics" (225).

Bonifácio's defense of constitutional monarchy as a desirable median term between chaotic republicanism and tyrannical absolutism inspires two questions. First, did he consider constitutional monarchy to be the best form of government *in the abstract*, or was his position *specific to Brazil*, in other words, to what extent was it derived from his views on the Brazilian people's character and democratic potential and from his understanding of Brazil's place in the hemisphere? And second, did Bonifácio's championing of constitutional monarchy extend to the Spanish American republics, and if so, to what degree? Regarding the first question, Bonifácio seems most interested in constitutional monarchy as a means to secure liberty in a specifically Brazilian (or more broadly American) context.

Recall that for Bonifácio, the "republican ideal" requires "bitter sacrifices," which he believed Brazilians might not be willing or able to make in the name of the Republic (203). Evaluating his co-nationals' democratic potential, Bonifácio writes that "Brazilian souls are not elevated enough to hear the strong cry of freedom, accompanied by a strength moderated by reason. The great mass of the people wants independence; but not for the sake of constitutional liberty" (208). Bonifácio suggests that his people's lack of political maturity and their limited civic dedication might be a function of poor education—a concern he shared with Spanish American contemporaries such as Andrés Bello, Domingo Faustino Sarmiento, and Venezuelan educator Simón Rodríguez (1769–1854). For Bonifácio, what is called for in addressing this lack of civic engagement, short of rule by a "republican aristocracy, or a government of the wise and honored," is a constitutional monarchy capable of reconciling individual liberty with social order—a balancing act that preoccupied Latin American intellectuals, including the four writers discussed at length in this book, throughout the nineteenth and into the twentieth century (*Projetos* 209). Bonifácio suggests elsewhere that there may be limits to what civic education can accomplish, presenting Ibero-American government (and here is where he extends his defense of constitutional monarchy to Spanish America) as circumscribed by a shared, pre-determined racial and civilizational character: "Men through whose veins Iberian blood flows are not made for the Republic, all the more so if they have some African blood mixed in; and if their religion is Catholic. It is on this basis that I conclude that the best system of government that Brazil can have is a tempered monarchy [*monarquia temperada*], with institutions that are analogous to those of Great Britain." In this way Bonifácio, anticipating the racial determinism that would come into vogue later in the nineteenth century with the publication of texts like the Comte de Gobineau's *Essay on the Inequality of Human Races* (1853–55), acknowledges the capacity of "Iberian blood" to place limits on both Brazil and its Spanish American neighbors in terms of representative institutions, civic dedication, and so on. That said, Bonifácio's focus and loyalties remain with Brazil, as illustrated by the fact that he makes this statement on a common Ibero-American heritage as part of a policy recommendation that is specific to Brazil. Moreover, it was Brazil that Bonifácio invoked as his poetic muse in his verses, which he wrote under the pseudonym of "Américo Elísio."[46] Ultimately, Bonifácio, unlike Bolívar and later Spanish American continentalists, was concerned with "the best system of government that Brazil"— not Spanish America, nor the whole of the continent—"can have" (227).

***

In this opening chapter I have presented the analytical model that will guide the discussion I present in this book. As we have seen, this model, grounded in what I view as Brazil's *necessarily problematic* position within Latin America, is defined on one side by Spanish American rhetorical identity projection, undertaken in defense of a two-tiered nationalism—what might also be termed continentalism or supranationalism—and on the other by a Brazilian affirmation of national singularity, which largely precludes the recognition of non-instrumental (i.e., historical, cultural, and otherwise fraternal) ties with Spanish America. In the chapters that follow I will apply this model to the work of four important Latin American essayists—José Enrique Rodó, Joaquim Nabuco, Alfonso Reyes, and Sérgio Buarque de Holanda. I begin with Rodó, whose *Ariel* (1900) inaugurated one of Spanish America's most important paradigms for interpreting Latin America's (supra)national reality. Rodó's understanding of Latin America—as united by a dedication to philosophical idealism and to humanistic values, by a common Greco-Latin and Iberian linguistic and cultural heritage, and by a shared program of continental and transatlantic reform—has intringuing implications for Brazil, as we shall see. And while the reception that greeted Rodó in Brazil was—and continues to be—substantially more muted than in Spanish America, Rodó nonetheless responded to the challenge of Brazil by addressing Brazilian-Spanish American relations in certain of his essayistic texts, and has been referenced by some Brazilian intellectuals, among these a young Sérgio Buarque de Holanda. The next chapter will, then, address the pervasive influence of Rodó's *arielista/americanista* interpretive paradigm in light of his attempts to fit Brazil into the Latin American *magna patria* as he understood it.

Chapter Two

José Enrique Rodó

"Iberoamérica," the *Magna Patria,*
and the Question of Brazil

> Yo creí siempre que en la América nuestra no era
> posible hablar de muchas patrias, sino de una patria
> grande y única; [. . .] cabe levantar, sobre la patria
> nacional, la patria americana, y acelerar el día en
> que los niños de hoy, los hombres del futuro, pre-
> guntados cuál es el nombre de su patria, no contes-
> ten con el nombre del Brasil, ni con el nombre de
> Chile, ni con el nombre de México, porque contes-
> ten con el nombre de América.
> — José Enrique Rodó
> "El Centenario de Chile"
> (speech given in Santiago, 17 Sept. 1910)

> La historia del Brasil y de la América Española
> son paralelas y sincrónicas [. . .] Desde el primer
> momento, tendimos a realizar un mismo ideal
> de libertad [. . .] Y si la raza y la historia y las
> instituciones nos confunden a los brasileños y los
> hispano-americanos, ¿qué queda capaz de trazar entre
> nosotros una línea de separación? ¿Acaso el idioma?
> —José Enrique Rodó
> From draft of unpublished speech (1910)

Uruguayan writer-critic José Enrique Rodó (1871–1917), best
known for essayistic texts like *Motivos de Proteo* (1909), *El
mirador de Próspero* (1913) and especially *Ariel* (1900), is
without question one of Spanish America's most influential
literary and intellectual figures.[1] *Ariel*, published to acclaim
throughout the Spanish-speaking world, "help[ed]," in the
words of Julio Ramos, "to formulate [. . .] one of the key

narratives of legitimation [. . .] propagated by literature at the
turn of the century" (232). Here, Rodó famously borrows and
reconfigures characters and themes from Shakespeare's late
comedy *The Tempest*—as well as from Ernest Rénan's *Caliban*
(1878), a "philosophical" sequel to the play[2] —to make an
argument for Latin American spiritual unity and political solidarity. Rodó's thinking exists at the crossroads of philosophical
idealism (primarily absorbed via French writers), Bolivarian
federalism, and Spanish American *modernismo*'s preoccupation
with Spanish literary and cultural inheritance.[3] His reflections
on the prospects for a Latin American *magna patria*, or over-
arching continental unity, and on US–Latin America relations,
as well as his classicizing though still exultant contribution
to *modernista* prose style, profoundly impacted later Spanish
American thinkers, including Alfonso Reyes, Pedro Henríquez
Ureña, and Leopoldo Zea, and provided the impetus for a collective turn from positivist modes of analysis in favor of a "new
continent-wide idealism."[4] The opposition Rodó presents in
Ariel between Latin America, identified with the "airy spirit"
Ariel and committed to high humanistic ideals, and Anglo-
America, identified with Shakespeare's "savage and deformed
slave" Caliban and characterized by utilitarianism and crass
materialism, was widely inherited, with *arielismo* joining José
Martí's idea of *nuestra América* as one of early twentieth-
century Spanish America's dominant intellectual paradigms.[5]
Rodó's criticism and journalistic writing made him a celebrity
in Spanish America during his lifetime and a defining figure in
Ibero-American letters thereafter, a necessary point of reference
for both his detractors and his defenders. Mario Benedetti's
judgment on Rodó is apt: "[I]n the first years of the [twentieth]
century, Rodó's example and influence were those of a pioneer.
Before him, only Martí had achieved a comparable continental
reception" (94).[6]

Rodó, then, remains an obligatory point of reference in Latin
American literary scholarship—and an essential object of study
for those interested in comparative approaches to Brazilian and
Spanish American literature and criticism. Rodó's importance,
not merely a function of his intellectual and popular impact in
Spanish America, is due quite concretely to the range of his
textual dealings with Brazil—Rodó wrote about Brazil, its

people, its foreign relations, and its potential role in the *magna patria* with a degree of specificity that Martí, for example, did not. In the essay "Iberoamérica" (1910), in the unpublished speech on which "Iberoamérica" was based, and in other short texts, Rodó attempts with some difficulty to fit Brazil into his vision of a continent united by a shared "Latin" idealism and commitment to classical values, by a Spanish-origin history and language, and by solidarity in the face of US military and economic expansion. Indeed, the conflict between Rodó's over-arching vision of a Latin American unity grounded in Romantic notions of shared national or supranational "genius," and Brazil's linguistic, political, and historical particularities vis-à-vis Spanish America, forced Rodó to adapt his views and make conceptual leaps in his Brazil-themed texts that are revealing of what I understand as his ultimately *hispanocentric* vision of Latin America—that is, Rodó's assumption that *América Latina* and *Hispanoamérica* are like terms, and that Brazil is effectively part of Spanish America. The differing reception of Rodó's work in Spanish America, where he was treated as an intellectual hero, and Brazil, where his interlocutors have been few and far between, also deserves attention.

The structure of this chapter is as follows: the first section describes the discrepancy between Rodó's canonical status in Spanish America—largely due to *Ariel*—and his muted reception in Brazil. The second looks to Rodó's use of terms such as *América, Hispanoamérica, América Latina,* and *nuestra América* as ordering concepts for his continentalist thought. Close attention is paid here to Rodó's tendency to generalize these terms in rhetorically extending the boundaries of Spanish America to encompass the whole of Latin America (including Brazil), in line with a projective tendency in Spanish American continentalist discourse described in the previous chapter and extending from Simón Bolívar's "Carta de Jamaica" forward. Moreover, the semantic ambiguities and contradictions attending Rodó's construction of a Spanish American *magna patria* will be discussed. The third and final section examines texts in which Rodó *specifically* addresses the topic of Brazil in Latin America. My analysis of the essay "Iberoamérica" (1910), the longer speech on which it was based, and the reflection "Cielo y agua" (1916) will demonstrate how Rodó's imperative to rhetorically incorporate Brazil into the *magna patria* challenges his preferred terminology and arguments, forcing him into logical contradictions and textual misinterpretations that include a telling misreading of Portuguese writer Almeida Garrett.

I. A *Maestro* in Spanish America, a Virtual Unknown in Brazil

Rodó's critical writing, beginning with *El que vendrá* (1896), reached a broad readership in Spanish America, with his pioneering 1899 study of *modernista* luminary Rubén Darío and especially *Ariel* (1900) making his reputation and earning him praise as a master of high idealism, literary elegance, and courageous intellectual resistance to the United States (Benedetti 46).[7] During his career as a consecrated writer (i.e., after the publication of *Ariel*), Rodó was routinely feted at regional conferences and meetings, as in Montevideo (1908) and Santiago de Chile (1910), and received tributes from younger Latin American writers, including a young Alfonso Reyes (1899–1959), who referred to the Uruguayan writer as "Maestro," and whom we will discuss in this book's fourth chapter.[8] And in 1908, Rodó's colleague, the Uruguayan philosopher Carlos Vaz Ferreira, placed *Ariel* alongside the four Gospels and texts by Diderot, Mill, Nietzsche, and Rodó's idol Rénan on a short list of fundamental books for philosophy students.[9]

If we trust Rodó's correspondence, he was genuinely surprised by the success "del dichoso *Ariel* que, con una buena fortuna que me asombra, todavía a estas horas provoca animados comentarios y levanta ecos de simpatía *en toda América*" (letter to Rafael Altamira, 29 Jan. 1908, Rodó, *OC* 1363; my emphasis). At the same time Rodó must have been quite pleased, since he repeatedly referred to *Ariel* as having been composed as an "obra de *acción* y propaganda," an essay he hoped would be read, since, "si el desempeño no es enteramente malo, creo que él puede hacer algún bien y sugerir ideas y sentimientos fecundos."[10] As Benedetti put it, by the early 1910s "one could almost say there was a cult of Rodó," with *Ariel* being read, discussed, and reprinted by young admirers as far away as Havana and Mexico City (68).[11] Rodó's ideas on Latin American unity and his distinctive literary and oratorical delivery, a "polish[ed] and burnish[ed]" style, *modernismo* with a "Parnassian finish," quickly seeped into Spanish American discourse (Brading 5).[12] In 1987, Carlos Fuentes—on the record as critical of Rodó—recalled the ubiquity of *Ariel*-inspired rhetoric in the oratory of his youth in Mexico during the 1940s and 1950s, noting that "[i]t was rare for the tremulous orators of our youth not to quote Rodó in their speeches: the topics of the spiritual versus the utilitarian, blithe Latin American Ariel fighting off brutish North American Caliban, beauty confronting ugliness, followed by a whole parade of simplistic dualisms (vulgar versus delicate, good versus evil, and so on) were facile, tempting devices for the young lawyer, politician, or journalist on the rostrum" (Prologue 14).

While Rodó's refined prose style and aestheticizing elitism have irked later generations of politically committed Spanish American writers,[13] the *arielista* paradigm has nonetheless elicited a number of critical responses in Spanish American and Latin Americanist circles, which effectively carry forward *arielista* discourse even while engaging it critically. One particularly influential response is found in Cuban poet and critic Roberto Fernández Retamar's *Calibán: Apuntes sobre la cultura en nuestra América* (1971), in which the author inverts Rodó's identification of Latin America with Ariel and the US with Caliban, identifying Latin America instead with the enslaved, apparently barbaric Caliban, whose story Retamar interprets as allegorical of the colonial condition. Retamar's analysis also serves as a point of contact between the Spanish American current of *Tempest* interpretation, begun with Darío and Rodó, and the very productive mid- to late twentieth-century use of Shakespeare's play in the Anglophone and Francophone Caribbean and in post-colonial studies, in such texts as Frantz Fanon's *Black Skin, White Masks* (1952) and Aimé Césaire's play *Une tempête* (1969) (Rodríguez Monegal, "Metamorphoses" 78–79). Richard Morse's magisterial study *O Espelho de Próspero* (Prospero's Mirror, 1988), authored by a US Latin Americanist but published in Brazil and most widely read among Luso-Brazilianists, constitutes another noteworthy response to Rodó. In the opening lines to the text, Morse defines his version of Prospero's *mirador* as a mirror (as opposed to a watch tower), and announces his aim to "reverse the mirror's angle" from Latin America back to the United States, showing the former to be "not [. . .] a victim, patient, or 'problem,' but [. . .] the mirror image in which Anglo-America may recognize its *own* sicknesses and its own 'problems'" (13–14; author's emphasis).[14]

In contrast to his immediate fame and long-term influence in Spanish America, Rodó's impact in Brazil has been muted. Very few Portuguese-language editions of *Ariel* have been published, and the number of Rodó-themed studies by Brazilian writers has been limited.[15] The critic-turned-historian Sérgio Buarque de Holanda (1902–82) referenced *Ariel* in two short articles, "Ariel" (published May 1920 in the *Revista do Brasil*), and "Considerações sobre o americanismo" (Considerations on Americanism, collected in *Cobra de Vidro*, 1944). While Buarque does not refer directly to Rodó in his most famous text, the interpretive essay *Raízes do Brasil* (Roots of Brazil, 1936), I contend that Rodó constitutes an unacknowledged presence in that text, as I will argue in this book's final chapter. The few additional Brazilian voices who have engaged Rodó over the years, with varying degrees of depth, include the poet Manuel Bandeira, sociologist and historian Vicente Licínio Cardoso, and Sílvio Júlio, a self-described "bolivarist" and the author of *José Enrique Rodó e o Cinqüentenário do Seu Livro "Ariel"* (José Enrique Rodó and the Fiftieth Anniversary of His "Ariel," 1954), in which he airs his frustration that so few in Brazil had read Rodó.[16]

In accounting for this muted reception, it seems intuitive to begin with language, which worked on a number of levels to channel Rodó's writing and influence toward a transatlantic Spanish-speaking public, and away from Brazil. Just as Brazilian texts have historically been incorporated into Lusophone circulation routes by virtue of their being published in cities like Rio de Janeiro, São Paulo, Lisbon, and Porto, so was Rodó's work more prone to circulate and have an impact in the Spanish-speaking as opposed to the Portuguese-speaking world. Rodó's own views and priorities, along with his publishing decisions and epistolary contacts, worked to compound the effects of language. Analysis of Rodó's correspondence as collected in the 1967 edition of his *Obras completas* shows nothing like an active desire to forge ties with Luso-Brazilian writers. It is striking that of his forty-six listed correspondents, forty-five were Spanish-speakers, none was Portuguese, and only one, the *gaúcho* critic João Pinto da Silva, was Brazilian. Pinto received two very brief letters from Rodó in 1914 (the second possibly dates from 1915), after sending the Uruguayan writer articles on his work, presumably material collected in the volume *Vultos do Meu Caminho* (Notable Persons along My Path; Rodó, *OC* 1474–75). Importantly, it was Pinto who initiated the exchange. While Rodó paid lip service in his response to Pinto's friendship as hopefully "contibu[yendo] al acercamiento de dos países [i.e., Uruguay y Brasil] entre los cuales *ni aun el idioma puede considerarse distinto*"—an interesting observation to which I will return—there is no evidence that he attempted to develop the relationship (*OC* 1474; my emphasis).

If Rodó's essayistic writing is any indication, his knowledge of Luso-Brazilian literature and society was quite limited, despite his country's entangled history and shared border with Brazil. Rodó's *Obras completas* contain no reference to any Brazilian writer with the possible exception of Euclides da Cunha, author of *Os Sertões* (Rebellion in the Backlands, 1902); his substantive knowledge of Lusophone letters seems limited to Luís de Camões's epic poem *Os Lusíadas* (The Lusiads, 1572), and Almeida Garrett's poetic gloss on the poet's life in his *Camões* (1825).[17] Rodó references Camões on a few occasions, in the article "Americanismo literario" (1895), as well as in *El mirador de Próspero* and *Motivos de Proteo*, though only in passing, in conjunction with other writers, and with no mention of Luso-Brazilian literature generally.[18] Rodó makes similarly decontextualized mention of Garrett in *Motivos,* offering a very questionable interpretation of a footnote from Garrett's *Camões* in "Iberoamérica" (1910)—as I will discuss in section 3 of this chapter (Rodó, *OC* 372, 419, 689). Rodó, then, effectively fell victim to the ignorance and antiquarianism Rubén Darío observed among Spanish-speaking intellectuals in his 1896 profile of Portuguese poet Eugénio de Castro. Referring to his colleagues' limited engagement with Luso-Brazilian letters, Darío writes: "Close to us there is a great country, the child of Portugal, whose spiritual manifestations are completely ignored in the rest of the continent; and there is [. . .] in Portugal and in Brazil a literature that is worthy of universal attention and of study by men of ideas and art. In *our Spanish America* [*nuestra*

63

América española], knowledge of Portuguese-language literature is reduced to the scant number of those who have read Camões, for the most part in poor translations" (*Los raros* 233; my emphasis).

Rodó's broad unfamiliarity with and seeming disinterest in Luso-Brazilian letters, coupled with his virtually non-existent correspondence with Lusophone writers, contrasts sharply with his detailed knowledge of and engagement with literature in Spanish, as reflected in numerous essays and in his vigorous attempts to establish relationships with Spanish-speaking writers beyond Uruguay.[19] A broad look at Rodó's critical and epistolary production shows him especially interested in spreading his ideas to Spain, gaining the approval of Spanish masters like Miguel de Unamuno and Leopoldo Alas (aka Clarín), and reaffirming cultural, linguistic, and historical ties between Spain and its former colonies—the "mil cachorros sueltos del León Español," as Darío put it in the poem "A Roosevelt" (*Obras completas* 5: 879). Moreover, Rodó clearly believed in a *raza española*, a transatlantic category that, in line with his theory of Spanish-Portuguese linguistic equivalence, would implicitly extend to the Luso-Brazilian sphere. As Rodó wrote in an October 12, 1900 letter to Unamuno, "[s]i pudiéramos trabajar de acuerdo aquí y allá, y llegar a una gran armonía espiritual de *la raza española*, ¿qué más agradable y fecundo para todos?" (*OC* 1379; my emphasis).

II. The *Americanista* Paradigm, Language, and the *Magna Patria*

At this point it becomes incumbent to ask how Rodó understood Latin America as an *idea*, and to ask how Brazil might fit into this scheme. As various critics have noted, the "*americanista* theme" was central to Rodó's writing and intellectual practice (Ardao, *Rodó* 8). In this chapter I will use the term *americanismo*, as opposed to the potentially misleading "Americanism," to describe Rodó's broad continentalist agenda and his concern with a Latin American identity that is effectively equivalent to "Spanish America," as signaled by his interchangeable usage of the terms *América, nuestra América, América Latina,* and *Hispanoamérica*. As we shall see, this usage, which Rodó deploys in rhetorically extending the boundaries of the *magna patria* beyond Spanish-speaking Latin America, reflects a broader tendency in Spanish American continentalist discourse to project a *hispanoamericano* identity onto apparently liminal territories like Brazil.[20]

Rodó's *americanismo* was informed by such factors as the 1898 US intervention in the Cuban independence war and subsequent incorporation of Cuba, Puerto Rico, and the Philippines into its sphere of direct influence (Pérez Petit 151–54), as well as Rodó's experience of Uruguay's fractious party politics around the turn of the twentieth century (Rodríguez Monegal, in Rodó, *OC* 27–35), and especially by the examples of Simón Bolívar, whom he idolized as the "representativo de la eterna unidad hispanoamericana," and a generation of mid-nineteenth-century exiled Argentine writers (among them Juan Bautista Alberti, Juan Carlos Gómez, and Juan Maria Gutiérrez), whom Rodó remembered as laboring to strengthen ties between the Spanish American republics, particularly in the Southern Cone (Rodó, *OC* 551). In his long 1912 essay on Bolívar, Rodó credits the Venezuelan-born independence leader with having an "inquebrantable fe" in "la natural hermandad de los pueblos hispanoamericanos," and he prophesies that "[c]on más o menos dilación, en una u otra forma, un lazo político unirá un día a los pueblos de *la América nuestra*" (*OC* 554–55; my emphasis). Rodó's reference in the same piece to Bolívar's brief flirtation with the idea of "arrolla[ndo] hasta la misma corte del Brasil las huestes imperiales, [y] funda[ndo] allí la república," which I discussed in the previous chapter, compels us to ask the question of Brazil's *specific role* in Rodó's vision of Latin America (550). If Rodó were an adherent to Bolivarian federalism, which was republican and generally hostile to Brazil's constitutional monarchy (1822–89), then he would logically be compelled to exclude Brazil from his project for a united *América Latina*, or to use Bolívar's preferred term, *América meridional*. On the other hand, Rodó's references to Brazil elsewhere, particularly when he discusses the *magna patria* as a cultural as opposed to political unity, indicate that he *was* interested in Brazilian participation in a Latin America united in terms of culture and shared ideals.

The critic Arturo Ardao perceptively notes that Rodó often conflated the idea of "Spanish America" with "Latin America," or even with "America" as a whole, and observes that, "[f]ollowing a certain tradition, Rodó uses *América* (sometimes specified as '*la nuestra*'), *América Latina, Iberoamérica, Hispanoamérica* and even *América Española* throughout his career as equivalent terms for the same continental community [. . .] [H]e used *Iberoamérica* exceptionally and for circumstantial reasons, though with the same meaning [as the other terms]" (*Rodó* 7n, author's emphasis). Significantly, it is in the essay "Iberoamérica" (1910) that Rodó's examination of Brazilian-Spanish American relations compels him to utilize the term *Iberoamérica*. Far from coincidental, I believe that Rodó was forced here to adopt a new term, one unique to his criticism, precisely to account for Brazil as a country that did not easily fit into *América* as he understood it. In the following paragraphs I will analyze some of Rodó's key descriptions of Latin America as a linguistic, historical, cultural, and political unity, and then examine how he applies these ideas in his Brazil-themed pieces.

Rodó was a lifelong believer in the Spanish American *magna* or *máxima patria*, that is, the idea that in Spanish America one's discrete national identity (as a Uruguayan, for example) could be productively reinforced by a broader regional or supranational identification. It may be useful to take a chronological look at Rodó's writing on the topic. In one of his earliest pieces, "El Centenario de Bolívar," published in 1883 in the student journal *Los primeros albores,* Rodó calls on individuals from the "varios pueblos de América" to honor Bolívar's memory by freeing those who are "esclavos todavía de la dominación de un poder extranjero" (qtd. in Pérez Petit 59). This seems a clear reference to Cuba and Puerto Rico, still Spanish colonies in 1883, and a possible additional reference to Brazil, to the extent that imperial Brazil had traditionally been understood by Spanish American republicans, beginning with Bolívar, as foreign and "Portuguese" as opposed to genuinely "American."[21] Indeed, Rodó later described Bolívar's views on Brazil in his "Bolívar" (1912), and it is not impossible that Rodó would have been aware of this aspect of Bolívar's thinking in 1883, thereby substantiating the idea that "El Centenario de Bolívar" contains an implied critique of Brazil's imperial government (Rodó, *OC* 550). In any case, the piece announces the idea of a broader Spanish American *magna patria*, which Rodó would develop and defend in his mature career.

"Por la unidad de América," an open letter to Manuel Ugarte dated April 1, 1896, is one of the adult Rodó's earliest *americanista* documents. Here Rodó mentions several ideas that he would develop later, and which, through Rodó, would become commonplaces in subsequent Spanish American discourse on national and continental identity. These include: Spanish America's congenital *"internacionalidad,"* an unfortunate "desconocimiento de América por América misma" and consequent need to "estrech[ar] los lazos de confraternidad" (this point having been addressed five years earlier by Martí in "Nuestra América"); the need to fulfill Bolívar's dream of creating a united "Meridional America" at the level of "ideales y [. . .] tradiciones"; and most importantly, the idea that Spanish America, projected outward to coincide with all of "los pueblos del Nuevo Mundo" represents a "patria común" (Rodó, *OC* 831–32; author's emphasis). Also in 1896, Rodó published "La nueva novela: A propósito de 'Academias' de Carlos Reyles" (*Revista Nacional* 25 Dec. 1896, 2: 273–76), a text in which he uses the work of a fellow Uruguayan writer as an occasion to reiterate the case for Spanish American participation in "universal" culture (an argument later taken up by Jorge Luis Borges and Alfonso Reyes, among others), and to reaffirm Spanish America's linguistic and "racial" ties to Spain (Rodó, *OC* 159–61). True to Ardao's observation on terminology, Rodó effectively limits the problem of "American" literature and culture in "La nueva novela" to a Spanish-speaking America he claims as "ours." Rodó writes: "[A]l lado del hijo fiel de *nuestra América*, que se reconoce vinculado de lo íntimo de su ser a los particularismos de determinada parcialidad humana, que lleva entre las cosas propias de su espíritu el reflejo de cierta latitud de la tierra, —está en nosotros el ciudadano de la cultura universal, ante el que se desvanecen las clasificaciones que no obedezcan a profundas disimilitudes morales, como ante un espectador de las alturas" (*OC* 161; my emphasis). At the same time as Rodó implicitly narrows the field of his discussion to Spanish America, his sweeping, universalizing rhetoric extends the scope of Spanish-speaking "our America" far beyond its formal geographical boundaries, such that the ideal of an integrated, transatlantic, Spanish-speaking cultural sphere may be described as an "inmensa red nerviosa que el genio de una misma civilización extiende *del uno al otro extremo del planeta, como por una universal confederación de las almas*" (*OC* 162; my emphasis). Here Rodó follows the example of Bolívar in amplifying Spanish American continentalist discourse's projective tendency, extending the category of "Spanish America" to correspond with "the whole of the New World (*todo el Mundo Nuevo*)" as Bolívar had it in his 1815 "Carta de Jamaica" ("Jamaica" 172). As we will see, Rodó used this approach to great effect in several texts, including *Rubén Darío* (1899) and *Ariel* (1900).

Turning to Rodó's enumeration of the bases for a nation's inclusion in the *magna patria*, our author concludes "La vuelta de Juan Carlos Gómez," a speech on the nineteenth-century Uruguayan writer given on October 8, 1905, with the following revealing *americanista* flourish: "Señores: Alta es la idea de la patria; pero en los pueblos de *la América latina*, en esta viva armonía de naciones vinculadas por todos los lazos de la tradición, de la raza, de las instituciones, del idioma, como nunca las presentó juntas y abarcando tan vasto espacio la historia del mundo, bien podemos decir que hay algo aún más alto que la idea de la patria, y es la idea de *la América*: la idea de *la América*, concebida como una grande e imperecedera unidad, como una excelsa y *máxima patria*, con sus héroes, sus educadores, sus tribunos; desde el golfo de México hasta los hielos sempiternos del Sur" (*OC* 513; my emphasis). Despite Rodó's juxtaposition here of the terms *América latina, máxima patria,* and *América* pure and simple—which suggests a flexibility that would allow for Brazil's inclusion—his list of criteria for participation, including Spanish language and republican government, as well as his enumeration of an exclusively Spanish American list of eminent "ciudadanos de la intelectualidad americana," imply a Spanish American focus for his comments, if not an explicit restriction of his envisaged *magna patria* to the Spanish American republics.

Rodó reprises much of the discussion from "La vuelta de Juan Carlos Gómez" in the appropriately titled short piece "Magna Patria" (1905). Here he declares that fractious regionalism amounts to "algo aún más pequeño que un fetichismo patriótico," and cites "comunidad del origen, del idioma, de la tradición, de las costumbres, de las instituciones, de los intereses, de los destinos históricos, y la contigüidad geográfica" as

reasons for Spanish Americans to reject a narrow provincialism in favor of a multilayered sense of identity that would, in
a fashion reminiscent both of Johann Gottlieb Fichte's argument in his *Addresses to the German Nation* (1807–08), and
of federalist discourse, allow the Spanish American citizen to
successively identify with his province, region, nation, and continent.[22] Rodó explains: "Patria es para los hispanoamericanos
la América española. Dentro del sentimiento de la patria, cabe
el sentimiento de adhesión no menos natural indestructible, a la
provincia, a la región, a la comarca; y provincias, regiones o co-
marcas de *aquella gran patria nuestra* son las naciones en que
ella políticamente se divide" (627; my emphasis). Rodó repeats
this identification of "our" *gran patria* with a specifically *Spanish* America in "El Centenario de Chile" (1910), probably his
most famous speech. Here Rodó, who was sent to the Chilean
capital with an official Uruguayan delegation to attend centenary festivities, proposes that in addition to honoring the anniversary of Chile's independence, the assembled dignitaries (which
incidentally included representatives from Brazil),[23] should
commemorate a "magno centenario" that would extend to the
whole of Latin America. However, as in previous pieces Rodó's
argument is grounded in an understanding of a specifically
Spanish-origin *magna patria,* as he indicates at the opening of
the speech's third paragraph: "Por lo que tiene de americano,
permitidme que conceda preeminencia a este carácter [america-
no o hispanoamericano] sobre el otro. Más arriba del centenario
de Chile, del de la Argentina, del de México, yo siento y percibo
el centenario de *la América española.*" Rodó then cites a list of
familiar unifying factors including "comunidad del origen, de
la tradición, del idioma, de las costumbres, de las instituciones
[. . .] y [. . .] todo cuanto puede servir de fundamento a la unidad
de *una conciencia colectiva*" (*OC* 570; my emphasis). On the
other hand, Rodó includes Brazil in his discussion of the need to
"magnify" (*magnificar*) and "spread" (*dilatar*) a (Latin) American "consciousness"—this despite his insistence on a set of historical, linguistic, and political commonalities to which Brazil
is seemingly unable to adhere (570–71). Indeed, Rodó affirms:
"[C]abe levantar, sobre la patria nacional, la patria americana, y
acelerar el día en que los niños de hoy, los hombres del futuro,
preguntados cuál es el nombre de su patria, no contesten con el

nombre *del Brasil*, ni con el nombre de Chile, ni con el nombre de México, porque contesten con el nombre de América" (*OC* 571; my emphasis). Brazil's ambiguous place in the *magna patria* as sketched out in "La vuelta de Juan Carlos Gómez," "Magna Patria," and "El Centenario de Chile" seems nothing if not simultaneously *necessary* and *problematic*.

Months before his death in 1917, Rodó again declared his faith in the *magna patria*, though here, in the article "Al concluir el año" (1916), he argues that foreign (i.e., European) observers tend to overstate Latin American unity and ignore local differences—a less radical version of Brazilian writers Manoel Bomfim and Mário de Andrade's critiques of Latin Americanism as outlined in the previous chapter. Rodó explains:

> Para la mirada europea, toda la América española es una sola entidad, una sola imagen, un solo valor. La distancia desvanece límites políticos, disimilitudes geográficas, grados diversos de organización y cultura, y deja subsistente un simple contorno, una única idea: la idea de una América que procede históricamente de España y que habla en el idioma español. Esta relativa ilusión de la distancia, que a cada paso induce a falsas generalizaciones, a enormes errores de lugar, a juicios de que no aprovechan, por cierto, las mejores entre nuestras repúblicas, tiene, sin embargo, la virtud de corresponder a un fondo verdadero, a un hecho fundamental y trascendente, que acaso los hispanoamericanos no sentimos todavía en toda su fuerza y toda su eficacia: el hecho fundamental de que somos esencialmente "unos"; de que lo somos a pesar de las diferencias, más abultadas que profundas, en que es fácil reparar de cerca, y de que lo seremos aún más en el futuro, hasta que nuestra unidad espiritual rebose sobre las fronteras nacionales y prevalezca en realidad política. (*OC* 1289)

In his description of the European "idea of an America that is the historical outgrowth of Spain and that speaks the Spanish language," Rodó gestures toward the differences in language and colonial origin he glosses over in earlier texts like "El Centenario de Chile," though his proviso in "Al concluir el año" that there exists a "true basis" of Latin American *essential* unity such that "we are essentially 'one,'" suggests that though differences may exist, these are for Rodó ultimately of secondary importance. This implies that while Brazil may be *Portuguese* in linguistic and historical terms, as indicated by Darío, Brazil is more broadly *Spanish* in language (Portuguese apparently equal to or a variant of Spanish) and in its history (Portugal as part of Spain) (*Los raros* 233).

This admittedly jarring idea of Brazil as an effectively Spanish-speaking nation amounts to more than willful over-interpretation of Rodó's argument: for Rodó, commonality of language, even if overstated by foreigners, is responsible for the deep fellow-feeling that is key to the maintenance of Latin American unity, and to his *americanista* vision generally. Here language becomes, as Johann Gottfried Herder put it in his *Essay on the Origin of Language* (1770), the "very symbol of tribal identity" (169). While this may register as somewhat contradictory given Rodó's earlier critique of European commentators' fixation on Spanish language as a privileged sign of Latin American unity, it is consistent with Rodó's understanding of language as not only a marker of shared identity, but as the vehicle by which national or supranational unity is achieved—a typically Romantic view of language and national literature as embodying a given people's unique character or "genius." As Rodó explains in "La enseñanza del idioma" (1910): "El idioma es a la personalidad colectiva de un pueblo lo que el estilo a la personalidad del escritor; [. . .] Un pueblo que descuida su lengua, como un pueblo que descuida su historia, no están distantes de perder el sentimiento de sí mismos y de dejar disolverse y anularse su personalidad." Further, Rodó specifically binds together his arguments for Spanish America's linguistic and historical unity, writing of the Spanish tongue that "esta lengua, para las naciones hispanoamericanas, no puede ser otra [que la española], fundamentalmente, que aquella que las vincula a la tradición humana de la civilización; que las vincula entre ellas mismas, manteniendo para lo por venir el lazo de una unidad preciosísima, y que, dentro de cada una de ellas, sirve de vínculo con el propio pasado y de expresión connatural a todos los accidentes de la vida" (*OC* 653).

Rodó paid particular attention to this theme during his final years—the same period in which "Al concluir el año" was written. In a February 28, 1913, letter to the Spanish Academy, in which he accepted the body's invitation for him to join as a corresponding member, Rodó discusses the role of the "gloriosa lengua castellana" as a bond (*vínculo*) capable of "estrech[ando] las relaciones entre España y la América" at the literary and fraternal levels (*OC* 1194). Rodó argues along similar lines in the article "El Centenario de Cervantes" (1915), referring alternately to *esta América nuestra* and *la América de habla española*, and presenting Spanish as the region's language and Cervantes as its "escritor-arquetipo" (*OC* 1210–11). Rodó writes: "[E]sa persistente herencia [latina y española] no tiene manifestación más representativa y cabal que la del idioma, donde ella se resume toda entera y aparece adaptando a sus medios connaturales de expresión las adquisiciones y evoluciones sucesivas. Confirmar la fidelidad a esa forma espiritual que es el idioma y glorificarla en el recuerdo de su escritor-arquetipo [i.e., Cervantes], es, pues, el modo más adecuado y más sincero con que *América* puede mostrar el género de solidaridad que reconoce con la obra de sus descubridores y civilizadores" (*OC* 1210–11; my emphasis). While this argument would certainly not have registered in Brazil (a country whose European "archetypal writer" would be Camões), this does not stop Rodó from marshalling Brazilian examples in defending his audacious argument that "América nació para que muriese Don Quijote." He elaborates: "Mientras se disipan en el aire los mentidos tesoros de la cueva de Montesinos, fulguran con deslumbradora realidad la plata de Potosí, el oro de México, *los diamantes y esmeraldas del Brasil*" (*OC* 1211–12; my emphasis).[24] Though Rodó may want to view Brazilians as fellow Latin Americans or even fellow Spanish Americans, the problem he fails to confront is that while Brazil may be endowed with great "treasures" (mineral, cultural, and otherwise), Brazilians seemingly insist on speaking Portuguese, a language they (along with linguists in general) consider distinct from Spanish. As we will see in the next section, Rodó, building on his comment on Spanish-Portuguese linguistic equivalence from his letter to João Pinto da Silva, arrives at a solution that might alternately be described as ingeniously bold or rather narrow-minded.

Turning to his major essays, one of Rodó's central concerns in *Rubén Darío* (1899) is to present the Nicaraguan writer against the backdrop of a literary tradition he refers to as "American," though which is unmistakably Spanish American. While Rodó praises Darío for his literary originality and for his role in renovating the Spanish language through his use of borrowed French terms and structures, he rejects the idea of Darío as a representative poet for Spanish America (a role he analogously presents Walt Whitman as playing for the United States), stating flatly at the opening of the essay that, "[i]ndudablemente, Rubén Darío no es el poeta de América" (*OC* 169). As in "La nueva novela," Rodó limits his discussion of the project to create a "free and autonomous" art to Spanish America, drawing exclusively on Spanish-language examples (with the exception of Whitman, whom he clearly defines as foreign) and speaking of the renovation of an identifiably Spanish language (169, 179, 189–90). Despite this frame of reference, Rodó is unwilling in *Rubén Darío* to abandon a continentalist rhetoric that presents Spanish America as extending beyond its borders to coincide with the whole of America—even at the risk of contradicting his opposition between Darío–*nuestra América* and Whitman–United States. Rodó writes:

> Confesémoslo: *nuestra América* actual es, para el Arte, un suelo bien poco generoso. Para obtener poesía, de las formas, cada vez más vagas e inexpresivas de su sociabilidad, es ineficaz el reflejo; sería necesaria la refracción en un cerebro de iluminado, la refracción en el cerebro de Walt Whitman. —Quedan, es cierto, nuestra Naturaleza soberbia, y las originalidades que se refugian, progresivamente estrechadas, en la vida de los campos. —Fuera de esos dos motivos de inspiración, los poetas que quieren expresar, en forma universalmente inteligible para las almas superiores, modos de pensar y sentir enteramente cultos [. . .] deben renunciar a un verdadero sello de *americanismo* original. (*OC* 169; my emphasis)

Moving to *Ariel*, here Rodó employs the same strategy he utilized in *Rubén Darío* of rhetorically projecting Spanish America onto the whole of the hemisphere. Rodó begins *Ariel* with his famous dedication of the text to "la juventud de América," though analysis of *Ariel* and of Rodó's broader *americanista* program confirms that his intended audience is found in the rising generation of Spanish American—and Spanish—writers and intellectuals (*OC* 206). Rodó makes several references in *Ariel* to America's "present," "destiny," and "life" (211–12, 224), though as in *Rubén Darío* he uses the *nuestra América/*

Norteamérica dichotomy to identify the former with a Spanish or Latin American "us" and the latter with a North American "them," as he makes clear in the following consideration on democratic revolution: "Hay, en la cuestión que plantean estos juicios severos, un interés vivísimo, para los que amamos—al mismo tiempo—por convencimiento, la obra de la Revolución, que en *nuestra América* se enlaza además con las glorias de su Génesis; y por instinto, la posibilidad de una noble y selecta vida espiritual que en ningún caso haya de ver sacrificada su serenidad augusta a los caprichos de la multitud" (*OC* 224; my emphasis). This specifically Spanish or Latin American frame is underscored by Rodó's extended contrast in *Ariel* between US–identified utilitarianism and Latin American idealism, which draws on Rubén Darío's earlier identification of the US with Shakespeare's Caliban from his 1894 article. Here Rodó admonishes a specifically Latin American public to avoid uncritical imitation of the United States, "esa democracia formidable y fecunda [. . ..] *allá* en el Norte" (*OC* 232; my emphasis). Rodó repeatedly affirms *nuestra América* as the point of reference for his analysis of the US, joining himself (or the Shakespearean Prospero, whom he recasts as an elder intellectual sage, and who functions as his narrating stand-in) and his audience in the idea of *nosotros*: "[L]a vida norteamericana no *nos* ofrece aún un nuevo ejemplo de esa relación indudable [entre lo material y lo espiritual], ni *nos* lo anuncia como gloria de una posteridad que se vislumbre. *Nuestra* confianza y *nuestros* votos deben inclinarse a que, en un porvenir más inaccesible a la inferencia, esté reservado a *aquella* civilización [i.e., los EEUU] un destino superior" (*OC* 242; my emphasis).

Rodó's lack of reference in *Ariel* to particular Latin American countries and his tendency toward sweeping continentalist rhetoric perhaps make it difficult to establish whether in this text "Latin America" is strictly synonymous with "Spanish America"—an important distinction in determining if Rodó intended his argument to apply to Brazil. However, his allusions to *Ariel* in his correspondence seem to make this point clear. In a March 20, 1900 letter to Unamuno, Rodó first describes *Ariel* as an "obra de *acción*" directed toward "la juventud de América," though he then specifies that his "America" is in fact that portion of the continent that looks to Spain as its "venerable home" (1375; author's emphasis). He explains: "La repercusión de la propaganda que yo quiero promover en esa España que todavía *consideramos* como el hogar venerable de *nuestra raza y nuestro espíritu* [. . .] significaría para mí muchísimo, porque daría a mi propaganda una sanción invalorable" (*OC* 1375; my emphasis). And in a January 29, 1908 letter to Rafael Altamira, Rodó mentions that *Ariel* is still "provoca[ndo] animados comentarios y levanta[ndo] ecos de simpatía en *toda América*," but then refers specifically to "las nuevas generaciones de *Hispanoamérica*" (1363; my emphasis).

These epistolary clarifications appear to disqualify Brazil from membership in the *magna patria*, unless Brazil can somehow be presented as looking to "Spain" as its European point of origin—a live possibility for Rodó, given his stated view of Spanish-Portuguese linguistic equivalence. This said, Rodó acknowledges the capacity for semantic misinterpretation in *Ariel*, foreshadowing his later discussion of European misconceptions of Latin America in the article "Al concluir el año" and providing an opening for a discussion of Brazil's ambiguous position with regard to the *magna patria*. While, as Ardao notes, Rodó lays claim to the idea of *americanismo* throughout his writing, Rodó observes at the opening of his discussion of the US in *Ariel* that this term is identified in Europe with North American utilitarianism, as "la fórmula de lo que ha solido llamarse [. . .] el espíritu de *americanismo*" (231; author's emphasis). This recognition of *americanismo*'s capacity for multiple, perhaps contradictory meanings seems to force Rodó in his following statements to refer to a specifically non-North American "Hispano-América" as the potential site of "una América *deslatinizada*" (232; author's emphasis).[25] Rodó also concedes that *América* need not be construed as equivalent to Spanish America, but might be defined as encompassing a hemispheric duality, as Ranke, Hegel, and Chevalier had proposed early in the nineteenth century, to be followed by Francisco Bilbao, José María Torres Caicedo and finally José Martí in later decades. In *Ariel*, this dualistic conception of *América* can be seen in Rodó's description of Latin and North America as "dos águilas" with the former representing Athens (or Latin America) and the latter Sparta (or the US) (233).

This dualistic conception of *América,* presented allegorically as "two eagles," and frequently described by Rodó (and Martí) in the opposition between *nuestra América* and *la otra América,* would become one of the more prominent features of Rodó's writing to be taken up by later Spanish American intellectuals. It is reasonable to suppose that the simplistic elegance of this racialized opposition between "Latins" and "Anglo-Saxons" or "Teutons," enshrined in the nineteenth century by writers in both the Old and New Worlds, and made urgent in Latin America by the consolidation of US geopolitical, economic, and military dominance over the hemisphere, is partially responsible for the attention given in Spanish American intellectual production to comparative US–Latin America analyses, at the expense of other approaches—including Luso-Hispanic comparativism. As will be shown in the next section, Rodó himself wrote relatively little on Brazil or on Brazilian–Spanish American relations, though what he *did* write is important in illustrating how the Uruguayan essayist was forced to adapt his *americanista* vision to a country that in many ways is marked as distinct from Spanish-speaking Latin America.

III. All of the Latin American Nations, including Brazil?

Over the course of his career, Rodó published a total of four texts that directly address Brazil. The first is a speech given on September 24, 1909 at Montevideo's Círculo de la Prensa (published the following day in the *El Día* newspaper), in which Rodó reflects on an impending border treaty with Brazil to regularize maritime access to the Río Yaguarón and the Laguna Merín (in Portuguese: *Jaguarão* and *Mirim*) on the Brazilian-Uruguayan border. The second, "Iberoamérica" (1910), is a truncated version of a speech Rodó would have given in Rio de Janeiro in 1910 in commemoration of the recently signed treaty, but for his last-minute removal from the Uruguayan delegation.[26] "Iberoamérica" was later published in the collection *El mirador de Próspero* in 1913, along with a third text, the eulogistic "Rio Branco: En ocasión de su muerte," which discusses the legacy of Brazil's highly influential foreign minister. Rodó's final published Brazil-themed text was "Cielo y agua" (1916), an impressionistic recollection of Rio de Janeiro and Guanabara Bay written as Rodó was beginning a maritime journey to Europe. This was published in the Argentine publication *Caras y Caretas* before being collected in Rodó's posthumous travel volume *El camino de Paros* (1918). It was en route to Europe, where he died in 1918 (in Palermo), that Rodó made his sole visit to Brazil, stopping very briefly in Brazilian ports along the way (Etcheverry 8). In addition to the aforementioned texts, Rodó's November 11, 1909 legislative speech on the treaty and his unpublished 1910 speech will be considered in demonstrating that while Rodó stated or implied on several occasions that he viewed Brazil as part of Latin America, his argumentation on the *magna patria*—as seen in major texts like *Ariel* and in his Brazil-themed pieces—may lead one to the opposite conclusion.

Despite the inconsistencies to be seen in Rodó's treatment of Brazil in relation to the *magna patria*, I am confident that if we could ask Rodó if he considered Brazil a part of Latin America, he would on balance have responded in the affirmative. He implied as much in "El Centenario de Chile" (1910), in which he declares that in the future, when asked about their nationality, Latin Americans "no contest[arán] con el nombre *del Brasil*, ni con el nombre de Chile, ni con el nombre de México, porque contest[arán] con el nombre de América" (*OC* 571; my emphasis). Rodó builds on this characterization in his unpublished 1910 speech and in "Cielo y agua," presenting Guanabara Bay (here a synecdoche for Brazil as a whole) as the "pórtico del continente," and writing that "[p]or este arco triunfal [de la bahía] debió de penetrar a la Atlántida soñada, para consagrarla en la historia, el genio latino. Aquí, aquí y no en otra parte, debieron de tocar las carabelas de la sublime aventura, y plantar el pendón y la primera cruz" (Etcheverry 21; Rodó, *OC* 1245).[27]

Rodó applies the fraternal language and *americanista* vision that typify his writing on Brazil in his September 24, 1909 speech, which he gave to a visiting delegation of Brazilian journalists and students. Rodó states that the treaty, "no sólo estrechará los *lazos fraternales* de nuestras dos naciones, sino que será en el tiempo *una gloria americana*."[28] José Enrique Etcheverry, author of *Rodó y el Brasil* (1950), notes a curious and important feature of Rodó's speech: instead of focusing exclusively on the treaty's reciprocal benefits for Uruguay and Brazil, Rodó "amplifies the resonance and significance of [the treaty], giving it an American transcendence" (12). This is consistent with the universalizing rhetoric that marks Rodó's writing on the *magna patria*, as well as the broader imperative felt by a number of Spanish American exegetes when confronted with the challenge represented by Brazil: to project a *hispanoamericana* identity onto that nation. Also following the general pattern, Rodó encounters a snag in attempting to describe Brazil as part of *América* writ large, and is forced to acknowledge the particularity of Brazilian history, which he writes has been "caracterizado, más que por violentas transiciones revolucionarias, por el ritmo de una firme y segura evolución" (Rodó, *OC* 1063).

The *americanista* framework within which Rodó approaches Brazil and the border treaty is likewise apparent in his November 11, 1909 speech to the lower house of the Uruguayan legislature (Rodó was a three-time legislator, 1902–05, 1908–11, and 1911–14). Here he argues for ratification, and anticipates the argument he would make in "Bolívar" (1912) regarding Latin America's prospects for long-term political unity (555). He states:

> América tiende, desde sus orígenes, por el pensamiento consciente de sus emancipadores, de los fundadores de los pueblos que la constituyen, a formar una confederación de naciones. Esta confederación de naciones será primero una confederación moral, una armonía de intereses, de sentimientos, de ideas. Será, algún día muy lejano, una gran unidad política, como lo soñaba el libertador Bolívar [. . .] Hechos como el que va a realizarse, manifiesten [. . .] que esa idea grandiosa no fue sólo una utopía nacida de las fiebres del genio; que hay en el fondo de esa idea el presentimiento de un porvenir, remoto quizá, pero seguro. (1132)

These speeches, then, show that Rodó placed Brazil squarely at the center of his continentalist project. However, Rodó seems aware of the fact that incorporating Brazil into Latin America—even rhetorically—presented certain problems, and he struggles in his writings and speeches that deal with Brazil's place in Latin America to incorporate Brazil into his vision of a continent united by a common (implicitly Spanish) origin and language, by a shared commitment to classical values, and by anti-imperialistic solidarity. Consequently, I believe that Etcheverry is mistaken in implying that Rodó *seamlessly* integrated Brazil into his *ameri-*

canista vision, and his claim that Rodó considered Brazil one of the continent's most representative nations likewise seems inaccurate (Etcheverry 25–26). Rodó—as with practitioners of Spanish American continentalist discourse generally—risked historical inaccuracy in folding Brazil into a Bolivarian narrative of republican independence struggle and projected confederation. This "bolivarization" of Brazil is of course problematic for historical reasons (Brazil gained its independence in 1822 as a constitutional monarchy, not via republican revolt against Spain; Bolívar refused to concede Brazilians the title of *americanos* and did not view Brazil as a continental partner), and moreover, for its potential to propagate a distorted view of Brazil's historical participation in Latin America, given Rodó's degree of influence in Spanish American letters.

The difficulties Rodó faced in incorporating Brazil into his vision of Latin America become particularly apparent in examining "Iberoamérica" and the longer unpublished speech on which it is based. As Ardao notes, the subject of Luso-Hispanic relations that Rodó set out to address in "Iberoamérica" forced him to abandon his preferred terminology (*América, nuestra América, Hispanoamérica*), in favor of *Iberoamérica*, a term that is unique to this piece and to the 1910 speech. It seems significant that it is precisely the question of Brazil's place in Latin America that prompts Rodó's terminological shift (Ardao, *Rodó* 7). After opening "Iberoamérica" by affirming that the South American people are defied by the "genio de una grande y única raza," Rodó declares:

> No necesitamos los sudamericanos, cuando se trata de abonar esta unidad de raza, hablar de una América latina; no necesitamos llamarnos latinoamericanos para levantarnos a un nombre general que nos comprenda a todos, porque podemos llamarnos algo que signifique una unidad mucho más íntima y concreta: podemos llamarnos "iberoamericanos," nietos de la heroica y civilizadora raza que *sólo políticamente se ha fragmentado en dos naciones europeas;* y aún podríamos ir más allá y decir que el mismo nombre de hispanoamericanos conviene a los nativos del Brasil. (Rodó, *OC* 689; my emphasis)

Here Rodó draws on an argument typical of iberianism, which we may succinctly define as a position that favors closer political, economic, or intellectual-cultural ties between Portugal and Spain—and by extension, between Brazil and Spanish America. Iberianists, among whom feature several prominent nineteenth- and early twentieth-century peninsular intellectuals (Antero de Quental, J.P. de Oliveira Martins, Juan Valera, and Miguel de Unamuno, for example), argue that a deeply rooted Iberian cultural unity, symbolized in the Roman-era designation *Hispania,* supersedes the peninsula's (apparently artificial) political division into two competing nation-states—Portugal and Spain.[29] Iberianists note that *Hispania* referred to the peninsula as a whole and was the ancestor of the terms *España/ Espanha* and *españoles/espanhóis.* According to the iberianist argument, any self-identified Iberian or Ibero-American may cite historical precedent in describing him/herself as "Spanish," and may cite "Spain" as his/her immediate or ancestral homeland.[30] Romantic-era contributions to historical linguistics likely inform this position: Herder's observation in his *Ideas for a Philosophy of the History of Mankind* (1784–91) regarding shades of racial and linguistic difference (with Portugal and Spain here representing, to paraphrase Herder, "different shades of the same great picture which extends through all ages and all parts of the earth") would prove useful in providing the historical and anthropological bases for the iberianists' project of political and cultural approximation (284).[31] Iberianists have frequently bemoaned the fact that the Spanish nation-state lays exclusive claim to the idea of "Spain" and to "Spanish" nationality, thereby depriving those excluded from the Castile-dominated political order of their "right" to these terms. This argument is premised on the confidence of iberianists—and as we shall see, of Rodó—that non-Castilian Iberians (Portuguese, for example) or Ibero-Americans (Brazilians, in this case) would view their "Spanish-ness" as a "right" to be claimed, as opposed to an inaccurate description to be cast off.

Rodó broadens his argument for Brazil as a part of a Spanish-identified *Hispanoamérica* in his unpublished 1910 speech, in which he argues that Portuguese and Spanish are essentially the same language ("dos matices de un solo idioma"), and that Brazilians are effectively fellow Spanish-speakers—an argument he would allude to in his 1914 letter to João Pinto da Silva. Rodó observes:

[Y]o nunca he podido acostumbrarme a considerar como dos lenguas distintas el portugués y el castellano. Las he considerado siempre más bien, como *dos modulaciones, como dos matices de un solo idioma.* Y esta relación de *semejanza intrínseca, de casi identidad,* se complementa con las vinculaciones históricas elocuentísimas [. . .] [L]a hermandad literaria del portugués es tal que la lírica española nació balbuceando un verso casi portugués, el dulce y gracioso verso de los Cancioneros; y en cambio, en el siglo de oro de la historia y las letras de Portugal, apenas hay poeta, apenas hay escritor que no cultive al mismo tiempo que el portugués, el castellano. El más grande de todos, Camoens, rimó *en lengua española* la parte más preciosa y pujante de su obra lírica. *Son, lo repito, dos [matices] de un idioma único.* Cuando los hombres de habla castellana, leemos u oímos pronunciar una frase en idioma portugués, nos parece que llega a nosotros una frase en nuestro propio idioma envuelta en un velo suave y matizado que filtrase su excesivo fulgor, o modulada por voz íntima que mitigase la rotundidad de bronce del idioma del Romancero. (qtd. in Etcheverry 23; my emphasis, Etcheverry's brackets around "matices")

Rodó's description of Portuguese as equivalent to Spanish, though distinct in "tone" and wearing a sort of linguistic veil (*velo suave y matizado*) that metaphorically works to smooth out the rough edges of the Castilian language and character, both recycles a literary figure from Herder,[32] and is typical of the metaphorical descriptions that have historically been employed to "explain" Portuguese relative to Spanish.[33] Rodó adheres to the iberianist pattern in his recourse to metaphor, in his invocation of differentiating linguistic and character traits (Luso-Brazilian softness and smoothness vs. Castilian and Spanish American hardness and robustness), and in his insistence on a hispanocentric speaking position ("Cuando los hombres de habla castellana, leemos u oímos . . ."), which forces Portuguese into the paradoxical situation of being both identical to Spanish and "Spanish with a difference," or as Rodó puts it, "two tones of the same language." While this argument for Brazilians as Spanish-speakers invites logical objections and risks inflaming Luso-Brazilian nationalism, it serves the critical function in Rodó's writing of grounding his program for Latin American unity. As we have seen, Rodó repeatedly defines Latin America as an ideal unity, a *magna patria* bonded by a common, specifically *Spanish* language and origin, among other elements. Confronted with evidence of Brazilian historical and linguistic difference, yet unwilling to abandon the idea of the *magna patria*, Rodó adopts a strategy on the more extreme end of the spectrum of identity projection described in this book's opening chapter. Instead of merely implying that Brazil is part of Spanish America, as he does elsewhere, here Rodó boldly affirms the "right" of Brazilians to declare themselves Spanish Americans in identity, heritage, and language. This assumes that Brazilians would want to identify themselves in this way, which a cursory examination of nineteenth- and twentieth-century Luso-Brazilian reflections on national identity would show to be far from a consensus view.

An additional problematic feature of Rodó's argument in "Iberoamérica" is found in the paraphrase that serves as its lynchpin, and which is taken from the Portuguese Romantic writer and liberal politician Almeida Garrett (1799–1854). Garrett's views on Portugal's political relationship with Spain were decidedly more cautious than Rodó implies, and he, unlike Rodó, did not equate cultural *iberismo* with political unionism. Rodó's choice of Garrett as opposed to a more sympathetic and solidly iberianist voice—such as Oliveira Martins, a hispanophile whose *História da Civilização Ibérica* (History of Iberian Civilization, 1879) was widely read in Spanish-speaking intellectual circles—along with his questionable interpretation of Garrett, underscores his broader unfamiliarity with Luso-Brazilian letters, as discussed earlier in this chapter. Rodó introduces Garrett in this way:

> [Y]o lo confirmo [que los portugueses y brasileños puedan llamarse de españoles] con la autoridad de Almeida Garret: porque, siendo el nombre de España, en su sentido original y propio, un nombre geográfico, un nombre de región y no un nombre de nacionalidad, el Portugal de hoy tiene, en rigor, tan cumplido derecho a participar de ese nombre geográfico de España como las partes de la Península que constituyen la actual nacionalidad española; por lo cual Almeida Garret, el poeta por excelencia del sentimiento nacional lusitano, afirmaba que los portugueses podían, sin menoscabo de su ser independiente, llamarse también, y con entera propiedad, españoles. (*OC* 689)

Rodó's knowledge of Garrett seems limited to his long biographical poem *Camões* (1825), which may have attracted Rodó because of his modest interest in the author of the *Lusíadas*. Then again, Rodó may have only had indirect knowledge of Garrett's poem: the Spanish writer-critic Juan Valera—whom Rodó read[34] —published an article on iberianism (part of a series) in the journal *El Contemporáneo* on December 6, 1861, in which he misreads Garrett in a manner that is strikingly similar to Rodó: "From the Spanish armed intervention in Portugal in 1847, the idea of the Iberian Union [. . .] spread and became commonplace and well-received in both countries. In Portugal, the most eminent men adopted it as their own [. . .] [T]he great poet Almeida Garrett said in the most famous of his works: 'Spaniards we are, and Spaniards we should be proud to be'" (231). It is worth noting that Valera's interpretation of Garrett conveniently reinforces the pro-unionist argument he (like Rodó) makes in the article, as well as reflects a broader interest in Luso-Brazilian culture (not shared by Rodó) on display in Valera's criticism and in novels such as *Genio y figura* (1897) and *Morsamor* (1899), which utilize Luso-Brazilian settings, motifs, and source materials.

The passage from *Camões* to which Rodó almost certainly refers in "Iberoamérica" is a footnote to the text's third canto, a marginal (though interesting) observation which reads as follows:

> Nem uma só vez se achará em nossos escritores a palavra "espanhol" designando exclusivamente o habitante da Península não português. Enquanto Castela esteve separada de Aragão, e já muito depois de unida a Leão, etc., nós e as outras nações das Espanhas, Aragoneses, Granadiz, Castelhanos, Portugueses e todos, éramos por estranhos e domésticos comummente chamados *espanhóis;* assim como ainda hoje chamamos alemão indistintamente ao Prussiano, Saxónio, Hanoveriano, Austríaco; assim como o Napolitano e o Milanês, o Veneziano e o Piemontês indiscriminadamente recebem o nome de italianos. A fatal perda da nossa independência política depois da batalha de Alcácer-Quibir, deu o título de reis das Espanhas aos de Castela e Aragão, que o conservaram ainda depois da gloriosa restauração de 1640. Mas Espanhóis somos, e de Espanhóis nos devemos prezar todos os que habitamos esta península. (Garrett 1: 432; author's emphasis)[35] [4]

A cursory look at this passage, at the rest of *Camões,* and at Garrett's broader oeuvre reveals Rodó (and Valera) to have clearly misrepresented Garrett's views. Garrett's reference to the "fatal loss of our political independence" with the Spanish monarch Felipe II's ascent to the Portuguese throne in 1580 (which inaugurated sixty years of dynastic union, frequently remembered as occupation in Portugal), makes his position clear: while some Portuguese (and by implication, Brazilians) may consider themselves geographically, historically, and culturally "Spanish" and may legitimately take an interest in Iberian culture, this does not make Luso-Hispanic political union desirable. Garrett underscores this distinction in his essay *Portugal na Balança da Europa* (Portugal in the Balance of Europe, 1830), mentioning Spain's "incessant desire" to annex Portugal, and denouncing the "mad, anti-national projects of some hallucinated Portuguese who [. . .] [wish] to promote and *nationalize,* if I may use this repugnant expression, the idea of union with Spain." Garrett concludes *Portugal na Balança* with a statement clearly designed to rally his Portuguese readers to his program of liberalizing national reform, declaring that Portugal must either achieve "true independence, that is, independence with liberty and the institutions to secure it, —or union with Spain" (1: 928–29; author's emphasis). Moreover, while Garrett acknowledges the common origin of the Spanish and Portuguese languages, he would have been quite uncomfortable with Rodó's argument for their effective equivalence. In his "Bosquejo da História da Poesia e Língua Portuguesa" (Sketch of the History of Portuguese Poetry and Language, 1826), Garrett argued that Portuguese and Spanish only reached a "complete state of perfection and character [as] erudite and civilized languages" once Portugal and Spain separated both politically and linguistically (1: 485). For Rodó, the essentially "Spanish" character of the Portuguese language serves as evidence for Brazil's eventual integration into a future Latin American political unity, whereas for Garrett, the health of Portuguese is tied to its cultivation as a separate, albeit related tongue, and to continued Luso-Brazilian political sovereignty. This implies Portugal's continued independence from the rest of the peninsula, and by implication, Brazilian independence from an (as yet unrealized) Spanish American federation of the type dreamed of by Rodó.

***

As an illustration of the stakes attending Rodó's characterizations of Brazil and its relationship to the idea of Latin America, the Uruguayan writer's misrepresentation of Garrett has been reproduced in the work of at least one other critic. In a 1918 article for *Hispania,* Aurelio M. Espinosa cited Rodó's discussion of Garrett as evidence that Brazil should be considered a Spanish American country, and that the term "Latin America" is deceptively vague, a position that apparently echoed Spanish philologist Ramón Menéndez Pidal (Espinosa 142–43). In this way, Rodó's influence allowed for Espinosa's misinterpretation of Garrett to enter into the quiver, so to speak, of arguments available for extending the rhetorical borders of Spanish America so as to comprehend Brazil.

Building on this idea of "stakes," it may be useful by way of conclusion to ask as to the significance of examining Rodó's efforts, illustrated in a few apparently minor pieces, to fit Brazil into the vision of a Latin American *magna patria* that he elucidated in his better-known texts. In my view, the significance is twofold: first, the question of Brazil affords us a unique and underexamined perspective on Rodó's writing, particularly his shorter critical prose, just as Brazil serves, I would argue, as a privileged point of entry for us to reexamine prevailing, hispanocentric definitions of Latin America, which from the publication of *Ariel* in 1900 have been profoundly influenced by Rodó—particularly in terms of the oppositions he draws between Ariel and Caliban, *nuestra America* and *la otra América,* and so forth. These dualisms work to obscure important cross-border relationships, whether configured along a North-South or Luso-Hispanic axis. And second, Rodó's status as a foundational figure in Spanish American essayistic and critical writing and in *continentalista* discourse makes the examination of his views on Brazil, along with his attempts to fit the country into his vision of the *magna patria* and his misreadings of Luso-Brazilian literary materials, vitally important if we are to understand how prominent Spanish American essayists have characterized and mischaracterized Brazil, and how their counterparts in Brazil have responded in their own characterizations of Brazil's relationship to Spanish America.

Moving across the Luso-Hispanic frontier, the next chapter will examine the case of another foundational figure, Brazilian writer-diplomat Joaquim Nabuco, whose ideas on slavery, government, and Pan-Americanism have exerted an appreciable influence on Brazilian intellectual life, and whose views on Brazilian–Spanish American relations, while not nearly as studied as the aforementioned aspects, provide us with a powerful example of one Brazilian writer's selective, partial approximation to Spanish America, mediated in this case by Nabuco's fear of his country's *sul-americanização,* or "South Americanization."

Chapter Three

Joaquim Nabuco

Monarchy's End and the
"South Americanization" of Brazil

Estamos no redemoinho republicano da América.
Somos um cadáver girando no sorvedouro da anarquia. Em tal estado devemos abandonar a sociedade ao seu destino ou fundar uma nova pátria no
estrangeiro, os que têm filhos? Se nada pode salvar
a nação, é preciso lutar para elevar socialmente a
minoria, a parte moral da sociedade [. . .] Temos,
pois, que ficar brasileiros, vendo o Brasil tornar-se
uma Venezuela, um México, uma Argentina, um
Chile; propriedade do déspota do dia. [5]
—Joaquim Nabuco
diary entry, 28 Feb. 1891

O Chile tinha um Governo forte como nós nunca
tivemos [. . .] Destruir um governo que tem dado os
mais admiráveis resultados para pôr em lugar dele
uma mera teoria, é ausência de senso prático. [6]
—Joaquim Nabuco
Balmaceda (1895)

Joaquim Nabuco (1849–1910) was one of late nineteenth- and
early twentieth-century Brazil's most important public intellectuals, active across the spectrum of journalism, politics,
diplomacy, and social activism during the later years of Brazil's
Second Empire (1840–89), and the early years of the Republic
that followed. Nabuco, the son of a prominent liberal politician
and a member of an aristocratic Pernambuco family with deep
roots in the northeastern sugar economy, made several important contributions to Brazilian intellectual history, including
the anti-slavery tract *O Abolicionismo* (Abolitionism, 1883); a

four-volume biography of his father, the statesman José Tomás Nabuco de Araújo, *Um Estadista do Império* (A Statesman of the Empire, 1898–1899); and a memoir, *Minha Formação* (My Formation, 1900). Among Nabuco's many lesser-known texts is *Balmaceda* (1895), originally published in Brazil as a series of newspaper pieces on Chile's Revolution of 1891, and a volume that contains some of Nabuco's most revealing and incisive critical prose. Nabuco regularly contributed to Brazilian newspapers and journals, served various terms as a *deputado* (i.e., member of the lower house of the imperial-era legislature) for Pernambuco, and was a leader of the Brazilian abolitionist movement; legal slavery was finally abolished in Brazil in 1888, in part due to Nabuco's persistent denunciations in the legislature, the press, and public rallies. As a member of Brazil's imperial and republican-era diplomatic corps, Nabuco represented his country in New York, London, Rome, and finally in Washington, DC as Brazil's first ambassador to the United States. In Washington, Nabuco cultivated close relationships with members of Theodore Roosevelt's administration and was a key Latin American supporter of US-sponsored Pan-Americanism. Nabuco was a contemporary and associate of several important Brazilian writers and public intellectuals, including Machado de Assis, Manuel de Oliveira Lima, Euclides da Cunha, and Eduardo Prado, and was a friend of the imperial family. At home and abroad Nabuco, nicknamed "Quincas o Belo" (Quincas the Handsome) for his good looks, polished charm, and Anglophile style, was an active member of high society, hobnobbing with kings, politicians, plutocrats, popes, society matrons, and writers, including Portugal's great nineteenth-century novelist Eça de Queiroz and Nicaraguan *modernista* poet Rubén Darío.[1]

Nabuco described himself in his memoir as a "dilettante," writing: "Sou antes um espectador do meu século do que do meu país" (*Minha Formação* 53; "I am more a spectator of my century than of my country"). Indeed, the cosmopolitan Nabuco was a regular visitor to Europe and occasionally wrote in French or English rather than his native Portuguese. And despite his abolitionist views, Nabuco at times described black Brazilians and other non-whites, particularly Chinese immigrants, with an appreciable prejudice, if not outright disdain. Bearing all this in mind, it is tempting to cast Nabuco as representative of

a closed, intellectually unoriginal and fundamentally conservative nineteenth-century Brazilian elite, in the mold of the cultural philistines and political cynics routinely lampooned by his
friend, the writer Machado de Assis (1839–1908)—one thinks
of characters such as Machado's charming boor Brás Cubas and
the affable but politically noncommittal Counselor Aires. I agree
with Jeffrey D. Needell that Nabuco "suggests something of [. . .]
the range, contradictions, and limits of elite [Brazilian] political thought" during his time, though it is both uncharitable and
misplaced to dismiss Nabuco as a mere well-connected member
of that elite (Needell 159). Nabuco participated in and observed
some of the most significant domestic and global events of his
time, including abolition, various Brazilian territorial disputes,
the rise of US hegemony in Latin America, and as I will discuss
at length in this chapter, the political and ideological conflict between monarchism and republicanism—a debate through which
we can uncover a good deal of Nabuco's thinking on Brazilian–
Spanish American relations and on Brazil's place in America.

Moreover, Nabuco was a very *public* intellectual, fully assuming what he considered his responsibility to speak for and
to the public, both literally (as in speeches) and through his
broader political, social, and literary engagement. Nabuco once
included in a parliamentary speech a simple but revealing statement on this theme, declaring: "Falo para cumprir um dever
público" (*OC* 7: 213; "I speak in order to fulfill a public duty").
Throughout his career Nabuco "spoke" to his readers, friends,
and colleagues, to allies and opponents alike, in newspaper
articles, pamphlets, books, and official documents, as well
as in private correspondence and diary entries. And although
Ferreira de Araújo once wrote of Nabuco that "in politics he
was always a case apart" (qtd. in Viana Filho, *Joaquim Nabuco*
210), Nabuco followed earlier imperial-era political figures
such as José Bonifácio de Andrada e Silva, "patriarch" of Brazilian independence, in advocating English-style constitutional
monarchy for Brazil as a median term between an apparently
chaotic republicanism and autocratic despotism—both of which
were amply on display, in the minds of many Brazilian observers, in nineteenth-century Spanish America, marked as it was by
civil strife and seemingly incessant party factionalism. Indeed,
Nabuco steered a middle course between the republicanism

of his more radical peers and the authoritarian tendencies of the imperial elite's more conservative elements, seizing on the ideas of English liberal utilitarians John Stuart Mill (1806–73) and Walter Bagehot (1826–77) in confronting what he understood as the threat of Brazil's "South Americanization" (*sul-americanização*), a fear he shared with monarchists such as Prado and da Cunha that Brazil, in abandoning a constitutional monarchy that had proved capable of balancing social order and individual liberty, would descend into the "republican whirlwind" of Spanish America. While Nabuco's late-period Pan-Americanism has received a good deal of scholarly attention,[2] the role played in his thought by the looming specter of Spanish America, particularly during the crucial 1889–95 period, which saw the end of the Empire and the birth of the Republic, has not. This chapter will seek to address this oversight, exploring how Spanish America constitutes a major albeit underexamined presence in Nabuco's writing—whether as an imagined site of "republican" disorder and despotism, as a source of economic and political competition, or after 1889, as the home of at least one "civilized" country whose government Nabuco viewed as worthy of emulation—Chile.[3]

In this chapter I will delineate Nabuco's evolving position on Brazilian government and Brazil's place in Latin America, moving from his pre-1889 defense of English-style constitutional monarchy to his agonized 1889–94 reflections on the implications of Brazil's abandonment of the monarchy and his 1895 defense in *Balmaceda* of Chile's "parliamentary republic" as a model for post-imperial Brazil. Despite the particularities of his thought, Nabuco, in observing Brazilian–Spanish American relations, conforms to a long-standing tradition in Brazilian essayistic discourse of selective, pragmatic approximation to the Spanish American republics, exhibiting a "hispano-skepticism" I described in this book's first chapter. Nabuco's defense of constitutional monarchy, though grounded in European ideas and examples, looks to Spanish America as an implied negative counterpoint to Brazil, as Nabuco's repeated references to the threat of Argentine economic competition and Paraguayan "tyranny" and "barbarism" attest. Like his Brazilian contemporaries Eduardo Prado, in his volume *A Ilusão Americana* (The American Illusion, 1893), and Euclides da Cunha, in the articles collected in *Contrastes e Confrontos* (Contrasts and Confrontations, 1907), and in contrast to countless Spanish American thinkers (José Enrique Rodó and Alfonso Reyes, among them), Nabuco rejected the idea that a common Latin American "essence" should inform Brazil's political institutions and foreign policy. Instead, he affirmed Brazil's familial bonds with Portugal, and posited "Latin America" as a geopolitical *construct* as opposed to a functional supranational identity for his country. Nabuco's diaries for 1889–94 show his agonized reaction to the 1889 overthrow of the Brazilian monarchy and the 1893 *Revolta da Armada* (Naval Revolt) that nearly overthrew the nascent Republic, with Brazil's seeming descent into turmoil appearing to disprove his earlier confidence in the country's ability to avoid South America's apparent propensity for failed republican government. With the advent in 1894 of civilian rule and Nabuco's reintegration into national political life, Nabuco reformulated his pre-1889 defense of constitutional monarchy around the model of Chile's "parliamentary republic," as a case of *de facto* parliamentary rule that struck him as both reminiscent of the Second Empire and as the continent's least "South American" (i.e., radical, despotic, unstable) government. Moreover, from his 1905 appointment as Ambassador to the United States, Nabuco presented Pan-Americanism as a pragmatic choice to be made in order to preserve Brazilian sovereignty and national identity. In gauging Nabuco's influence in Brazilian intellectual life, we should note that thinkers like Prado and da Cunha would radicalize Nabuco's hispanoskepticism in their own reflections on 1889, and that in terms of foreign policy, Nabuco's pragmatic Pan-Americanism would become a hallmark of later Brazilian diplomacy.[4] Moreover, and though it falls outside the purview of this chapter, Nabuco's interpretation in *Minha Formação* of northeastern plantation life, in which he simultaneously rhapsodizes over the apparent warmth of the master-slave relationship and condemns slavery as a practice, would be developed by various Brazilian thinkers, including Gilberto Freyre in his influential, monumental study *Casa-grande e Senzala* (The Masters and the Slaves, 1933), and to a lesser extent, Sérgio Buarque de Holanda in his interpretive essay *Raízes do Brasil* (Roots of Brazil, 1936).[5] On the other hand, Nabuco's thoughts were squarely opposed to thinkers like Martí and Rodó (recall their ideas of *nuestra América* and the *magna patria*, respectively), who grounded supranationalist arguments for Latin American unity in notions of a common Latin American "essence," which they defined in racial, linguistic, and historical terms, and in opposition to the example and actions of the United States.

The structure of this chapter is as follows. After briefly summarizing Nabuco's early career, I will lay out his pre-1889 argument for English-style constitutional monarchy as the best means for Brazil to preserve liberty, prosperity, and national unity in the face of Spanish America's apparent republican disorder. Acknowledging Nabuco's debt to English liberal utilitarianism, I will show how he adapts ideas from Mill's *Considerations on Representative Government* (1861) and Bagehot's *The English Constitution* (1867) to the Brazilian and South American context. Further, I will address Nabuco's arguments against slavery, contending that Nabuco saw abolition as a necessary means for Brazil to *reinforce* and *reform* imperial institutions and maintain its economic and strategic position relative to neighbors such as Argentina. Additionally, I will point out some of the more contradictory and troubling features of Nabuco's abolitionism—namely, his references to African-descended slaves as potentially corrupt, degenerate, and dangerous, as well as the language of racial purity and naked prejudice he deploys in his staunch opposition to Chinese immigration to Brazil. In the third section, I will describe the challenge posed by the Revolution of 1889 and by Brazil's adoption of republican government, citing extensively from Nabuco's diaries and correspondence to demonstrate how between 1889 and 1894 he wrestled with Brazil's "South Americanization." In the chapter's fourth and final section, I will turn to 1895's *Balmaceda*, showing how Nabuco used Chile's Revolution of 1891 to argue to a Brazilian reading public that in a republican age and hemisphere and in the absence of a viable imperial alternative, Brazil must choose between dysfunctional militarism (represented by dictators like José Manuel Balmaceda in Chile, and by implication, early republican Brazil's military leaders, the *marechais*), and Chile's example of a well-ordered aristocratic republic. With *Balmaceda*, Nabuco offers what for him serves as a solution to the problem of "South Americanization," arguing that even in a disordered South America, educated, morally upright elites like the Chilean and imperial-era Brazilian aristocracies can and must govern effectively, and that Brazil must choose to emulate the exceptional Chilean model of government if it is to prosper. A fascinating text and a valuable historical document, *Balmaceda* has received surprisingly little critical attention, an oversight I will attempt to remedy.[6] In the chapter's conclusion, I will tie Nabuco's position in *Balmaceda* to the pragmatic Pan-Americanism he adopted in his final years, during which Nabuco argued that despite recent US interventions in the Caribbean and Central America—most notably in 1898, at the outbreak of the Spanish-American War—a US-led system of continental arbitration represented a better means for Brazil to maintain its autonomy than the prospect of renewed European intervention in the region on the order of the imperial powers' "scramble for Africa." Finally, I will briefly reassert the distinction between Nabuco's pragmatic, selective approximation to Spanish America and Rodó's whole-hearted culturalist embrace of a Latin American *magna patria*, as described in the previous chapter.

I. The Formation of a Monarchist and Abolitionist

Joaquim Nabuco was born in 1849 into one of the principal families of Brazil's interlocking political, economic, and cultural elites. His paternal and maternal families had deep roots in the northeastern sugar economy, and had been active in Brazilian politics since the colonial period. His father, José Tomás Nabuco de Araújo, was one of "the foremost statesmen of the Empire," and served as a deputy, senator, Minister of Justice, and a member of Emperor Dom Pedro II's Council of State (Needell 160–61). The younger Nabuco would later narrate his father's life in the four-volume *Um Estadista do Império*, which long remained the authoritative history of the Second Empire, a period the younger Nabuco termed the *Grande Era Brasileira*, or "Great Brazilian Age" (*OC* 3: viii).[7]

Nabuco's familial connections and history virtually "predestined" him for a prominent public role (Iglésias 6). As his biographer Luiz Viana Filho puts it, the young Nabuco was a self-conscious child of privilege, a *principezinho*, or "little prince" (*Joaquim Nabuco* 16–17). Nabuco spent his first years with his godparents at Massangana, a small Pernambuco plantation. In *Minha Formação*, Nabuco writes ambivalently about slavery's mark on his plantation childhood. On the one hand, he credits it with providing the initial inspiration for his entry into the abolitionist movement, stating that slavery "decidiu, estou certo, do emprego ulterior de minha vida" (182; "decided, I am certain, what I would later do with my life"). Of special importance was an apparent encounter he narrates with a young runaway slave, who Nabuco claims begged his godparents to buy him so that he could escape a cruel master. "Foi êste," Nabuco writes, "o traço inesperado que me descobriu a natureza da instituição com a qual eu vivera até então familiarmente, sem suspeitar a dor que ela ocultava" (*OC* 1: 181; "This was the unexpected element that allowed me to discover the true nature of the institution I had lived with until then, without suspecting how much pain it concealed").[8] On the other hand, Nabuco's evocation of Massangana and of plantation life generally is nostalgic in the mode of José Lins do Rego's novel *Menino de Engenho* (Plantation Boy, 1932) and fellow *pernambucano* Freyre's characterization of the strong emotional ties that bound master and slave in *Casa-grande e Senzala* (1933)—indeed, in an introduction he wrote to Nabuco's memoir, Freyre seizes on the allegedly "humanitarian, sentimental, kind" elements of slavery as described by Nabuco (*Minha Formação* 14). Nabuco tells of his godmother as practicing a relatively benign, "particular form" of slavery, one that could only exist in the older plantations, where master-slave relations went back generations. While abolition in 1888 was of course to be applauded, Nabuco, lamenting the end of what he saw as a key component of his pastoral childhood, nonetheless credits slavery with "espalha[ndo] por nossas vastas solidões uma grande suavidade" ("spreading a great softness across the solitude of our vast country"), and describes the slave's affection for a kindly master as "um dos mais absolutos disinterêsses de que o coração humano se [tem] mostrado capaz" (*OC* 1: 181–82; "one of the most absolute examples of disinterested love of which the human heart has been capable").

At eight years of age, Nabuco joined the rest of his family in Rio de Janeiro, the imperial capital, where he was quickly placed on the track open in nineteenth-century Brazil to elite males, a path he shared with the majority of his generation of Brazilian intellectuals. After being enrolled in a Friburgo boarding school in 1859, Nabuco transferred to the elite Colégio Dom Pedro II in 1860 (Carolina Nabuco 10; Viana Filho, *Joaquim Nabuco* 20–21; Iglésias 6–7). Viana Filho reports that the young Nabuco excelled at literature, history, and philosophy, though his early "passion" was poetry. His poetic aspirations mirrored those of countless other members of Brazil's Romantic-era elite, with Nabuco writing "odes to Mexico and Poland, two nations that were fighting for their independence, and later translat[ing] Schiller's 'Maria Stuart.' After these attempts he undertook a more ambitious effort, publishing a luxurious edition of an ode entitled *O Gigante da Polônia*" (The Giant of Poland) (*Joaquim Nabuco* 22–23; Iglésias 6; Carolina Nabuco 11–12). Nabuco's early poetic efforts were not especially well received, eliciting a negative (though characteristically polite) review from a young Machado de Assis in the *Diário do Rio de Janeiro*.[9] During this period Nabuco also embarked on a journalistic career and began articulating his liberal political views in student journals. After matriculating at the São Paulo law faculty in 1866, Nabuco began writing in the daily *Ipiranga* and founded the journals *A Independência* and the *Tribuna Liberal,* which he and his student friends used to oppose the conservative government then in power in the legislature (*Minha Formação* 33; Sodré 230; Viana Filho, *Joaquim Nabuco* 27). Moreover, Nabuco was elected *orador* ("orator") of the student-run Ateneu Paulistano and wrote a philosophical response to the question of whether one is justified in killing a tyrant in order to secure public liberty, using Charlotte Corday's 1793 assassination of radical French republican Jean-Paul Marat as his "principal example" (Carolina Nabuco 13). Nabuco's response, a tentative "yes," is indicative of the pains he would take in his later thinking to balance a utilitarian concern for social welfare with a defense of individual liberty. Nabuco transferred to Recife's law faculty in 1869, and it was there that he incidentally earned his reputation as a well-dressed "dandy," and was given his nickname "Quincas o Belo" (Viana Filho, *Joaquim Nabuco* 34–35).

As Nabuco approached the completion of his studies, his broadly liberal thinking began to coalesce around two ideas, both of which would inform his vision of Brazil's place in the Americas: a defense of English-style constitutional monarchy and a pro-abolitionist position. I will address both in the next section. It was during his legal studies that Nabuco began reading Walter Bagehot, a failed English politician and early editor of *The Economist*, who in 1867 published *The English Constitution*, a study of English parliamentary government. During his time in Recife, Nabuco published the pamphlet "O Povo e o Trono" (The People and the Throne) under the pseudonym "Juvenal da Decadência Romana" (Juvenal of the Roman Decadence), using Bagehot's ideas to criticize Emperor Dom Pedro II's abuses of power, namely, his 1868 decision to invite legislative conservatives to form a government despite a liberal parliamentary majority. This signaled Nabuco's long-term willingness to critique the Emperor in the interest of reforming and consolidating imperial institutions—a milder version of what José de Alencar (1829–77), a conservative Brazilian politician and journalist (and more memorably, an important Romantic-era novelist), had done in 1865–66 in his pseudonymous open "Letters to the Emperor."[10] While in Recife, Nabuco also began writing a long, unfinished manuscript entitled *A Escravidão* (Slavery)—the forerunner to 1883's *O Abolicionismo*—and he volunteered to defend an escaped black slave accused of murder. While, in Francisco Iglésias's words, Nabuco's legal defense "horrified his relatives and friends," his success in saving the slave's life (he was sentenced to life in prison) was "in itself a victory, since the death penalty was [normally] imposed in such cases. This was a preview of an [abolitionist] career that would be above all else very difficult, since it would contradict entrenched, local economic interests" (Iglésias 9; Carolina Nabuco 19–20).

Upon completing his law degree in 1870, Nabuco drifted between a brief and unhappy career as a lawyer and more political journalism. Throughout the 1870s Nabuco collaborated with several newspapers, writing on philosophy, literature, and politics, and defending English-style constitutional monarchy in a polemic with *A República* (Sodré 235–36, 246–47n138, 257, 306). For our purposes, however, it was Nabuco's 1873–74 European trip (his first) that stands out during this period. There Nabuco would get his first look at French and English institutions, helping to solidify his preference for the English model as the best guarantor of order, liberty, and unity for Brazil. In the following section, I will outline Nabuco's argument for constitutional monarchy, which was strongly influenced by his reading of Bagehot—and indirectly by Mill—and secondarily, by his first-hand look at French and English government.

II. The Ends of Constitutional Monarchy

In 1870 a group of Brazilian intellectuals, including several of Nabuco's peers, signed a republican manifesto that argued that Brazil's monarchy was an aberration "in its essence and in practice antithetical and hostile to the rights and interests of the American states," and a model that appealed to neither Europeans nor Americans: "To Europe we appear as a monarchical democracy that neither inspires confidence nor provokes loyalty. To America we seem a democratized monarchy in which the people's instinct and force are outweighed by the sovereign's arbitrariness and omnipotence." In a rebuke of the idea that Brazil's political difference and distance from its neighbors constituted a benefit for the country, whether pragmatic or in terms of autonomy of national identity, the manifesto concluded by arguing for the Republic as a means to place Brazil "in fraternal contact with all peoples, and in democratic solidarity with the continent of which we are part" (qtd. in Djacir Menezes 517).

With some in the younger ranks of Brazil's intelligentsia arguing that the Empire was antithetical to national prosperity, particularly in an American context, how did Nabuco come to the opposite conclusion? As Nabuco relates in his correspondence, his defense of constitutional monarchy was not motivated by a slavish reverence for imperial majesty, but was the result of a pragmatic decision made in the interest of fostering individual and collective liberty as he understood these concepts. In a November 1888 letter to Domingos Alves Ribeiro, Nabuco notes that "[a]lthough I have no faith in a Brazilian republic, I have no desire to support the monarchy against democracy in our present phase of feudalism and the quasi-vassalage of the working classes. All of my efforts are bent toward making the monarchy the creator and the protector of the only democracy that we can have in Brazil, that of the people themselves." And as he wrote in 1898, "I was and am a Monarchist, but that is a secondary and accidental characteristic as far as I am concerned; the basic and increasingly strong characteristic was another [. . .] 'liberal'" (qtd. in Carolina Nabuco 182, 239).[11]

As an Anglophile, Nabuco was relatively unique among his peers, many of whom venerated the political and cultural example of revolutionary France, as did the character Paulo in Machado de Assis's political and romantic satire *Esaú e Jacó* (Esau and Jacob, 1904). Nabuco spoke skeptically of this Francophile tendency in an 1880 speech, asserting of the typical Brazilian, "o que êle lê, é o que a França produz. Êle é pela inteligência e pelo espírito cidadão francês; nasceu parisiense, [. . .] vê tudo como pode ver um parisiense desterrado de Paris" (*OC* 11: 43; "what he reads is what France produces. Intellectually and spiritually he is a French citizen; he was born Parisian [. . .] he sees everything as a Parisian exiled from Paris"). Breaking with this trend, Nabuco was from his student days attracted to English thinkers and especially English political theory. Nabuco specifically credited Bagehot's *The English Constitution* with convincing him of two ideas: first, that English cabinet government (i.e., government by a committee of legislatively nominated ministers) is superior to the presidential system as practiced in the US and France, and by implication, as *mis*practiced in Spanish America; and second, that the power of the crown should be essentially ceremonial, its function properly "dignified," as opposed to "efficient," to cite Bagehot's distinction.

Bagehot defines the cabinet system as follows: "A Cabinet is a combining committee—a *hyphen* which joins, a *buckle* which fastens, the legislative part of the State to the executive part of the State. In its origin it belongs to the one, in its functions it belongs to the other" (68; author's emphasis). For Bagehot, this organic linkage of the legislative and executive powers in the cabinet system is advantageous in that a cabinet can dissolve itself and call for new legislative elections once the government has ceased to work effectively. By contrast, presidential democracies compel voters to elect a new government at regular intervals and divide the government into separate (and in Bagehot's view, antagonistic) legislative and executive parts. This, for Bagehot, "weakens the whole aggregate force of Government—the entire imperial power; and therefore it weakens both its halves" (74). As Nabuco explains, in a presidential system such as the United States, the executive and legislative branches "guerreiam-se implacavelmente, como dois partidos rivais" (*Minha Formação* 42; "make war against each other implacably, as two rival parties").

Another important feature of Bagehot's argument is his distinction between the "efficient" part of government, which he identifies with the cabinet-led lower house of Parliament (in England, the House of Commons) and the "dignified" part, which he identifies with the monarchy. Each part has a specific role to play in the effective functioning of government: the crown captures the imagination and loyalty of the governed, particularly the lower classes, whom Bagehot understood to be receptive to pompous display and incapable of grasping how government "really" works: "The ruder sort of men [. . .] are uninterested in the plain, palpable ends of government; they do not prize them; they do not in the least comprehend how they should be attained [. . .] The elements which excite the most easy reverence will be the *theatrical* elements—those which appeal to the senses, which claim to be embodiments of the greatest human ideas, which boast in some cases of far more than human origin" (63–64; author's emphasis).[12] It is the cabinet, appointed by a legislature that is in turn elected by a limited number of male property-holders, which does the actual governing.[13]

The monarchy's ceremonial function, especially important for Bagehot because he believed that the majority of his day was "scarcely more civilised than the majority of two thousand years ago" (62), would later be studied from a much different political angle by Marxist historian Eric Hobsbawm, who understands it as a collection of "invented traditions" (to cite his rather successful term), and by co-religionist Raymond Williams, who described *The English Constitution* as, "in its way a superb piece of demystification, but of a rather special kind: demystification in order to mystify [. . .] [Bagehot] saw and approved the whole panoply of the British State as a means of creating deference in its subjects" (*Culture and Materialism* 89).[14]

While Nabuco may not be quite as strident as Bagehot concerning the "natural" human inequality that allowed the political elite to "mystify" the masses, he believed that a certain level of inequality was a fact, that elite status generally correlated with a superior moral profile, and that sensible political moderation was a characteristic feature of the *boa sociedade* ("good society") to which he belonged (*Minha Formação* 62–63). Further, and as will be shown, in Nabuco's writing, questions of race, class, and nationality often intersected with the idea of relative political capacities, with the caricatured figures of the indigenous and black, the poor, and the Spanish American (and especially the Paraguayan, racialized by Nabuco as indigenous), whom he characterized as prone to destructive political fanaticism, military despotism, and anarchy. By contrast, Nabuco viewed Brazil's rich, white, and affluent "good society" as an educated, patriotic, and "moral" minority, naturally inclined toward a pragmatic political moderation that would balance order and liberty in the context of evolving yet essentially stable governing institutions. As he wrote in *Minha Formação*, the "espírito *cosmopolita* ou, antes, *mundana,* caracteriza-se pela compreensão das soluções opostas dos mesmos problemas sociais, pela tolerância de tôdas as opiniões, [. . .] pela idéia [. . .] de que acima de quaisquer partidos está a *boa sociedade.* Êsse modo de ser, em política, não é necessàriamente eclético, nem, ainda menos, céptico; é sòmente incompatível com o fanatismo, isto é, com a intolerância, qualquer que ela seja" (*OC* 1: 40–41; author's emphasis; "the *cosmopolitan*, or rather, *worldly* spirit is characterized by an understanding of opposing solutions to given social problems, by a tolerance for all opinions, [. . .] by the idea [. . .] that above and beyond any party is the *good society.* This way of being, in politics, is not necessarily eclectic or skeptical; it is merely incompatible with any fanaticism or intolerance").[15]

Though Nabuco agreed with Bagehot on monarchy's "ceremonial" usefulness, and the need for an organic connection between the legislature and executive, his position also owes a great deal to John Stuart Mill, particularly as concerns the connection between a people's character and its government, and regarding the progressive democratization of governing institutions. Mill, one of the principal architects of liberal utilitarianism in England, argues in his *Considerations* for a two-way relationship between a people's character and its government, with the people's "good" or "bad" traits manifesting themselves in good or bad governments, and correspondingly raising or lowering the level of public morality. Mill believed that a well-organized representative government can and should promote the elevation of the masses, and he contended that the best way to achieve this was by allowing the nation's constitution (written, or unwritten as in Britain) to *evolve* so as to make government and society ever more representative. For Mill, "[t]he first question in respect to any political institutions is, how far they tend to foster in the members of the community the various desirable qualities, moral and intellectual" (226). Nabuco upheld these views in his early legislative career, arguing in a April 29, 1879 parliamentary speech for the Brazilian constitution as an essentially progressive, "grande maquinismo liberal" ("great liberal machine"), and noting that, "em todos os países a tendência liberal é alargar o direito do voto e não restringi-lo" (*OC* 11: 38, 46; "in all countries the liberal tendency is to extend the right to vote, not to restrict it").[16] To this end, Nabuco the legislator advocated a series of concrete liberalizing reforms, including direct election to the Senate, religious freedom, extension of the vote, and most famously, abolition of slavery (Carolina Nabuco 41–44).

However, Mill cautions that while an entirely representative democracy should serve as an ideal, a people's democratic evolution "may be stopped short at any point in their progress, by defective adaptation of their government to that particular stage of advancement" (231). Like Mill and Bagehot, Nabuco believed that Brazil would in time evolve from a constitutional monarchy with limited representative institutions into a representative democracy organized as a republic. He said as much in an 1889 speech in Buenos Aires, given shortly before the republican revolution, stating that while "some day we shall be a Republic," he opposed "ideas before their time, [. . .] the Republic before the Brazilian people are prepared to govern themselves" (qtd. in Carolina Nabuco 191). Nabuco and his fellow "aristocratic liberals" feared that premature adoption of the Republic might lead to civil war and despotism—frequently cited as typically "Spanish American" ills by Brazilian commentators, Nabuco included. The key for a young nation like Brazil, to Nabuco's mind, was to slowly and steadily open its political institutions to the people, or he put it, "conservar do existente tudo o que não seja obstáculo invencível ao melhoramento indispensável" (*Minha Formação* 121; "preserve of what exists all that is not an invincible obstacle to indispensable improvement"). Prior to 1889, Nabuco believed that for the foreseeable future the monarchy would continue to play the useful role of winning the loyalty of the *povo* ("people"), thereby allowing reformers like Nabuco to steer the ship of state without undue interference from the masses he was (paradoxically) trying to enfranchise.

In sum, Nabuco was convinced by Bagehot specifically and liberal utilitarianism generally of the "superioridade prática do governo de gabinete inglês sobre o sistema presidencial americano" ("practical superiority of English cabinet government over the American presidential system") and of the fact that "uma monarquia secular, de origens feudais, [. . .] como é a inglesa, podia ser um governo mais direto e imediatamente do povo do que a república" (*Minha Formação* 45; "a centuries-old monarchy, feudal in origin [. . .] as in England, could be a more direct and immediately popular government than the Republic").[17] Nabuco's Millian interest in progressively enlarging participatory rights as Brazilian political culture matured might entail long-term adoption of the Republic, but in his opinion, the constitutional monarchy would in the mean time provide the valuable service of checking popular rule (through royal prerogatives, voting restrictions, and so on), which it "sells" to the people through the majesty of its monarchical trappings. This is important in upholding the "order" side of the liberty/order equation, since Nabuco (following Mill and Bagehot) believed that the apparently impulsive *povo* would misguidedly value liberty over order if given premature control of government.

Nabuco's ideas were confirmed during 1873–74, when he had the opportunity to observe English and French government. While in France Nabuco attended the deliberations of the National Assembly, and felt a strong attraction to Adolphe Thiers, a political survivor who had been active in the governments of Louis Philippe, Napoleon III, and finally the Third Republic. By the 1870s Thiers was a center-right republican, who as President (1871–73) used his powers to crush the 1871 Paris Commune.[18] Nabuco's admiration for Thiers seems grounded in what he interpreted as Thiers's ability to see past ideological divisions and "mant[er]-se como o fiel da balança entre os parti-dos" ("function as a scale's fulcrum, balancing the parties"). This apparently allowed France under Thiers to avoid the twin dangers of dictatorship (as under Napoleon III) and proletarian radicalism and disorder (as in the Commune). However, Nabuco is quick to remind readers of his memoir that this did not make him a "republicano de princípio; pelo contrário" (*OC* 1: 52; "republican in principle—to the contrary"). In Nabuco's opinion, liberalism in Brazil would remain best served by a constitutional monarchy modeled on Great Britain. Drawing a specific parallel between Europe and Brazil, Nabuco argues that "[a]ntes de tudo, o republicanismo francês, *que era e é o nosso*, tem um fermento de ódio, uma predisposição igualitária que logicamente leva à demagogia [. . .] ao passo que o libera-lismo, menos radical, não só é compatível com a monarquia, mas até parece aliar-se com o temperamento aristocrático [. . .] A intolerância é, ou era, o característico do republicanismo agressivo francês, e a intolerância é uma fobia da liberdade e do mundo" (*Minha Formação* 61–62; my emphasis; "above all else, French republicanism, *which was and is ours*, has an odor of hatred to it, an egalitarian predisposition that logically leads to demagogy [. . .] whereas liberalism, which is less radical, not only is compatible with the monarchy, but seems an ally of the aristocratic temperament [. . .] Intolerance is, or was, characteristic of aggressive French republicanism, and intoler-ance is a phobia toward liberty and the world"). As for English government, Nabuco visited Parliament at least once during his 1873–74 European trip, and was impressed by the British ju-dicial system, which in *Minha Formação* he pronounced fairer than the United States judiciary (*OC* 1: 113–14).[19] This impres-sion was no doubt influenced by his visit to the US as an attaché to the Brazilian legation, during which he witnessed the fall-out of the disputed 1877 presidential election between Rutherford B. Hayes and Samuel J. Tilden, in which the Republican Hayes lost the popular vote but was given the presidency by a congres-sional committee in an 8–7 party-line vote.[20]

While Nabuco's argument for constitutional monarchy in *Minha Formação* makes little direct reference to Brazil as a specifically South American nation, it is clear that he had the Spanish American comparison in mind when developing it. See, for example, the following statement from *Minha Formação* on the advantage of a monarch (as opposed to a popularly elected president) as head of state, which contains a probable reference to Brazil's neighbors: "Eu via claramente nessa não-eletividade o segredo da superioridade do mecanismo monárquico sobre o republicano, condenado a interrupções periódicas, que são *para certos países* revoluções certas" (*Minha Formação* 47; my emphasis; "I clearly saw in this unelectability the secret of monarchy's superiority to the Republic, [the latter being] condemned to periodic interruptions, which represent clear revolutions *for certain countries*"). Here Nabuco may be drawing on Mill, who argues in his *Considerations* that in imperfect and immature representative systems like Greece (or Brazil), a king serves as a better head of state than an elected president. Mill writes:

> In the modern kingdom of Greece [. . .] it can hardly be doubted, that the [parliamentary] place-hunters who chiefly compose the representative assembly [. . .] keep up the idea of popular rights, and conduce greatly to the real liberty of the press which exists in that country. This benefit, however, is entirely dependent on the coexistence with the popular body of a hereditary king. If, instead of struggling for the favours of the chief ruler, these selfish and sordid factions struggled for the chief place itself, they would certainly, *as in Spanish America*, keep the country in a state of chronic revolution and civil war. (259–60; my emphasis)

Given the extent of Nabuco's involvement in the abolitionist movement between 1879 and 1888, it makes sense that a good part of his written defense of constitutional monarchy and his corresponding distrustful comments concerning Spanish American republicanism would appear in the context of the debate over slavery. In *O Abolicionismo* (1883), a series of articles originally printed in the anti-slavery publication *O Abolicionista*, Nabuco makes various negative references to Spanish America, both implied and explicit. Nabuco argues for slavery's negative impact on all aspects of Brazilian society (in terms of "commerce, religion, poverty, industry, Parliament, the Crown, the State"),[21] and presents abolition as part of a project of "reform within the monarchical system," that is, as a means to revitalize the Empire, which he feared was straining under slavery's corrupting influence (*Intérpretes* 1: 26). Specifically,

Nabuco argues that slavery has destroyed the people's faith in government, which leads to the worst men being attracted to politics and getting elected to office. Parliament's consequent mediocrity and weakness allow the Emperor to overstep his authority, filling the vacuum at the expense of representative institutions, as in the 1868 legislative switch. Though Nabuco, ever-sympathetic to the royal family, contended that "[o] Imperador não tem culpa, exceto, talvez, por não ter reagido contra essa abdicação nacional, de ser [. . .] tão poderoso que nenhuma delegação da sua autoridade [. . .] conseguiria criar no país uma fôrça maior que a Coroa" (*OC* 7: 173; "the Emperor is not to blame except, perhaps, for not having reacted to this national abdication, [and] for being so [. . .] powerful that no delegation of his authority [. . .] could create a force greater than the Crown").

Nabuco also focuses on the fact that slaves were not considered citizens by Brazil's Constitution. As such, one of the benefits of abolition would be to "[d]ar um *cidadão* mais ao rol dos brasileiros" (*OC* 7: 176; author's emphasis; "place another *citizen* on the roll of Brazilians"). In this way abolition would gradually widen the scope of civic participation and bring what Nabuco viewed as a disenfranchised, corrupted, and potentially rebellious slave population under the auspices of a morally edifying constitutional monarchy. After all, as Mill argued, "[t]he maximum of the invigorating effect of freedom upon the character is only obtained, when the person acted on either is, *or is looking forward to becoming,* a citizen as fully privileged as any other" (254; my emphasis). It was in this spirit, perhaps, that Nabuco addressed would-be supporters of African descent in a November 1, 1884 campaign speech: "Peço os votos de todos os descendentes de escravos, de todos os homens de côr, porque estou trabalhando pela sua causa, e porque, apesar de não haver entre nós o preconceito que desonrou a democracia norte-americana, [. . .] *é preciso que a raça negra se convença de que ela ainda tem no futuro de nosso país grandes transes por que passar, grandes dificuldades, desigualdades e opróbios que vencer, e de que a justiça que ela terá de receber no futuro* será medida pelo interêsse e pelo amor que nesta geração houver mostrado pelos seus irmãos de cativeiro" (*OC* 7: 279; my emphasis; "I ask for the vote of all those descendents of slaves, of all men of color, because I am working for you, and because, while there is not among us the prejudice that has dishonored the North American democracy [. . .] *the black race must be convinced that it still has great obstacles to overcome, great difficulties, inequalities and injuries to overcome and that the justice it will receive in the future* will be measured by the interest and love that this generation will have shown toward its brothers in captivity"). In short, Nabuco argued that by freeing the slaves and putting them on a path to full (or fuller) participation in Brazilian society, the country's civic consciousness, whose development had been stunted by slavery, would be strengthened, along with Brazil's representative institutions (279). Or as Nabuco put it, "[e]ssa reforma [. . .] de nós mesmos, do nosso caráter, do nosso patriotismo, no nosso sentimento de responsibilidade cívica, é o único meio de suprimir efetivamente a escravidão da constituição social. A emancipação dos escravos é portanto apenas o comêço de um *Rinnovamento*" (217–18; author's emphasis; "this reform [. . .] of ourselves, of our character, of our patriotism, of our sense of civic responsibility, is the only effective means of removing slavery from the social constitution. The emancipation of the slaves is therefore only the beginning of a *Rinnovamento*"). Nabuco's implication that slavery oppresses free Brazilians as much as it does actual slaves seems sincere, though it is tempting to characterize Nabuco's as an argument that could only be made by someone whose social status was as far removed as possible from that of a slave. Indeed, Machado de Assis parodied this elitist strain of Brazilian abolitionism in *Esaú e Jacó* (1904), in the character Paulo, who makes an anti-slavery speech that could conceivably have been inspired by Nabuco's argument in *O Abolicionismo*. Paulo grandiloquently declares: "Abolition is the dawn of liberty, [. . .] the black emancipated, it remains to emancipate the white" (91).

Nabuco lays out three main anti-slavery arguments in *O Abolicionismo*, the second of which bears directly on Brazilian–Spanish American relations and appeals to national pride as well as a standing fear among nineteenth-century Brazilian intellectuals and political leaders of regional revolt and separatism—threats commonly associated with Spanish America. Here Nabuco argues for abolition, "[p]orque a escravidão é um pêso enorme que atrasa o Brasil no seu crescimento *em comparação com os outros Estados sul-americanos* que a não conhecem; porque [. . .] êsse regímen há de forçosamente dar em resultado *o desmembramento e a ruína do país*" (*OC* 7: 100; my emphasis; "because slavery is a great weight that holds back Brazil's growth *in comparison to the other South American States* that do not have it; because this state of affairs will necessarily result in the *dismembering and ruin of the country*"). Further, Nabuco references two countries at opposite ends of the continent's developmental and civilizational spectrum as he understood it: Paraguay and Argentina. First, he compares the slaveholding status quo in Brazil to the substantial human and political costs of the War of the Triple Alliance (1864–70), in which Brazil, Argentina, and Uruguay allied against an expansionist Paraguay led by dictator Solano López. Nabuco writes that slavery "é uma escola de desmoralização e inércia, de servilismo e irresponsabilidade para a casta dos senhores, e que fêz do Brasil *o Paraguai da escravidão*" (6; my emphasis; "is a school of demoralization and inertia, of servility and irresponsibility for the class of landowners who have made Brazil *the Paraguay of slavery*"). Somewhat paradoxically, Nabuco later argues that without slave labor, Brazil's colonial development would have been impossible, and that Brazil would have taken on the undesirable features of its southwestern neighbor. He warns: "Suprima-se mentalmente essa raça e seu trabalho, e o Brasil não será, na sua maior parte, senão um território deserto, quando muito *um segundo Paraguai*, guarani e jesuítico" (21; my emphasis; "If one mentally subtracts this race and its labor, most of Brazil becomes nothing more than an uninhabited territory, largely *a second Paraguay*, Guarani and Jesuit"). Here Paraguay is invoked as a barbaric backwater, a society whose example of indigenous primitivism and Jesuit reaction (recall the importance of the Jesuit *reducciones* in colonial Paraguay) Brazil is lucky to have avoided thus far, and should avoid in the future.[22]

Regarding Argentina, Nabuco warns that failure to abolish slavery will compromise Brazilian growth relative to its southern rival, whose impressive late-nineteenth-century economic development Nabuco ascribes to the waves of free European immigrants then flooding into Buenos Aires. Nabuco argues that in contrast to African-descended slaves, who have apparently

been corrupted by generations of captivity and forced labor
(and possibly by inherent racial inferiority), as well as undesirable Chinese immigrants, whom Nabuco pejoratively terms
chins, "white" immigration "tra[z], sem cessar, para os trópicos
uma corrente de sangue *caucásico* vivaz, enérgico, e sadio, que
po[de]mos absorver sem perigo, em vez dessa onda chinesa,
com que a grande propriedade aspira a viciar e corromper ainda
mais a nossa raça" (218; my emphasis; "continually brings to
the tropics a stream of living, energetic, and healthy *Cauca-
sian* blood, which we can absorb without risk, instead of this
Chinese wave, with which the great property holders seek to
further damage and corrupt our race"). As a side note, Nabuco's
opposition to large-scale Chinese immigration constituted one
of the recurring themes of his 1879 parliamentary speeches, and
one of the more curious, disturbing and—if one thinks of his
impassioned opposition to slavery—paradoxical aspects of his
writing. Nabuco, possibly reflecting his roots in the northeastern
sugar economy as well as an individual or inherited prejudice,
argued against the southeastern coffee planters who favored the
use of Chinese laborers, contending that Chinese immigration
would forestall serious consideration of abolition, as well as
contribute to the *mongolização* ("mongolization") of the country.[23] Moreover, he argued that it would prove economically
unsuccessful for landowners to have it both ways on the labor
issue, contending in an October 8, 1879 speech that "o trabalho
livre é incompatível com o trabalho escravo" (*OC* 11: 74; "free
labor is incompatible with slave labor").[24]

Returning to Argentina, Nabuco speculates that the Argentine
government, "se devesse ter uma política maquiavélica, inve-
josa e egoísta, deveria desejar ao Brasil [. . .] trinta anos mais de
escravidão" (*OC* 7: 206; "if it sought to follow a Machiavellian
policy, jealous and egotistical, would desire [. . .] thirty more
years of slavery for Brazil"). Nabuco presents Argentine growth
not only as an economic problem for Brazil, but also as a threat
to Brazil's political and territorial integrity, tying the country's
rivalry with Argentina to the fear that Brazil's southern provinces might secede, and possibly join their southern *gaucho* neighbors in a trans-Platine republic: "Guardando nós a escravidão, e
tendo a República Argentina paz, este será dentro de vinte anos
uma nação mais forte, mais adiantada e mais próspera do que o

Brasil, e o seu crescimento e a natureza do seu progresso e das suas instituições exercerá sobre as nossas províncias do Sul o efeito de uma *atração desagregante* que talvez seja irresistível" (207; my emphasis; "If we do not abolish slavery, and if the Argentine Republic remains peaceful, Argentina will within twenty years be a stronger, more developed and more prosperous nation than Brazil, and its growth and the nature of its progress and that of its institutions will have for our southern provinces a possibly irresistible *disaggregating attraction"*).[25]

In short, Nabuco considered slavery a pervasive, multi-dimensional threat to the Second Empire—"o fratricídio de uma raça, [. . .] o patricídio de uma nação" (387; "the fratricide of a race, [. . .] the parricide of a nation"), as he put it in a November 30, 1884 campaign speech—and he presented abolition as a vital reform for preserving the constitutional monarchy he saw as Brazil's best hope for ensuring national prosperity.[26] The overthrow of the monarchy by insurgent army officers on November 15, 1889, seventeen months after Princess Isabel signed the *Lei Áurea* (Golden Law) abolishing slavery, forced Nabuco toward a profound reconsideration of his vision of Brazilian nationhood and the country's place in the Americas, as we shall see in the next section.

III. Monarchy's End and the Threat of "South Americanization"

A few short months off of his abolitionist victory, the events of November 15, 1889 came as a shock to Nabuco (Vianna Filho, *Joaquim Nabuco* 172–73; Carolina Nabuco 184–86; Salles 137). The critic José Veríssimo characterized the Nabuco of this period in quixotic terms in a 1900 review of *Minha Formação*, writing that in 1889 Nabuco was a "politician of a regime that had suddenly been overthrown. He was the regime's devoted servant and believer, had served as its strange knight errant in its final days, and was deeply hurt by the fall of institutions that seemed linked to the fortunes of the country, of his family, and most of all of his father, who [for the younger Nabuco] incarnated these" ("O Sr. Joaquim Nabuco" 89).

Closely identified with the now-defunct Empire, and despite his years spent railing against one of its bedrock institutions (slavery), Nabuco was precluded from continuing his political career during the early years of the Republic, though at least some in the new regime apparently wished for him to return to the diplomatic service (Carolina Nabuco 240). Nabuco carried on as a journalist and polemicist, quickly publishing two pamphlets explaining why he would remain a monarchist and would not serve as an elected official under the new order (Salles 137–42).[27] Further, in 1891 he began publishing articles in the *Jornal do Comércio* and *Jornal do Brasil* on topics like "Republican Illusions" and "Militarism in Brazil" (Carolina Nabuco, 199–200). As Sodré reports, Nabuco's articles "inspired heated debates," leading to the storming of the *Jornal do Comércio*'s editorial offices on December 16, 1891 by a mob apparently calling for Nabuco's head (Sodré 296).

In addition to putting his political career on hold, and complicating (though certainly not stopping) his journalistic involvement, the Revolution of 1889 forced Nabuco to engage in a profound reexamination of his core political beliefs. Nabuco may have held (following Mill and Bagehot) that constitutional monarchy in Brazil would eventually give way to the Republic, but he also believed that Brazil in 1889 was not yet mature enough to make this transition.[28] To his mind, until such time as Brazil could naturally evolve into a republic, "the monarchy would play a necessary tutelary role in granting liberty, which though it existed in Brazil without the appropriate social conditions [emancipation, etc.], was nonetheless a central element in the formation of a nation. Ultimately, this seemed a slow, delicate process of perfection and education, prone at every instant to succumb to an adverse environment" (Salles 142).

As Salles implies, for Nabuco, Brazil and Spanish America were subject to a common South or Latin American "environment" that placed certain limits on their national development and political institutions. From early on, Nabuco subscribed to the idea that Brazil and the Spanish American republics, occupying the same landmass, were subject to certain shared developmental influences, among which was an unfortunate difficulty in establishing free, ordered societies. Importantly, Nabuco occasionally made reference in his writing to Latin America *as an idea*, though not in the same sense as the Spanish American continentalists. Nabuco tended to invoke it as a geopolitical concept—particularly early on—and was certainly versed in the Latin/Anglo-Teutonic dichotomy popularized by Hegel, Ranke, and Chevalier, as demonstrated by the title of his "Post-Scriptum" to *Balmaceda*, "A Questão da América Latina" (The Question of Latin America). However, this does not mean that Nabuco believed that Brazil and Spanish America had the same essential "Latin" character—quite the opposite. Nabuco, a believer in collective character and prototypical group "tendencies" or "traits" as defining factors in national development, argued that if Brazil were tied to another nation at the level of *gênio* ("genius"), that nation would be Portugal, a point he makes plain in an 1888 speech given, appropriately enough, at the Gabinete Português de Leitura (Portuguese Reading Room) in Rio de Janeiro. Here he addresses the Portuguese community in attendance as follows: "Sòmente num sentido consentirei em chamar o Brasil país estrangeiro para vós, no sentido de sermos uma nacionalidade política distinta. Nós nos constituímos em nação independente, ou melhor, diversa da vossa, porque tal era a lei da formação social da América" ("Only in one sense will I concede that Brazil is a foreign country to you [i.e., the Portuguese], in that we are a distinct nationality in political terms. We constituted ourselves independently, or rather, diversely from you, because this was the law of America's social formation"). This transatlantic Luso-Brazilian commonality of history, language, and character leads Nabuco to conclude that "até o dia infalível da nova Restauração"—that is until the Day of Judgment, or indefinitely—"Portugal e o Brasil formar[ão] uma só nacionalidade tão certo como êles hão de sempre falar uma só língua" (*OC* 11: 41, 50; "Portugal and Brazil will form a single nationality just as they will always speak the same language").[29]

Since for Nabuco each South American nation has its own unique history, informed by the interactions of distinct peoples subject to similar (though not identical) environmental conditions, these nations will presumably possess distinct collective consciousnesses or identities, with Brazil and the Spanish American republics representing the continent's two major identitarian blocs.[30] Nabuco built on these ideas in later texts, arguing in a 1904 report he submitted on behalf of Brazil as his country's representative in a boundary dispute with British

Guiana that "Brazil, prior to the proclamation of its independence, was already a conscious and homogeneous nation, [and
consequently] it was able to maintain its mighty physical mass
intact when independence came, while the unity of Spain's
crumbled" (qtd. in Carolina Nabuco 292; Dennison, *Joaquim
Nabuco* 132).[31] Throughout his life, Nabuco seems to have held
firm in this distinction between a South American *environment*
in which Brazilians share, and the idea that Brazilians nonetheless possess a unique national *consciousness* that distinguishes
them from their neighbors. Though as we will see, the events
of 1889 and the chaos of the early Republic, which recalled
for Nabuco the turbulent history of post-independence Spanish
America, forced him to consider the possibility that Brazilians
and Spanish Americans might not be so different after all, and
that they might share a common despotic and violent character
which would predispose them equally toward civil strife and
dictatorship.[32]

For Nabuco, Brazil's constitutional monarchy, like its plantation economy or its prolonged experience of slavery, was a key
formative element of the country's unique national character. In
Nabuco's reading of history, from 1822 to 1889, with the partial
exception of the agitated Regency period (1831–40),[33] imperial
Brazil alone among its republican neighbors managed to overcome the anti-democratic pull of the land through the imple-
mentation of a system that had been proven in theory (by the
English liberal utilitarians) and empirically, through Nabuco's
personal observation, to be the best available model for fostering liberty in an inhospitable South American environment.
The construction of imperial institutions by earlier generations
of public-minded nation-builders like Nabuco's father had
set Brazil down a unique historical path, so Nabuco believed,
which with time would imply further differentiation in character
from Spanish America. The overthrow of the monarchy forced
Nabuco to consider a number of troubling questions: why had
Brazil forsaken the constitutional monarchy? Did the fault lie
in Brazil's environment, in its national character, or in circum-
stance? Was Brazil more "South American" than Nabuco had
previously thought, and if so, did this imply a necessary reconsideration of Brazil's relationship to its neighbors? Nabuco's
diary entries and letters from 1889 to 1894 (the period of mili-

tary rule by the *marechais* Deodoro da Fonseca and Floriano Peixoto) provide revealing evidence of his agonized struggle to answer these questions.[34]

In a July 31, 1890 letter to the Baron of Rio Branco,[35] Nabuco combines a dystopian vision of Brazil's future—marked by military dictatorship, financial ruin, and eventual disunity—with a sense of profound personal frustration and helplessness. He writes: "Entramos na série de governos pessoais militares e daí virá a degredação do exército, a bancarrota pela ladroeira e pela especulação, como nas demais repúblicas do mesmo tipo, o governo nos 'Estados' de verdadeiros caudilhos, cercados de uma *quadrilha* de analfabetos, e por fim o desmembramento, se o sentimento nacional não reagir à última hora [. . .] Esse espetáculo me nauseia e não tenho vontade de assistir a ele até o fim" (*OC* 13: 188; author's emphasis; "We have entered into a series of personalist military governments and from this will stem the degradation of the army, bankruptcy due to theft and speculation, as in the other republics of the same type. Government in the 'States' will be in the hands of true caudillos, all surrounded by a band of illiterates, and we will finally see the dismembering [of the country], if national feeling doesn't intervene at the last minute [. . .] This spectacle nauseates me and I don't have the stomach to watch it until the end").[36]

This letter conveys the bleakness with which Nabuco viewed Brazil's immediate future, which he saw as hijacked by unruly, uneducated, and "illiterate" masses who had been irresponsibly radicalized and mobilized by insurgent army officers and republican activists—a nightmare scenario feared by conservative and "aristocratic liberal" thinkers from Edmund Burke to Jacob Burckhardt to José Ortega y Gasset.[37] However, if Nabuco's writings from the period are to be trusted, he oscillated between the feeling of helplessness he expresses in his letter to Rio Branco and a compulsion to act, to speak out as a representative of what he described in *Minha Formação* as the "good society," the well-mannered coalition of reasonable, affluent parliamentary liberals and conservatives who, along with Dom Pedro II, had given Brazil decades of relative political stability. The latter sentiment is displayed in a February 28, 1891 diary entry, in which Nabuco writes:

> "Nós estamos atravessando uma crise," diz-se no Brasil. Engano! Estamos no redemoinho republicano da América. Somos um cadáver girando no sorvedouro da anarquia. Em tal estado devemos abandonar a sociedade ao seu destino ou fundar uma nova pátria no estrangeiro, os que têm filhos? Se nada pode salvar a nação, é preciso lutar para elevar social-mente a minoria, a parte moral da sociedade [. . .] Temos, pois, que ficar brasileiros, vendo o Brasil tornar-se uma Venezuela, um México, uma Argentina, um Chile; propie-dade do déspota do dia. É como se o mundo voltasse a ser fetichista ou canibal! Mas por isso mesmo que foi o nosso destino nascer neste período, nos séculos futuros a América Latina há de ser *civilizada* ou não ser latina; o nosso dever consiste em manter na minoria o nível moral superior ao político, dissociar o desenvolvimento moral da incurável estagnação política. (*OC* 2: 34–35; author's emphasis) [7]

Despite Brazil having been thrust into "America's republi-can whirlwind," Nabuco holds firm in his belief that its future depends on maintaining the "moral" level of the minority (that is, the *boa sociedade*), which is based on the assumption that the political elite is by virtue of its privileged position more moral than the masses. For Nabuco, the consequence of failure would be Brazil's descent to the status of "a Venezuela, a Mexico, an Argentina, a Chile," a disastrous possibility he presents as tan-tamount to a return to primitive "fetishism" or "cannibalism." The placement of Brazil in the same category as these Spanish American republics implies for Nabuco not only a loss of politi-cal stability and legitimacy, with Brazil becoming "the property of the despot of the day," but also a surrender of Brazil's unique national identity. Nabuco warns that in spite of Brazil's appar-ent similarities to Spanish America, made manifest by 1889, "[w]e must, then, remain Brazilians." The question Nabuco leaves unanswered is how to place Brazil on the right path, whether through a restored monarchy or through some kind of reconciliation with the republican regime.

For the duration of the presidencies of Deodoro and Floriano, Nabuco was moderately active in the monarchist opposition, and he was in any case unwilling to compromise with the Republic. He spent time abroad (in Argentina and in Europe, where he visited the royal family in exile), and dedicated much of 1893 and 1894 to organizing his father's archive, which he then drew

on to write the monumental biography *Um Estadista do Império*, which as Salles and other critics have noted, Nabuco used
in order to make the case for the superiority of the Brazilian
constitutional monarchy over the disorder of Spanish American
republicanism (195, 200–01).[38] Nabuco's private political judg-
ments remained severe during the initial, *marechal*-led phase of
the Republic (1889–94), and indeed, his criticism can be seen
as part of a broader trend of rapid disenchantment with the new
regime among elite Brazilian intellectuals and political actors,
both monarchists and republicans. This disenchantment was
captured by the imperial and early republican-era politician
Joaquim Saldanha Marinho, in his oft-cited statement, "this is
not the Republic of my dreams" ("Esta não é a República dos
meus sonhos"). For his part, Nabuco continually struggled with
the problem of Brazil's apparent "South Americanization,"
which he describes in diary entries written on October 16 and
17, 1893 in the midst of the naval revolt:

> Como o Brasil se sul-americanizou depressa, e com que
> fúria! [. . .] Agora as guerras civis de todo gênero! E quem
> se salvará deste mergulho? [. . .] [E]ssa gente se está sacri-
> ficando por fanatismo, os que não são pagos nem forçados
> por um Floriano, que não se sacrificaram por um Pedro II!
> Como isto é sul-americano, como se vê a degradação típica
> deste infeliz hemisfério—ao lado do despotismo bestial, o
> republicanismo imbecil do paraguaio! (October 16, 1893;
> *Diários* 2: 67–68) [8]

> Cada vez me convenço mais de que a civilização no Brasil
> acabou com a monarquia. O que há são restos dela. O que
> se vê é extraordinário. Não há mais princípio que detenha
> ninguém, nem pressão social que impossibilite os piores
> atentados. Que o país que desfaça em pedaços e depois de
> se desfazer caia cada um deles na mais completa miséria e
> abjeção, que importa [. . .] A classe de homens que governam
> é inverossímil, os processos de governo uns torpes, outros
> indignos, outros ridículos. Copiam os decretos da coleção
> sul-americana, dos estados de sitio orientais [i.e., uruguaios],
> argentinos, bolivianos, que sei eu? A adulação dos jornais
> ao ditador é tão grosseira como a dos guaranis do Paraguai.
> (October 17, 1893; *Diários* 2: 68) [9]

These entries are notable not only for Nabuco's palpable
anger, frustration, and fear for himself and his family, but

moreover for the extraordinary conceptual associations he makes. Nabuco identifies a series of negative character traits (fanaticism, despotism, ignorance, stupidity) with the apparently ascendant Brazilian lower and middle classes, which he racializes as indigenous and links to republican ideology and to a "collection" of failing or failed Spanish American states—most notably Paraguay.[39] By implication, Nabuco links the positive values of moderation, democracy, experience, and intelligence with his own upper class, with constitutional monarchy, and with the idea that Brazil is fundamentally *distinct* from its neighbors, a country with far more in common with England than with Bolivia or Peru. These sentiments were exacerbated by rumors during the 1893 revolt that Argentina had sold Floriano a warship, an act that would run counter to the established logic of Brazilian-Argentine rivalry, one of the bedrock assumptions of imperial-era nationalist discourse.[40] This sends Nabuco in an October 19, 1893 entry into a fit of patriotic fury marked by racial and class prejudice. He writes:

> Na República não há noção de honra nacional, nem tradições internacionais, nem sentimento de pátria [. . .] A República, seja como for, uma só ou muitas, independentes ou tributárias, prósperas ou falidas, com brasileiros ou com chins, contanto que seja a República. É a moral dos roleteiros em ação. O Brasil tornou-se uma casa de tavolagem, e os chamados republicanos não passam de ratoeiros barateiros [. . .] desse antro político. (*Diários* 2: 72) [10]

The notion of Brazil's necessary rivalry with Argentina, which Nabuco had put in the service of emancipation in *O Abolicionismo*, returns in this passage, as he sees the specter of transnational South American republicanism challenge Brazil's standing system of alliances.[41]

Of all Nabuco's diary entries and correspondence for 1889–94, perhaps the best distillation of his struggle with Brazil's "South Americanization" is found in an 1893 letter to André Rebouças, an old abolitionist colleague. In this letter, which Nabuco transcribes in his diary, he again hits on what he considers the deeper, troubling implications of the present republican disorder—that Brazil's national character may be no different from that of its neighbors, and that Brazil might be just another

"South American" nation: a violent, petty, unstable, and ungovernable land overrun by mobs in the thrall of despots and generals.[42] He laments:

> Nossos pais sabiam criar e conservar, nós só soubemos destruir e dissolver. Acabamos com tudo, até com a memória deles. Em que é que esta guerra civil se diferencia das outras guerras civis da América? Os que se batem de um e outro lado julgam ter uma bandeira clara, o direito por si, *exatamente como acontece em todas as guerras sul-americanas.* Cada lado está certo de ter razão, de estar morrendo por uma causa nobre e nacional por excelência, e assim as gerações passam, vertendo o seu sangue por uma série de causas nacionais, que todas impedem o país de consolidar-se de caminhar um passo. A confiança dos nossos republicanos parece ser que estas guerras não se repitam, *como antes era que eram impossíveis com os nossos hábitos e a nossa docilidade.* Os acontecimentos os desmentem cada dia e quanto mais desmentidos, mais afirmativos eles se tornam. É preciso ter uma indignação de jovem com uma experiência de velho para se poder dizer a verdade a esta infame república. (October 20, 1893; *Diários* 2: 73; my emphasis) [11]

As we will see in the next section, Nabuco would in the coming years remain a harsh critic of the Republic, taking advantage of the advent of civilian government in 1894 to mount a more public and sustained critique, and using events elsewhere on the continent to indirectly attack Brazil's republican leadership and to propose a new model for post-imperial Brazil based on Chile (a country that, conveniently enough, shares no border with Brazil), and which Nabuco viewed as the continent's least "South American" nation.

IV. *Balmaceda*: Chile's "Parliamentary Republic" as a Solution for Brazil

With the elevation of the civilian Prudente de Morais to the presidency of Brazil in 1894, Nabuco took on a more prominent public role, writing overtly political journalism, as in his "Political Notes" in the *Comércio de São Paulo* in 1895–96. Further, Nabuco contributed a series of articles to the *Jornal do Comércio* between January and March 1895 that responded

to the Chilean writer-politician Julio Bañados Espinosa's exhaustive—and exhausting—two-volume account of the Chilean
Revolution of 1891, *Balmaceda: Su Gobierno y la Revolución
de 1891* (1894). Nabuco's articles, collected under the title
Balmaceda, were apparently well-received by Brazilian readers, though José Veríssimo is said to have noted, "with a certain
malice, that Nabuco was a 'republican in Chile.'" Veríssimo
took issue with Nabuco on several points in his 1895 review
of *Balmaceda,* and at least one other critic found Nabuco's enthusiasm for Chile misplaced, commenting that Nabuco should
"cross the Andes" and "serve the [Brazilian] Republic" (Viana
Filho, *Joaquim Nabuco* 204, 206). And Martín García Mérou,
the Argentine writer whose pathbreaking *El Brasil intelectual*
(1900) was discussed in Chapter 1, and who seems to have
been an associate of Bañados Espinosa, described Nabuco's
monarchist instincts in 1900 as a form of "auto-suggestion" that
predisposed him to a biased and inaccurate—that is, anti-Bal-
maceda—viewpoint (272). In García Mérou's reading, "Nabuco
condemned [José Manuel] Balmaceda *a priori* [. . .] and he
substantiated his position by reading documents that confirmed
his instinctive error" (277; author's emphasis).

Despite its marginal place in Nabuco's collected writings,
Balmaceda is important for multiple reasons. In addition to
representing some of Nabuco's most incisive critical prose,[43]
Balmaceda saw Nabuco use Chile as the site for an implicit
critique of the Brazilian republican leadership in the manner of
Tomás Antônio Gonzaga's satirical *Cartas Chilenas* (Chilean
Letters, 1789), themselves modeled on Montesquieu's *Lettres
persanes* (1721).[44] In the anonymous *Cartas*—attributed to
Gonzaga, a figure in the aborted 1789 *inconfidência mineira*
revolt—the narrator Critilo describes the despotic governorship
of one Fanfarrão Minésio in a fantastical version of colonial
Chile, in what amounts to a satire of the Portuguese governor
of Minas Gerais, Luís da Cunha Pacheco e Meneses. Gonzaga's argument in the prologue to his *Cartas* for the value of
"translating" the text to Portuguese from the "original" Spanish
describes what I strongly believe was Nabuco's intent in writing
Balmaceda—to denounce by negative example: "Just as a Don
Quixote can banish the madness of Knights Errant from the
world," Gonzaga writes, "so can a Fanfarrão Minésio correct

the disorder of a despotic Governor" (26). In carrying forward the thematic parallels between the *Cartas* and *Balmaceda*, several of Gonzaga's specific criticisms of Minésio's governorship match up with what we will see are Nabuco's objections to José Manuel Balmaceda's presidency in Chile: Minésio does not respect legislative authority, he ignores legal precedent, awards favors and delegates power to supporters, appeals to the worst instincts of the people, and rejects enshrined "aristocratic" customs in favor of a mode of comportment the author demonizes as crass and plebian.[45] The general spirit and ideological orientation of Gonzaga's attack further approximate the two texts, underscoring the argument that Gonzaga's *Cartas* clearly served as a model for Nabuco. As Sérgio Buarque de Holanda notes, Gonzaga's critique, despite its revolutionary appearance, is aimed at defending a local status quo under threat from new elements in power: "The revolt of this *inconfidente* amounts to, at its core, an aristocrat's resentment" (*Tentativas* 229). What Buarque writes for Gonzaga in 1789 is likewise true for Nabuco in the years following 1889. Buarque explains:

> The tyranny of Cunha Menezes is unjust [for Gonzaga] not because it seeks to maintain a transitory, unsustainable order in power, but precisely because it allows for the scandalous ascension of new elements who are incapable of accommodating themselves to the good, worthy customs of the past. It is to this sudden ascent of uncultured men [. . .] that the poet takes as a personal offense. (227)

Aside from its compelling parallels with the *Cartas Chilenas*, *Balmaceda* merits our consideration because in it Nabuco offers a solution to the problem of Brazil's "South Americanization" announced in his diary entries and correspondence from the years following the 1889 declaration of the Republic. In *Balmaceda*, Nabuco mounts a vigorous defense of the "constitutionalists," that is, the supporters of Chile's powerful legislature who went to war with and defeated José Manuel Balmaceda (President, 1886–91), a reform-minded executive with dictatorial leanings who clashed with Congress in seeking greater leverage to make appointments and develop the national economy. Balmaceda's defeat after a brief armed struggle led to the installation of a "parliamentary republic" in Chile, in which the legislature dominated a largely ceremonial president. This system, which strongly favored the entrenched landed aristocracy whose interests were represented in the legislature, though not technically amounting to parliamentary rule, nonetheless took on features of that system (notably legislative supremacy), and would remain in place until 1925.

Drawing on Mill and Bagehot's theories of the evolution of political institutions, Nabuco argued that Chile had for decades been peacefully developing toward a *de facto* parliamentary democracy even before the disruption represented by the Revolution of 1891. He strongly critiqued Bañados Espinosa's interpretation of events using, interestingly enough, the same legalistic criteria employed by the Chilean writer in his account, and attacking Balmaceda as an aspiring dictator who by usurping legislative authority had threatened to undo decades of moderate, effective government by a morally responsible aristocratic elite. Further, Nabuco offers his readers the example of Chile as a South American state that, while nominally republican, embodies what he considers the best aspects of constitutional monarchy as practiced during Brazil's Second Empire, a period Nabuco was busy celebrating in his concurrent book project, *Um Estadista do Império*. These were qualities like legislative supremacy, rule of law, judicious balancing of order and liberty, and leadership by a moral, modernizing (and wealthy) elite, whom Nabuco believed would progressively expand the scope of political participation to an ever-greater share of the public. As Nabuco argued, "[a]s circunstâncias faziam assim do balmacedismo o núcleo de uma nova fundação política, e, se de fato a oligarquia pesava sôbre o país, as massas deviam inclinar no conflito para o lado do Govêrno" (*OC* 2: 79; "circumstances made *balmacedismo* the nucleus of a new political foundation, and though in fact the oligarchy weighed on the country, the masses nonetheless leaned in the conflict toward the side of the Government [i.e., Congress]"). In the following paragraphs, I will contextualize Nabuco's position against the backdrop of the 1891 Chilean Revolution and its divergent historiographical interpretations. I will then offer a detailed analysis of Nabuco's argument in *Balmaceda*, paying particular attention to how the text functions as a program for overcoming Brazil's "South

Americanization," and to Nabuco's description of Chile as a model for post-imperial Brazil.

While the 1891 revolution has been overshadowed by Chile's tumultuous twentieth-century history, particularly the 1973 military coup that toppled Salvador Allende's democratically elected government and installed a military dictatorship under Augusto Pinochet, it has nonetheless been subject to debate among historians and other exegetes. "Constitutional" interpreters like Nabuco have criticized Balmaceda for bypassing the legislature and upsetting decades of hard-won stability along with the delicate balance of power,[46] while others, including generally left-leaning Chilean "economic" historians like Luis Vitale, Alfredo Jocelyn-Holt Letelier, and Armando de Ramón, have defended Balmaceda as a failed modernizer whose attempts to bring progressive reform to Chile and to open the political process were foiled by an entrenched aristocracy in control of the legislature, themselves held in the thrall of foreign, especially British, economic interests. The presidential cause also found an early defender in *modernista* poet Rubén Darío, who had met Balmaceda while living in Chile and was a colleague of Bañados Espinosa at the Chilean journal *La Época*. In two short prose pieces on the subject, Darío presents Balmaceda as a tragic figure caught between a cruel elite and the masses, writing: "Balmaceda, whether trusting or misled, forgot that his government stood between two forces that if they are in all places irreconcilable, are in Chile terribly devastating: above, the millionaire; below, the masses, the penniless" (*OC* 4: 1150). Noting the charges made against Balmaceda and his cause, Darío calls upon Bañados Espinosa to tell "the story of Balmaceda [. . .] who defend[ed] himself from his enemies with his vigorous intelligence, with his steely character, and with the conviction of his ideas. Many have attacked him fiercely, and he has used his silence as a weapon" (1155–56).

José Veríssimo takes a middle view in an 1895 review of Nabuco's *Balmaceda*, published after Bañados Espinosa had effectively answered Darío's call for him to write the history of the deposed regime. Veríssimo charges Nabuco with misreading Bañados Espinosa's text and the 1891 revolution itself, and with oversimplifying the conflict between Balmaceda and the

Chilean Congress. Further, he casts Balmaceda as a politician sincerely interested in reforming Chile's "social constitution," whose efforts were undermined by his failure to recognize that Chile was not ready for these changes, and he charges Nabuco with faulty legal reasoning in his critique ("A Revolução Chilena" 37). For Veríssimo, Balmaceda did not commit a crime, but made a fundamental strategic and historical mistake: "Balmaceda's error or crime (in politics only the defeated are criminals) is not entirely an error committed against legality, since he had the law on his side, but [. . .] worse than a crime, was an error [. . .] To attempt [transformative political reform] was more a violation of the national will than it was of Chile's political rules." However, Veríssimo sides with Nabuco in condemning Balmaceda's dictatorial behavior, and states that "this, whatever the rightness or nobility of Balmaceda's cause, is enough to dishonor and defame him" (40, 43).

In recent decades, an "economic" interpretation of the Revolution of 1891 that is generally sympathetic to Balmaceda's reformist impulses and is critical of the entrenched interests represented by the Congress seems to have become dominant. Vitale, for example, casts Balmaceda as an economic nationalist, dismisses the pro-legislature faction as a "seditious campaign," and argues that "[t]he fundamental cause of the 1891 civil war was the crisis in [Chile's] relations with Great Britain, occasioned by Balmaceda's nationalist policies [with regard to nitrates and trade]. The opposition between this political project, which sought to halt the process of Chile's semi-colonization, and British interests (along with those of its junior partner, the Chilean bourgeoisie) was the principal cause of the war" (274, 277, 281). More recently, Jocelyn-Holt Letelier has argued that Balmaceda, and not the legislative elite, understood the benefits of using Chile's nitrates-based wealth to "reaffirm the State and make it the axis and channeling agent of growth in the increasing complexity [of Chilean society]. Behind Balmaceda's program of public works was the idea of national economic growth that would come to benefit everyone" (30). Along the same lines, de Ramón speculates that "the success of Balmaceda's government would have led to renewed cultural, social, and even economic growth, while the triumph of Congress in 1891 limited political life to a salon or club intrigue, with resources and power becoming [or remaining] concentrated in a small part of Chilean society." In this context, Balmaceda becomes "another Chilean leader," as perhaps was the case of Allende in 1973, "who chose suicide once he had lost the battle against his enemies" (121, 231).

As we have seen, Nabuco was very much interested in progressive national reform—that is, "progressive" in the context of his nineteenth-century liberal monarchism, and provided this reform could be achieved without undue social turmoil or infringement of individual freedoms. However, in his account of events in Chile, Nabuco presents Balmaceda as insufficiently reformist to offset the negative effects of his uprooting of the standing political order and his alleged disregard for individual liberty. [47] Nabuco barely mentions Balmaceda's economic and infrastructure policies, though to be fair, these are also given short shrift by Balmaceda partisan Bañados Espinosa, whose argument focuses on asserting the legal grounds for Balmaceda's government and defending his personal character (Bañados Espinosa 2: 657). Adhering to a strict "constitutionalist" position, Nabuco contends that while one could make the argument along with Bañados Espinosa (and the aforementioned "economic" historians) that Balmaceda acted in the *spirit* of prior reformist presidents in his dealings with a strong-willed legislature, Balmaceda should ultimately be condemned for undermining the hard-won legitimacy of Chile's representative institutions, and for infecting them with "the South American dictatorial genius," as he put it. Nabuco, noting "the pride Chileans had in their political stability," writes:

> Na Revolução de 1891, pode-se afirmar, o antigo espírito chileno, os Portales e os Montts, estariam resolutamente com a sociedade contra Balmaceda. A tarefa de achar antecedentes para êste pode tentar os eruditos do seu partido, mas é de todo baldada. Balmaceda irrompe na História chilena, como uma aparição imprevista; é uma evocação, pode-se dizer, na presidência do Chile, do *gênio sul-americano da ditadura* que nunca havia penetrado nela. Justificá-lo como estando dentro da linha seguida pelo país desde 1833, é fazer ato de cepticismo. A sua defesa pode ser radical, democrática, científica, como se queira, mas não pode ser histórica, conservadora, constitucional, *sobretudo tomando-se a Constituição como a soma das conquistas tácitas feitas pelo espírito*

> *das instituições sobre a letra do foral.* (*OC* 2: 15, 19; my
> emphasis) [12]

For Nabuco, Balmaceda's undermining of the prevailing
political order is especially egregious because of the unfavorable conditions he believed South American nation-states faced
(whether because of environment, history, or civilizational or
racial factors) in establishing stable institutions and in balancing
order and liberty. Revisiting one of the principal themes of his
1889–94 diary entries, and referring specifically to Balmaceda's
alleged moves to replace Chile's existing political parties with a
new, single party under his control, Nabuco argues:

> Em *nossos países*, onde a nação se mantém em menoridade
> permanente, as liberdades, os direitos de cada um, o patrimô-
> nio de todos, vivem resguardados apenas por alguns princí-
> pios, por algumas tradições ou costumes, que não passam de
> barreiras morais, sem resistência e que o menor abalo deita
> por terra. A êsses países, onde a liberdade carece do amparo
> do poder, onde a lei é frágil, não se adaptam instituições que
> só pode tolerar uma nação como a norte-americana, cuja
> opinião é uma fôrça que levaria de vencida qualquer govêrno,
> cujos partidos são exércitos que dentro de horas se levanta-
> riam armados sob o comando de seus chefes, e que, por isso
> mesmo, se respeitam como duas grandes potências. (*OC* 2:
> 37; my emphasis) [13]

Nabuco flavors his critique of Balmaceda with several ideas
borrowed from Bagehot, revealing the enduring influence of
liberal utilitarianism on his thinking. In addition to comparing
Balmaceda at one point to England's King Charles in his battle
with Parliament (*OC* 2: 15–16), Nabuco revisits Bagehot's
discussion of cabinet government, casting Balmaceda and his
allies as "um gabinete pretendendo governar sem as Câmaras
e invocando para isso fragmentos arqueológicos ou postulados
da ciência moderna" (43; "a cabinet attempting to govern without the Chambers [of Congress] and invoking as justification
archeological fragments or postulates of modern science").
Accordingly, for Nabuco the Chilean legislature was justified
in dissolving Balmaceda's rebellious "cabinet" by force, since
Balmaceda failed to recognize what Bagehot described as the
cabinet's organic linkage to the legislature: it is formed *from* the

legislature, and is therefore responsible *to* it. As Nabuco puts it, "[u]m Presidente de República que não convoca o Congresso [. . .] não é mais um Poder constitucional [. . .] é um ditador que se sente o único poder no país" (50; "A President of the Republic who does not convene Congress [. . .] is no longer a constitutional power [. . .] but a dictator who feels himself to be the only power in the country").

Further, in *Balmaceda* Nabuco articulates his lingering preference for constitutional monarchy over republican government—though writing only months after the end of military rule in Brazil, he hedges his bets. In one passage, which makes clear reference to Dom Pedro II's abdication in 1889, Nabuco limits his argument to the realm of the theoretical, writing that, "[a] monarquia *seria* infinitamente mais humana do que a república, *se* o sentimento que tem feito tanto monarca abdicar, de preferência a aceitar a guerra civil, *fôsse* reputado indigno de um presidente" (*OC* 2: 56; my emphasis; "a monarchy *would be* infinitely more humane than a republic, *if* the feeling that has caused so many monarchs to abdicate, that is, in order to avoid civil war, *were* considered undignified in a president"). Elsewhere Nabuco borrows Bagehot's argument for the superiority of non-elective, preferably royal heads of state to make the implied case for the preeminence of leaders like Dom Pedro II over Balmaceda and the Brazilian *marechais*: "Nos *chamados governos presidenciais* o presidente está muito mais adstrito ao jugo partidário do que nas repúblicas parlamentares, onde êle representa o papel de um soberano constitucional, cingindo-se à vontade das maiorias" (22; my emphasis; "In *so-called presidential governments* the president is much more closely tied to the yoke of the party than is the case in parliamentary republics, where he plays the role of constitutional sovereign and is tied to the will of the majority"). And referring specifically to Latin America, Nabuco describes Balmaceda as making a failed, "retrograde" attempt to substitute a presidential system that he viewed as regionally untenable for the proven success of Chile's *de facto* parliamentary system: "Por mais singular que seja essa revelação, [. . .] de que o futuro do Chile depende de substituir pelo sistema norte-americano, *nunca ensaiado com sucesso em povo latino* [. . .] é incontestável que a êle Balmaceda pertence a iniciativa dêsse movimento retrógrado" (112; my emphasis; "As strange an idea as it may sound, [. . .] that the future of Chile would depend on the imposition of the North American system, *never before successfully adopted by any Latin people*, [. . .] it is undeniable that Balmaceda is responsible for this retrograde movement"). Finally, and echoing Mill, Nabuco compares the Chilean aristocracy to its English counterpart, describing it as comprising Chile's most moral, most capable citizens, and as a broadly progressive-minded group working toward gradual democratization. Nabuco writes that "[a] aristocracia chilena [. . .] tem alguma coisa do espírito nacional da aristocracia inglêsa; mantém-se em contato, em comunhão de interêsse, com as camadas populares, e procura de cada vez mais apoiar-se nelas. Os processos da Ditadura tornavam-se odiosos ao povo, nesse estado de espírito" (80; "the Chilean aristocracy [. . .] has something of the English aristocracy's national spirit; it keeps in contact with, and shares the interests of, the popular classes, and increasingly looks to these for support. The processes of the dictatorship became odious to the people, given this state of affairs").

For our purposes, however, the most significant feature of Nabuco's argument in *Balmaceda* is the solution he offers by way of his analysis of Chilean politics to the problem of Brazil's "South Americanization." Nabuco's first task in this regard is to establish the transferability to Brazil of the lessons of Balmaceda's presidency and of the Revolution of 1891. While Nabuco warns early in *Balmaceda* that the differences between the Chilean and Brazilian revolutions outweigh the similarities (*OC* 2: 5), I believe that he is again hedging his bets, inoculating himself in the event that Prudente de Morais's civilian administration (1894–98) were to give way to renewed military rule. In fact, Nabuco draws comparisons between Chile and Brazil on several occasions, as fellow South American nations (see Nabuco's discussion of *nossos países*—"our countries"), and moreover, as countries that have to his mind evinced a unique, admirable dedication to ordered government and personal liberties in an unfavorable Latin American environment (37).[48] Nabuco expresses his admiration for Chile in the following terms:

> Por Chile senti sempre grande admiração. Há mais energia nacional, quer me parecer, nessa estreita faixa comprimida entre a Cordilheira e o Pacífico do que em todo o resto da

América do Sul. Sem nenhum pensamento de desconfiança
contra o nosso vizinho do Prata [i.e. Argentina] que nos faça
cultivar, por motivo político, a amizade do Chile, temos,
para procurar essa amizade, as mais elevadas razões que se
possam dar entre dois países. Não sei que homem de espírito
disse, há anos, que só encontrara duas nações organizadas e
livres na América Latina: *o Império do Chile e a República
do Brasil.* Apesar de sermos nós (a história dirá se apesar
da monarquia, se devido a ela) a sociedade, sem exceção
alguma, mais igualitária do mundo, e de ser o Chile, pelo
contrário, uma aristocracia política, tínhamos a mesma con-
tinuidade de ordem, de govêrno parlamentar, de liberdade
civil, de pureza administrativa, de seriedade, decôro e digni-
dade oficial. Um e outro govêrno eram exceções genuínas na
América do Sul, saliências de terra firme entre ondas revoltas
e ensangüentadas. (*OC* 2: 8; author's emphasis) [14]

Further, Nabuco draws explicit parallels between the figures of Balmaceda and the *marechais*, comparing the deposed
Chilean president and Floriano Peixoto in *A Intervenção Estrangeira Durante a Revolta de 1893* (Foreign Intervention
during the Revolt of 1893), an 1895 volume dealing with the
Revolta da Armada, and something of a companion piece to
Balmaceda.[49] Finally, Nabuco celebrates the Chileans (or at
least, the congressionalists) as political pragmatists who, like
Thiers in France, were able to put ideology aside and recognize
the value of Brazil's constitutional monarchy: "Republicanos
de instinto e educação, os chilenos acolhêram simpaticamen-
te o 15 de Novembro como a data final do ciclo republicano,
com a intuição prática do seu temperamento positivo, a obra
democrática e nacional da monarquia no Brasil—obra singular
de paciência, constância, desinterêsse e patriotismo, que ficará
sendo, na atmosfera agitada e convulsa deste século na América
Latina, um fenômeno quase inexplicável" ("Republicans by
instinct and education, the Chileans celebrated on November
15th [1889] the end of the republican cycle, and with the practical intuition that is the product of their positive temperament,
[they celebrated] the democratic and national achievement of
the Brazilian monarchy—a singular act of patience, persistence,
disinterestedness, and patriotism, that will remain, in the agitated and convulsive context of Latin America in this century,
an almost inexplicable phenomenon") (*OC* 2: 9).

Having over the course of *Balmaceda* established the relevance of events in Chile for Brazil, as well as having presented his indictment of the now deposed Chilean president, Nabuco proceeds in the volume's "Post-Scriptum," evocatively titled "A Questão da América Latina" (The Question of Latin America), to expand the scope of his discussion outward, offering a solution to Brazil's "South Americanization" that makes specific reference to the Spanish American republics as a group. Here Nabuco repeats perhaps the most fundamental maxim of liberal utilitarianism as applied to politics: that choice of government should not be determined by ideology, but should be a pragmatic decision made in light of a desire to "obter para o [. . .] país o maior grau possível de liberdade" (*OC* 2: 137; "obtain for the [. . .] country the greatest possible degree of liberty*"*). Theoretically this should allow Brazilians a choice between constitutional monarchy and the Republic, yet by 1895, Nabuco, perhaps sensing that a restored Brazilian monarchy was unlikely, viewed the operative choice as between a parliamentary and presidential republic. The year 1889 had also forced Nabuco to retroactively revise his view of the solidity of Brazil's now-defunct constitutional monarchy. No longer a system that could absorb great social changes on the order of abolition, as implied in *O Abolicionismo*, Nabuco now presents the Second Empire as much more fragile, held together by the exceptionalism of Dom Pedro II as a capable "modern sovereign," an idea Mill and Bagehot, both skeptics of kingly ability, would not have seconded. Nabuco argues:

> Se tivemos a liberdade na monarquia, foi só porque o poder se continha a si mesmo. Isto era devido à elevada consciência nacional, que por herança, educação, e seleção histórica, *os soberanos modernos quase todos encarnam*. O respeito à dignidade da nação, o desejo de vê-la altamente reputada no mundo, era natural na monarquia, que era o govêrno pela fôrça moral sòmente. (*OC* 2: 138; my emphasis) [15]

Nabuco does not close the door entirely on monarchy in *Balmaceda*, arguing that if Brazil were to restore it, the United States would not use the Monroe Doctrine as a basis for objection (*OC* 2: 141). Further, Nabuco acknowledges that the fall of the monarchy has convinced him of the fact that Brazil is "parte de um sistema político mais vasto" ("part of a broader political system"), that events in other Latin American republics have a bearing on Brazil, and that the Latin American states are subject to certain common political forces (139, 142). However, in contrast to the agonized tone of his 1889–94 diary entries, in which he oscillates between environmental and national character-based explanations for Brazil's "South Americanization," in his "Post-Scriptum" Nabuco ridicules environmental determinism in its extreme form: "Muitos acreditam mesmo que se trata de uma fôrça cósmica, como se o oxigênio e o azôto formassem na América uma combinação especial dotada de vibrações republicanas" (140; "Many truly believe in a cosmic force, that, like oxygen and nitrogen, would come together in America in a special compound that gives off republican vibrations"). [50] Instead, he settles on a fairly hopeful, Millian explanation of history *itself* as the driving force behind a nation's character traits and choice of government. He describes Brazil as a nation "*criada na paz e na moleza da escravidão doméstica e da liberdade monárquica, enervada por uma ausência total de perigo em mais de cinqüenta anos, habituada* à atenção [do] Imperador" (138; my emphasis; "*raised* in the peace and mildness of domestic slavery and monarchical liberty, *enervated* by a total lack of danger for more than fifty years, *accustomed* to the attention of the Emperor"). In other words, Brazil's allegedly unique national characteristics (mildness, love of liberty, peacefulness, etc.) are for Nabuco largely the products of its unique history, and can be preserved into the future if the Brazilian people (or at least its governing elite) choose a form of government amenable to these traits.

In short, "South Americanization" for Nabuco need not signify the annulment of Brazil's national specificity, through it *does* imply that Brazil must choose its political models from among those variations of republican government practiced by its neighbors. As Nabuco observes, somewhat ironically, "[c]om efeito, ninguém procura justificar a nossa transformação republicana por motivos tirados das condições e conveniências do nosso país, mas sòmente pela circunstância de estar o Brasil na América. Dêsse modo o observador brasileiro, para ter idéia exata da direção que levamos, é obrigado a estudar a marcha do Continente" (*OC* 2: 139–40; "in effect, no one seeks to justify our transformation into a republic with reference to our state or to the favorable conditions of our country. Rather, they will refer exclusively to the fact of Brazil being in America. In this sense the Brazilian observer, if he wants to know the direction we will travel, is obliged to study the march of the Continent"). Nabuco reprises the choice between "Paraguayan tyranny" and the Chilean "parliamentary republic," referring to the former in the context of 1889, and writing that "a tirania paraguaia reviveu em nós na ponta das mesmas baionetas e lanças que a derribaram" (*OC* 2: 139; "the Paraguayan tyranny was reborn among us on the tips of the same bayonets and lances that destroyed it [in 1870]"). As for Chile, he describes the country as "ainda que de raça espanhola [. . .] uma exceção [. . .] um capricho de ordem moral na formação da América do Sul, como há aparentemente tanto capricho na sua estrutura geológica" (137; "though of Spanish race [. . .] an exception [. . .] a caprice of the moral order of South America's formation, just as there appears to be so much capriciousness in its geological structure").[51] Further, Nabuco writes that Chile's unique governing model has served it as an "escola de educação, da influência sã, varonil, patriótica" (139; "a source of education, of healthy, manly, patriotic influence"), capable of raising the moral level of the population.[52] In sum, Nabuco contends in the "Post-Scriptum" that Chile's *de facto* parliamentary democracy has contributed to its enviable status as the least "South American" of the South American republics, as an aristocratic, pragmatic, pseudo-English "caprice"—an ideal site onto which Nabuco can project his desire for Brazil's continued orderly, liberalizing, and aristocracy-guided political evolution as a unique nation-state. For Nabuco, the choice for Brazilians between idealized Chilean "civilization" and caricatured "Paraguayan" barbarism should be clear.[53]

***

During the latter half of the 1890s, Nabuco distanced himself from his colleagues in Brazil's monarchist opposition, abandoning the political abstentionism he advocated in "O Dever dos Monarquistas" (The Duty of the Monarchists, 1895) and warming to the idea of renewed government service. As he theorized in *Um Estadista do Império*, "[c]ada revolução subentende uma luta posterior e aliança de um dos aliados, quase sempre os exaltados, com os vencidos" (*OC* 3: 30; "all revolutions entail subsequent conflict, and the alliance of one of the allied parties, almost always that of the fanatics, with the defeated"). By the late 1890s, Nabuco seemed convinced that the time for reconciliation between republicans and monarchists had come, as he reveals in a March 26, 1897 letter to Rebouças: "A pátria é assim mesmo, é preciso não recusá-la nesses momentos em que ela se torna selvagem e hedionda, porque essa manifestação é o resultado e a expressão de causas anteriores acumuladas, é o êrro das gerações passadas que dá o seu fruto" (*OC* 13: 275; "This is how the country really is, and we must not abandon it in those moments in which it becomes savage and repulsive, because this is the result and expression of accumulated historical factors, it is the error of past generations bearing fruit"). The new president, Manuel Ferraz de Campos Sales, was inaugurated in 1898, and he was eager to bring Nabuco into his government regardless of his monarchism, which was by then largely consigned to the realm of the theoretical. Indeed, Nabuco seems to have sufficiently reconciled himself to the reality of a republican Brazil to half-joke about the country's state—still quite precarious, in his opinion—and his own prospects for renewed public service in an August 19, 1898 letter to Hilário de Gouvêa:

> [M]uita gente [está a] dizer que vou ser [. . .] ministro. Realmente seria um terremoto! Pobre país! é tudo que lhe posso dizer. Como a nossa sorte é a mesma da Espanha, do Peru, do Uruguai! Que destino nos está reservado? Não sente você, porém, que já se trata de nós; que já temos o cheiro da boa prêsa, senão, ainda do cadaver que as ondas vão atirando para a praia, onde o espreitam os abutres? Para que lhe escrever neste tom? (*OC* 13: 289) [16]

In 1899 Nabuco accepted a position representing Brazil in a border dispute with British Guiana, which would lead to assignments as minister to Great Britain in 1900, and as Brazil's first ambassador to the United States, a post he would hold from 1905 until his death in 1910. While in Washington, Nabuco would put into action his preference for US-led Pan-Americanism over Brazil's earlier policy of maintaining closer ties to Europe and largely ignoring its diplomatic relations with

Spanish America. As Nabuco made clear in the "Post-Scriptum" to *Balmaceda*, he viewed this shift as a necessary, pragmatic choice for Brazil, and an extension of his call in *Balmaceda* for Brazil to model itself on Chile's "parliamentary republic": "A manutenção de um vasto continente em estado permanente de desgovêrno, de anarquia, é um fato que dentro de certo tempo há de atrair forçosamente a atenção do mundo [i.e., Europa e os EUA], como afinal a atraiu o desaproveitamento da África" (*OC* 2: 140; "A vast continent in a prolonged, seemingly permanent state of misgovernment, of anarchy, will within a certain amount of time necessarily attract the attention of the world, just as the misuse of Africa eventually did").[54] Further, Nabuco acknowledged the growing interest of the United States in Latin America in a March 14, 1899 letter to Rui Barbosa, tying this to the US's gradual abandonment of the constitutional framers' caution against making foreign alliances and engaging in colonial activity: "Ninguém dirá que a política e a diplomacia brasileira podem ser hoje as mesmas coisas que eram quando a Federação Americana ainda se conformava ao conselho dos seus fundadores de não ter colônias, nem querer aliados" (*OC* 14: 10; "No one would argue that Brazilian policy and diplomacy can be the same today as they were when the American Federation still adhered to the advice of its founders not to have colonies, nor to seek out allies").[55] That said, Nabuco seems to have genuinely believed that the Monroe Doctrine was not intrinsically interventionist (a position at odds with José Martí and José Enrique Rodó, as we saw in this book's second chapter), though he acknowledged and opposed instances in which the US government interpreted the doctrine as condoning foreign intervention.[56] Nabuco further contended that it was in Latin America's interest to adopt *monroismo* and to cultivate better relations with the United States—possibly before Washington forced the issue. As Nabuco argued in a 1906 speech, "the preliminary step for the formation of the American conscience is that the Latin Republics look to the part the United States had and has to play in guarding the Monroe Doctrine as in no way offensive to the pride and dignity of any of them, but, on the contrary, as a privilege which they ought to support" (Joaquim Nabuco et al. 15). As Viana Filho notes, "it was tolerable to Nabuco that the United States pretended to be 'the queen of the American chessboard,'" because, Nabuco reasoned, US domination was more benign than that of Europe, and was more conducive to international peace and rule of law (Nabuco, "The Share" 57). Moreover, while the Americans were showing themselves apt to intervene in Central America and the Caribbean, Brazil seemed to Nabuco too large and too distant to represent a likely target for intervention (Viana Filho, *Joaquim Nabuco* 303).[57] While Nabuco's embrace of Pan-Americanism won him friends in the United States, most notably Elihu Root (Secretary of State, 1905–09), his position distanced him from some erstwhile allies in the Brazilian diplomatic corps, including Manuel de Oliveira Lima and Rio Branco, a former monarchist and Brazil's Minister of Foreign Relations from 1902 to 1912.

In sum, Ferreira de Araújo's characterization of Nabuco as a "case apart" in Brazilian politics seems apt when one contrasts the republicanism of many of Nabuco's peers to his staunch advocacy of English-style constitutional monarchy, his embrace of Chile's "parliamentary republic," and his impassioned late-period Pan-Americanism. If we take a broader view and properly contextualize Nabuco's seeming eccentricities, we see that in fact his evolving position on Brazil's place in America is remarkably consistent with a tradition of Brazilian hispano-skepticism and selective approximation to Spanish America that dates at least from José Bonifácio and was exemplified in Nabuco's generation by Euclides da Cunha, Eduardo Prado, and others. Following Bonifácio and drawing on the ideas of Walter Bagehot and John Stuart Mill, Nabuco defended constitutional monarchy as the best available means for Brazil to balance order and liberty while maintaining territorial integrity and a unique national identity. He was concerned about Brazil's relationships with its neighbors, whether in terms of Argentine competition or Paraguayan "tyranny"—particularly after the fall of the monarchy in 1889 brought his fear of the country's "South Americanization" to the fore. Far from conceding Brazilian participation in a supranational Latin American *magna patria* as advocated by Spanish American thinkers like Simón Bolívar, Rodó, and Alfonso Reyes (who will be addressed in the following chapter), Nabuco championed Chile's "parliamentary republic" precisely because Chile struck him as the *least* "South American" of nations, the *least* like the continent's array of apparently dysfunctional presidential democracies, and the *most* like Brazil's Second Empire. While Nabuco was fond of commenting on the arbitrariness of one's nationality and down-played his own patriotism, his frame of reference remained staunchly national throughout his career. Even when broaching the most international of questions, Nabuco seemed convinced of the need to "remain Brazilian."

Alfonso Reyes

Culture, Humanism, and Brazil's
Place in the American Utopia

> La red invisible de la lengua—una lengua, sin
> embargo, tan cercana y tan parecida a la nuestra—
> ha resultado una telaraña de acero lo bastante
> resistente para contribuir con eficacia a mantener la
> unidad de este inmenso continente metido dentro de
> otro: la nación brasileña. Acabada ya la formación
> del pueblo, la primera evolución nacional, la red se
> afloja ahora lo bastante para volverse permeable.
> Permeable hasta cierto punto, claro está.
> —Alfonso Reyes
> "Sobre la reforma de la ortografía portuguesa"
> (1931)

> El aprovechamiento de una tradición no significa
> un paso atrás, sino un paso adelante, a condición de
> que sea un paso orientado en una línea maestra y no
> al azar.
> —Alfonso Reyes
> "Atenea política," speech given in Rio de Janeiro
> (1932)

It is difficult to properly convey the extent of the contribution
of Alfonso Reyes (1889–1959) to Mexican, and more broadly,
Latin American thought, if only because of the monumental
written record he left in the twenty-six volumes of the Fondo de
Cultura Económica edition of his *Obras completas* (1955–93).
Reyes's complete works present a maddeningly diverse collection of essays, journalism, speeches, and assorted pieces
on Mexican, Latin American, European, and classical Greco-
Roman literature and history. Taken as a whole, Reyes's work

reads as a refreshingly non-hierarchical series of reflections on the history of ideas, politics, diplomacy, travel, language, gastronomy, philosophy, and innumerable other topics. Reyes devoted whole volumes to writers like Góngora, Goethe, Mallarmé, and the Mexican *modernista* poet Amado Nervo; wrote his own poetry (including a poetic rewriting of the legend of Iphigenia); and penned mountains of letters, book reviews, sketches, and anecdotes, along with a Spanish translation of most of Homer's *Iliad*. Among the preferred topics of Reyes's essayistic and critical prose were the defense of culture, the role of the humanistic intellectual, and Latin America's utopian vocation—all three of which betray the strong, formative influence of José Enrique Rodó on his thinking. Reyes is perhaps less well-known than his generational colleagues José Vasconcelos (1882–1959), who wrote the polemical and nearly unclassifiable essay *La raza cósmica* (1925), and Martín Luis Guzmán (1887–1976), author of *El águila y la serpiente* (1928), a novel of the Mexican Revolution. Nonetheless, Reyes is recognized as a thinker of great range and depth, a perceptive critic, and a writer of great clarity and elegance. His best-known contributions are invariably his essays, among which stand out the early, impressionistic "Visión de Anáhuac" (1915), the classically minded "Discurso por Virgilio" (1932–33), the much-anthologized "Notas sobre la inteligencia americana" (1936), and "Pasado inmediato" (1939), a historical synthesis of the Mexican Revolution. In addition to his work as a writer, Reyes served as Mexico's ambassador to Brazil from 1930 to 1936, and wrote a number of essayistic and creative pieces dealing with the country, in which he addressed themes ranging from colonial Brazilian history and the Portuguese language to the physical and human landscape of Rio de Janeiro. By applying Reyes's overarching cultural and humanistic preoccupations to his thinking on Brazil and to the texts he wrote while in the country, we can gain a sense for how Brazil featured in Reyes's vision of Latin America as a *category*, and more specifically, as an ideal space, an *Última Tule* (Ultima Thule) that would couple the supranational ties of Rodó's *magna patria* with a distinct utopian vocation.

The structure of this chapter is as follows. I will first present a brief summary of Reyes's life, arguably as varied and energetic as his writing. This will serve to contextualize Reyes against the formative influences of the Ateneo de la Juventud (in which he participated along with Pedro Henríquez Ureña, Antonio Caso, and other young Mexico City–based intellectuals), the Mexican Revolution, and Reyes's career as a diplomat and expatriate author writing to a Mexican and broader Ibero-American public. In sections two through four I will describe in detail Reyes's aforementioned three major thematic preoccupations (the defense of culture, the humanist's public role, and Latin America's utopian vocation), so as to demonstrate in the chapter's fifth and final section how Reyes would apply these perennial concerns to his thinking on Brazil. While critics like Carlos Monsiváis may complain that Reyes has on the whole not received sufficient scholarly attention, his relationship to Brazil has spawned a number of scholarly reflections, with Fred P. Ellison, James Willis Robb, and others contributing several articles (and in Ellison's case, a book) on Reyes's "Brazilian" writings and his relationships with prominent Brazilian intellectuals, including the poets Manuel Bandeira, Ronald de Carvalho and Cecília Meireles.[1] Though the popularity of this theme or sub-theme in Reyes scholarship may seem unlikely—after all, the pieces Reyes dedicates to Brazil form a small portion of his overall work—it makes a certain amount of sense: as a diplomat, Reyes lived for a longer time in Brazil than he did in France or Argentina, and spent nearly as much time in Brazil as he did in his beloved Spain. Indeed, Ellison argues, "it is fair to call Reyes a Mexican 'Brazilianist,' [. . .] as a non-Brazilian scholar whose work focuses on the country" (*Alfonso Reyes e o Brasil* 15). While there is a bit of anachronism in Ellison's contention (the term *Brazilianist* most commonly refers to US-based social scientists and historians who have studied Brazil since the Cold War era), he is correct to the extent that Reyes's interpretations of Luso-Brazilian literature, history, and culture make important—if underappreciated—contributions to the fields of Luso-Brazilian and comparative Luso-Hispanic studies.

I will argue in this chapter that scholars concerned with Reyes's relationship to Brazil can build on the important contributions made by Ellison, Robb, and others, who have elucidated many of Reyes's biographical and textual connections to Brazil, by shifting focus to give priority to the question of how the *idea* of Brazil fits into Reyes's conception of Latin America, and his broader worldview. To this end I will offer extensive discussion of Reyes's thoughts on language (particularly the Portuguese language's relationship to Spanish), and of his ambivalent identification of Brazil with *Última Tule*, the title of Reyes's most substantial collection of continentally themed texts.[2] Finally, I will return to the phenomenon of Spanish American identity projection that I identified in this book's first chapter, arguing that despite Reyes's affection for and knowledge of Brazil, as well as the priority he gave in his writing and public life to the bridging of cultural differences, he retains a fundamentally hispanocentric vision of the country, repeatedly incorporating Brazil at the rhetorical and conceptual levels into a scheme for continental utopia strongly indebted to Rodó and grounded in the notion that Latin America is the inheritor of a Greco-Latin tradition Reyes understood as mediated through a specifically *Spanish*-origin language, history, and cultural identity. Let us begin at the start of Reyes's life and career, in the northern Mexican city of Monterrey.

I. Reyes, a "Many-Tentacled Octopus"

Alfonso Reyes,[3] born in Monterrey in 1889 into a large and affluent family, moved to Mexico City to complete his education and graduated with a law degree in 1912 (his thesis would eventually be published in volume 26 of his *Obras completas* as *Teoría de la sanción*). As Reyes noted in 1939, in early twentieth-century Mexico law was the preferred course of study for young literature-inclined men such as himself, as was the case for a number of generations in Latin America before the establishment of independent university literature departments and academic programs in the region.[4] As a young man, Reyes established himself as part of the capital's intellectual vanguard, participating in the Sociedad de Conferencias, a group founded in 1907 and later reorganized as the Ateneo de la Juventud and then the Ateneo de México. The group, centered on the Dominican expatriate Pedro Henríquez Ureña (1884–1946), nicknamed "Sócrates"[5] for his role as an intellectual mentor, featured several of Mexico's future intellectual luminaries, including the philosopher Antonio Caso (1883–1946) and José Vasconcelos, future educator, Minister of Public Education (1921–24), failed presidential candidate, and inventor of the term *raza cósmica*.[6] While the *ateneístas* maintained a varied list of intellectual interests and priorities, their program "en pro de la cultura intelectual y artística"[7] cohered around Rodó's *arielismo*, proposed a critical reappraisal of Mexico's (and by extension, Spanish America's) peninsular and Greco-Latin heritage, and demonstrated a broad concern with fostering open public debate in the twilight years of the dictatorial Porfirio Díaz regime (1877–1911).[8] Theirs was a youth-driven, soul-searching campaign waged along similar lines as those of Portugal's *Geração de 70* (Generation of 1870) and Spain's *Generación del 98*.[9] In the particular cases of Reyes and Henríquez Ureña, these interests were coupled with a strong affinity for ancient Greek—a language that, along with Latin, had over the second half of the nineteenth century been weeded out of Mexico's educational system by influential positivists attached to the *porfiriato*.[10] For Reyes and Henríquez Ureña, "the cultivation of the humanities constitute[d] one of Mexican culture's best traditions, which allowed for Mexico's connection with Spanish [. . .] and moreover, with universal culture" (García Morales 73). As with their idol Rodó, the *ateneístas* uniformly affirmed philosophical idealism over positivism, implicitly aligning themselves against its cadre of intellectual proponents in the Díaz government, collectively known as the *científicos*. As García Morales notes, "the young men [of the *Ateneo* group], in their search for new ideals, almost instinctively read the authors that had been rejected by the positivists," including Schopenhauer, Anglo-American pragmatists, Henri Bergson, and Rodó, whose defense of high humanistic culture, along with his ideas on Latin America's classical and peninsular heritage and his call for regional solidarity, made a deep impression on Reyes and his colleagues (173).[11] Santiago Castro-Gómez writes:

> The function of the *ateneístas* [was] thus to reestablish the historical continuity [in the nation's cultural and intellectual development] that had been interrupted by Mexican positivism, and to reject the alienating quality of its cultural policy. This implied the reinforcing of the humanistic values that were a part of [Mexico and Latin America's] cultural *ethos*, and the demonstration that, as a depository for these values,

Latin America [had] a new, as yet unheard message for the
world. Latin America [had] something to say that the Anglo-
Saxon West had not yet said. (qtd. in Pineda Franco and
Sánchez Prado 55; author's emphasis)

The young Reyes was no supporter of Díaz or the *científicos*,
though he had personal and philosophical reasons for not being
as publicly opposed to the regime as many of his colleagues,
some of whom, with the fall of the *porfiriato* and the beginning
of the Mexican Revolution in 1910, leaped to the defense of
one or another revolutionary faction. His father was Bernardo
Reyes, a *porfiriato*-era general, governor of the state of Nuevo
León, and briefly Díaz's Secretary of War (1900). While Bernardo Reyes was very much a member of the Porfirian regime,
his opposition to the orthodox *científico* camp made his position awkward, and by 1909–10 he was contemplating a coup
attempt. After he led a failed uprising against the brief government of Francisco I. Madero (President, 1911–13), General
Reyes was imprisoned, and on February 9, 1913 was gunned
down by government troops after a brief escape from the
Mexico City jail where he had been held (García Morales 104,
239, 241). Shortly thereafter, Mexico's new leader, Victoriano
Huerta (1913–14) consented to Alfonso Reyes's appointment to
the Mexican legation in Paris after he refused a position as the
dictator's private secretary.[12] While *ateneístas* like Vasconcelos
and Guzmán cast their lots with the factions fighting for control
of the country, Reyes and his family were granted passage to the
safety of Paris. With the outbreak of World War I, Reyes was
forced to again relocate, this time from Paris to Madrid, a dramatic journey described in some of the articles later collected in
Las vísperas de España (1937).[13]

In Paris, Reyes began the diplomatic career he would pursue
for most of his adult life (and under various Mexican presidents), representing Mexico in France, Spain, Argentina, and
most importantly for our purposes, Brazil. Upon his definitive
return to Mexico and retirement from diplomacy in 1939, Reyes
helped found the Colegio de México (initially named the Casa
de España and established under President Lázaro Cárdenas as
a refuge for Mexico's many exiled Spanish republican intellectuals) as well as the Colegio Nacional. Both remain important
educational institutions today. I will now turn from the circum-

stances of Reyes's life to the major themes that mark his writing and record of public engagement.

II. Moderation, Continuity, and the Defense of Culture

Central to the *ateneísta* program was the idea—championed by Reyes throughout his career—that universal, humanistic (read as "Western" or "European") culture belonged to the world, and was not just reserved for those living in London, Paris, or New York. For Reyes and his colleagues, a space for free intellectual exchange could be constituted anywhere, including Mexico City—hence the group's choice of the term "Atheneum" to describe their organization. As Reyes wrote in his first book-length publication, *Cuestiones estéticas* (1911), "[c]reo, firmemente, que 'toda villa es Atenas,' siquiera a ratos" ("Horas áticas de la ciudad" [1910]; *OC* 1: 161). In Reyes's case, this idea was rooted in more than an ideal of equal access to culture. Following Rodó, Reyes argued that Mexico—as with the rest of Latin America—was necessarily connected to universal, humanistic culture, as well as to the classical tradition embodied in the original Athens. Drawing on Romantic notions of language's role in embodying national "genius" (which Rodó and Reyes absorbed from Herder via Rénan), Reyes and company contended that this connection was achieved for Mexico and Spanish America through the binding force of Latin and its neo-Latin successor, Spanish.[14] Affirming in the 1941 essay "Ciencia social y deber social" that "el lenguaje engendra una conducta" (*OC* 11: 118), Reyes defended the specific importance of Latin as a "point of reference" and "flag" by which Mexico and Latin America might realize their philosophical, political, and cultural links to the wider world.[15] Rejecting localized forms of nationalism as spiritually impoverishing, Reyes asked rhetorically, "¿[q]ué diría Platón del mexicano que anduviera inquiriendo una especie de bien moral sólo aplicable a México?"[16] For Reyes, the possibility of constituting "Athens" in Mexico City, Havana, or Rio de Janeiro compelled Latin American intellectuals to defend the continuity of humanistic learning and culture whenever and wherever they came to live and work, and to promote intellectual dialogue across languages, traditions, and geo-political contexts.

While it may be tempting to take a simplistic historical view and understand the *ateneístas* as the intellectual forerunners of the Mexican Revolution, or alternately, as mere products of it, Reyes himself warned against making this sort of assumption, and called for a more dynamic understanding of the relationship between his intellectual circle and the Revolution. In his essay "Pasado inmediato" (1939), he notes:

> [L]a Revolución Mexicana brotó de un impulso mucho más que de una idea. No fue planeada. No es la aplicación de un cuadro de principios, sino un crecimiento natural. Los programas previos quedan ahogados en su torrente y nunca pudieron gobernarla. Se fue esclareciendo sola conforme andaba; y conforme andaba, iba descubriendo sus razones cada vez más precisas [. . .] La inteligencia la acompaña, no la produce. (*OC* 12: 185–86)[17]

Beyond the biographical factors (i.e., the violent death of his father)[18] that militated against Reyes joining Vasconcelos, Guzmán, and other former colleagues in actively supporting one or another revolutionary cadre, Reyes was philosophically disinclined to advocate for change through violent struggle: first, because of his championing—understandable for a classicist and a disciple of Rodó—of the value of moderation or concord, which he identified with the Greek term *homonoia*, and which he defended in politics, personal conduct, and art; and second, as a result of what he viewed as the potentially tragic consequences of violent upheaval for the continuity of culture—a preoccupation Reyes shared with, among other eighteenth- and nineteenth-century "classical liberals," Swiss cultural historian Jacob Burckhardt.[19] In a prose reflection written shortly after Reyes's death, Octavio Paz (1914–98) described his fellow Mexican poet, critic, and national exegete as "one who loved moderation and proportion, a man for whom all things, even action and passion, should resolve themselves in equilibrium, [who] knew that we are surrounded by chaos and silence" ("Jinete" 280). Reyes insisted on the ideas of "[a]greement, concord, equilibrium" as means to achieve a greater level of personal and collective freedom through the fusion of the ethical and the aesthetic (285). Paz explains:

> For Reyes, form was not a covering or an abstract measure but rather the moment of reconciliation in which discord is transformed into harmony. This harmony's true name is liberty: fate ceases to impose limits from without, and is intimately, voluntarily accepted. Ethics and aesthetics intertwine. (281)

Paz, perhaps bothered by the political implications of characterizing his friend as valuing order as a principal precondition for liberty (the classical definition of conservatism), makes sure to qualify Reyes's moderation as an "aspiration" (*voluntad de concierto*) rather than an end in itself, and presents Reyes's position in dialectical terms and using visceral language (287). For Paz, Reyes was aware of the mutual dependence to be observed between the aesthetic and ethical orders one constructs for oneself (and bequeaths to the following generations), and the surrounding chaos. For "Don Alfonso":

> Concord is not a concession, a pact or a compromise but rather a dynamic play [*juego*] of opposing forces, concord between being and the *other*, the reconciliation of movement and repose, the coinciding of passion and form. The crush [*oleada*] of life, blood's back-and-forth flow, the hand that opens and the hand that closes: giving and receiving and giving again. Concord, the central, vital word. Neither brain, nor womb, nor sex, nor mouth: heart. (287–88; author's emphasis)

In his tribute, which captures much of Reyes's particular intellectual personality, Paz tries to show that his friend's seemingly staid worldview is in fact more dynamic than Reyes himself would have us believe, and that his core value of "harmony" or "concord" (*concordia*) is too all-encompassing to be exclusively a mental product. Indeed, as Reyes reveals in his own writing, he did not view the mind and the ideas it receives and transmits as static, cold, or prohibitively rationalized. While for Reyes *inteligencia* rather than *corazón*, as Paz would have it, steers the ship, so to speak, of individual and collective action, it takes on affective qualities in so doing.[20] Reyes makes this clear at a key moment in his poetic tribute to the Argentine writer Ricardo Güiraldes (1886–1927), when he says of their friendship that "[n]unca se dio una amistad tan parecida a una idea," with "idea" suggesting an ideal state of intellectual exchange and shared humanistic commitment rather than an emotionless or superficial bond (qtd. in Alicia Reyes 165). Further, in his piece "Notas sobre la inteligencia americana" (1936), Reyes explains his preference for the notion of an "American intelligence" over American "culture" or "civilization," both of which, for Reyes, can be reduced to discrete academic discourses or inherited traditions. What Reyes is after is more universal:

> Hablar de civilización americana sería [. . .] inoportuno: ello nos conduciría hacia las regiones arqueológicas que caen fuera de nuestro asunto. Hablar de cultura americana sería algo equívoco: ello nos haría pensar solamente en una rama del árbol de Europa trasplantada al suelo americano. En cambio, podemos hablar de la inteligencia americana, *su visión de la vida y su acción en la vida*. Esto nos permitirá definir, aunque sea provisionalmente, el matiz de América. (*OC* 11: 82; my emphasis)

As for Paz's implied fear that Reyes might be mistaken for a philosophical conservative, this is shown to be misplaced, as long as we draw a (perhaps overly schematic) distinction between Reyes's broadly liberal political views and his political temperament, which from all appearances was decidedly more cautious and skeptical. This internal division between ideology and personality led Reyes to champion the core components of the liberal-democratic program—individual freedoms, representative institutions, mutual understanding, and international peace—while aiming a good deal of his most serious criticism at what he saw as the shortcomings of this same model, as well as the failings of his left-leaning compatriots, particularly those who would sacrifice moderation and dialogue for a revolutionary violence he viewed as often more destructive than constructive. Here Reyes joins his epistolary partner, the Spanish philosopher José Ortega y Gasset (1883–1955), whose analysis in *La rebelión de las masas* (1929) can be read somewhat against the grain as an argument in favor of preserving liberal democracy from mass politics and from the ideological poles of the far right (fascism) and the far left (communism).[21] Reyes's reading of nineteenth-century French history in his 1919 article

"La Francia contemporánea," provides an illustrative example of his tendency to critique left-leaning positions in the name of a consensus-based view of politics and culture. Alphonse de Lamartine (1790–1869), the French Romantic poet who briefly led the Second Republic in 1848, comes in for harsh criticism from Reyes as a result of what he considered Lamartine's excessive faith in popular rule: "Los profetas suelen ser guías peligrosos," Reyes warns. Further, "Lamartine confía en la democracia; y la democracia se entrega a un salvador providencial, y sacrifica a Napoleón III las libertades tan penosamente conquistadas" (*OC* 4: 528). Jules Ferry (1832–93), a former Mayor of Paris, Prime Minister, and Minister of Foreign Affairs, and a decidedly less charismatic figure than Lamartine, receives a more positive evaluation from Reyes, precisely because of his pragmatic moderation—a trait that as we saw in the previous chapter, Joaquim Nabuco celebrated in another nineteenth-century French politician, Adolphe Thiers (1797–1877). Reyes writes: "Respetuoso para la libertad, [Ferry] nunca quiso confundirla con la anarquía" (*OC* 4: 531). Ferry may not have been as magnetic a figure as Lamartine, but he reinforced democratic institutions, and for Reyes this is what counts. This judgment is consistent with the message Reyes put forth in a remarkable November 18, 1939 speech, "Esta hora del mundo," in which he reflects on the world's troubled state and warns that liberal democracy, in seeking to confront the fascism of Nazi Germany and Mussolini's Italy, might fall victim to ideological polarization and transform itself into an agent of the very totalitarianism it has dedicated itself to defeat. Reyes's speech deserves to be quoted at length, as an illustration of his view of the cyclical ebb and flow of ideological and historical currents, as well as for its continued timeliness:

> La democracia liberal resulta blanda por principio. Con el "dejar hacer" no se detiene un ataque. Las llamadas potencias democráticas se debaten en compromisos imposibles, buscando una solución para la cual haría falta un genio como el de Santo Tomás, capaz de conciliar a Aristóteles con la Iglesia [. . .] La corteza democrática, adelgazada ya por efecto de tales antinomias (exaltación nacional y exacerbación capitalista), cae como una máscara y descubre detrás una cara que gesticula y enseña los colmillos. Esta cara,

> modelada en parte por esas fuerzas que llamo antinomias,
> y en parte por imitación del adversario [. . .], es el Estado
> totalitario que busca su filosofía en el racismo [. . .] Y las lla-
> madas potencias democráticas, a menos que la contingencia
> histórica las asista, pueden quedar eliminadas entre el tor-
> bellino cambiante. (*OC* 11: 242)

While Reyes laments lack of dialogue between a polarized
right and left, he ultimately sides with the latter:

> Aquí los antiguos proponen el justo medio como criterio
> de verdad, la armoniosa combinación de ambas tendencias
> [. . .] ¡Felices aquellos que transcurren en épocas de co-
> secha, de frutos, de síntesis! ¿Y aquéllos, nosotros, cuyo
> momento corresponde, como un tiempo matemático o como
> un "tempo" musical, a [. . .] diferenciaciones y corrientes
> intercelulares? A nosotros no nos queda más que consultar
> nuestra conciencia y escoger de acuerdo con ella, que esto
> es sonar bien el sueño de la vida [. . .] *Nuestro brazo para
> las izquierdas:* cualesquiera sean sus errores en defecto o
> exceso sobre el lecho de Procusto de la verdad pura, ellas
> pugnan todavía por salvar el patrimonio de la dignidad
> humana, hoy tan desmedrado, hoy tan amenazado. (*OC* 11:
> 253; my emphasis)[22]

Reyes's views on democracy are effectively summarized in
his 1943 "Prólogo" to a Spanish translation of Swiss historian
Jacob Burckhardt's posthumous *Reflections on Universal History* (1905). Here Reyes breaks with prevailing interpretations
of Burckhardt, casting him not as an anti-democratic conservative, but as a self-critical liberal. Reyes writes: "[c]uando se
le escapan a Burckhardt algunas protestas contra la palabra
'democracia,' debemos entender que no van dirigidas contra el
ideal democrático del bien común, que era su credo fundamental, sino contra todo procedimiento de abandono a los impulsos
ciegos" (*OC* 12: 110).[23] The distinction I have drawn between
Reyes's liberal political views and his more conservative political temperament takes us a long way toward explaining his
repeated protests against the costs of revolution, whether in
Mexico or abroad, particularly in terms of the loss of cultural
patrimony and continuity. Closely related to Reyes's faith in
homonoia was his belief in culture as an intrinsic good and as
the product of centuries of "good education" and "good will"

between men. Sebastiaan Faber makes the connection between Reyes's idea of culture and the concept of *Bildung*, which Reyes inherited from German idealism and which can be understood as "the slow process through which the individual, from his particular position, comes to fulfill the promise of his humanity, conceived in universal terms" (Pineda Franco and Sánchez Prado 16). As Reyes argued in 1932's "Atenea política":

> [L]a idea de continuidad, de cultura, de unificación de la inteligencia en el seno de su propia sustancia, nada tiene de común con lo que la gente llama pasatismo, derechismo, reacción u otras nociones de este jaez que hemos dejado a media calle antes de llegar a esta sala, porque ellas pueden corresponder a realidades inmediatas, pero no tienen cara filosófica con que presentarse. No se trata aquí de querer traducir el presente hacia el pasado, sino, al contrario, el pasado hacia el presente. El aprovechamiento de una tradición no significa un paso atrás, sino un paso adelante, a condición de que sea un paso orientado en una línea maestra y no al azar. (*OC* 11: 195–96)

In his 1942 essay "Posición de América," Reyes condenses his position in defense of cultural tradition, noting that while it may be possible to define culture as a thing in itself, in reality it "only exists in the transmission of its contents," or in other words, in its successful transfer to future generations.[24] Moreover, Reyes argues along with Burckhardt that the preconditions for culture—peace, democratic dialogue, unobstructed circulation of individuals and ideas—are easily disrupted by periods of instability, such as those occasioned by the Mexican and Russian revolutions, by the Spanish Civil War, and by the two World Wars—all of which occurred during Reyes's lifetime. While Reyes was not against revolutions *per se*, as a man of cautious political instincts he tended to focus on their unintended negative effects, what he termed in another context "the intrusive shadow that accompanies and at times obscures every thought."[25] For Reyes, the possibility that culture might fall victim to revolutionary violence was an objectively negative cost of violent political change, regardless of the justice or injustice of the revolution itself. As he wrote in an early reflection on the Russian Revolution:

> Toda gran revolución es un gran ejemplo: unos la imitan,
> otros la adaptan, otros se curan en salud [. . .] Pero la paz se
> ha dado en la tierra a los hombres de buena voluntad. Y la
> buena voluntad—este bien absoluto de Kant—es uno de los
> más raros frutos de nuestro huerto. ("La revolución rusa"
> [1919]; *OC* 4: 491)

Further, and in terms of Mexico's specific cultural heritage, Reyes wrote in his 1915 "Visión de Anáhuac" that, even as he acknowledged the continuity of Mexican history: "Hay que lamentar como irremediable la pérdida de la poesía indígena mexicana. Podrá la erudición descubrir aislados ejemplares de ella o probar la relativa fidelidad con que algunos otros fueron romanceados por los misioneros españoles; pero nada de eso, por muy importante que sea, compensará nunca la pérdida de la poesía indígena como fenómeno general y social" (*OC* 2: 29). Some years later, while living in Rio de Janeiro as Mexican ambassador to Brazil, Reyes made a similar observation for that country's indigenous poetry, noting in "Poesía indígena brasileña" (1933) that "[d]e aquella primitiva poesía sólo vestigios se conservan, recogidos en distintas épocas" (*OC* 9: 86). For Reyes, cultural artifacts are not only the products of generations of accumulated intellectual effort, but as the Romantics affirmed, are objects to be revered, and are possessed of a great symbolic force that can be applied to present-day projects of individual, national, and even continental construction and renovation.

In substantiating Reyes's dynamic view of cultural objects, we may cite "La poesía del Archivo," from the first series of *Simpatías y diferencias* (1921), in which Reyes writes: "Los eruditos curiosos leen los viejos manuscritos más allá de las letras; y en los bordes carcomidos por la humedad, y en esas manchas, que van del tono café de las hojas secas al tono morado de las lombardas—verdaderos hongos del papel—, adivinan tal vez una historia de reclusión en los sótanos del convento, cuando cayeron sobre la aldea, durante el año de tantos, estos o los otros salvadores de la patria, poco afectos a las antiguallas" (*OC* 4: 74). Texts like "La poesía del Archivo" illustrate their author's tendency, beyond simple reverence, to fetishize old books and documents. This, along with Reyes's half-ironic rejections of the value of utility in favor of a life of readerly ease,[26] has put him in the crosshairs of critics (generally those who criticize Rodó as well) who accuse Reyes of connoisseurship and an apolitical, ivory tower elitism.[27] While Reyes certainly did revere his books, housing his sizeable collection in a library revealingly dubbed the "Capilla Alfonsina," his appreciation for cultural objects and consequent anxiety over their preservation during periods of revolutionary turmoil were not merely grounded in a concern for his own sensory enjoyment. Again, for Reyes cultural objects (along with language) serve as vehicles through which a people can mine its own past so as to construct a more authentic and satisfactory collective identity in the present. Fired by Rodó's *Ariel* (1900), and to a lesser extent, José Martí's "Nuestra América" (1891), Reyes and many of his essay-writing contemporaries championed this project, particularly during the tumultuous 1920s and 1930s. As Reyes observed in general terms in "Atenea política" (1932), "[t]odos debiéramos estar convencidos de que la manera de asegurar el presente es asimilar el pasado" (*OC* 11: 194). And regarding his own work, Reyes explained in an August 5, 1922 letter to Antonio Mediz-Bolio that he originally conceived of his early essay "Visión de Anáhuac" as part of a larger project entitled *En busca del alma nacional*, which he describes as a would-be exegetic text, which might have occupied a place in the tradition of Miguel de Unamuno's *En torno al casticismo* (1902), Sérgio Buarque de Holanda's *Raízes do Brasil* (Roots of Brasil, 1936), and Octavio Paz's *El laberinto de la soledad* (1950).

> La *Visión de Anáhuac* puede considerarse como un primer capítulo de esta obra, en la que yo procuraría extraer e interpretar la moraleja de nuestra terrible fábula histórica: buscar el pulso de la patria en todos los momentos y en todos los hombres en que parece haberse intensificado; pedir a la brutalidad de los hechos un sentido espiritual; descubrir la misión del *hombre mexicano* en la tierra, interrogando pertinazmente a todos los fantasmas y las piedras de nuestras tumbas y nuestros monumentos. Un pueblo se salva cuando logra vislumbrar el mensaje que ha traído al mundo: cuando logra electrizarse hacia un polo, bien sea real o imaginario, porque de lo real y lo imaginario está tramada la vida. La creación no es un juego ocioso: todo hecho esconde una secreta elocuencia, y hay que apretarlo con pasión para que suelte su jugo jeroglífico. (*OC* 4: 421–22; author's emphasis)

Reyes's insistence that the destruction of culture represents a tragic if unintended consequence of revolution underscores his appreciation for those who would contribute to the "building" of national and universal culture, even against the backdrop of the violence and chaos that attend convulsive social change. He made this appreciation clear in a July 5, 1924 "Despedida a José Vasconcelos," in which he tied Vasconcelos, Mexico's outgoing Minister of Public Education, to his *porfiriato*-era predecessor, the historian and educator Justo Sierra (1848–1912)—a favorite of the *Ateneo* group:

> Los verdaderos creadores de nuestra nacionalidad—no siempre recordados en nuestros manuales de Historia—han trabajado, bajo las amenazas del furor y de la violencia, con esfuerzos siempre interrumpidos, oponiendo una constante voluntad de bien a los incesantes asaltos del error. ¡Oh Justo Sierra! De medio siglo en medio siglo, otro más se deja caer, exánime, y entrega el mensaje al que ha de seguirlo. Y éste es el hilo patético que mantiene nuestra seguridad como pueblo civilizado. Felices los que siembran la buena semilla que da el pan para todos. Beatos los que no escatiman su vida, porque ésos se salvarán. (*OC* 4: 442–43)[28]

That same year, Reyes addressed Mexico's P.E.N. Club, noting the challenges posed by years of turmoil to his fellow Mexican writers in their efforts to preserve cultural continuity:

> Habéis vivido todos estos años sometidos a rudas pruebas. La continuidad—base única de la cultura—, la continuidad de vuestros trabajos era interrumpida todos los días por el sobresalto y la violencia [. . .] ¡Qué pocos se salvan! (*OC* 4: 433)

As we will see in the following section, the cultural continuity Reyes sought to defend was intimately linked to his broader humanistic program. In opening a thematic "parentheses" to this chapter, I will in the following paragraphs explore how Reyes understood humanism generally, arguing for Reyes as a powerful precursor to what in recent years has been dubbed "critical humanism."

III. Critical Humanism, the Public Intellectual, and the Example of Reyes

One of the labels most frequently applied to Alfonso Reyes is that of "humanist."[29] Reyes's humanism is often linked to his reputation for considerable erudition, his command of a broad range of languages and literatures, and his alignment with a broadly idealist (or more specifically, *arielista*) reading of Latin American history and culture as grounded in Greco-Roman antiquity. For certain scholars, these aspects of Reyes's intellectual personality have proved problematic. Responding to the post-structuralist critique of coherent national cultures and to post-colonial critics' arguments that "high" or "universal" culture is predicated on uneven development, exploitation, and the silencing of marginalized regions or groups, Adela Pineda Franco and Ignacio M. Sánchez Prado, for example, have identified Reyes's humanism with an earlier era in which culture could be valued uncritically as an end in itself—a period that has evidently come to an end. They observe in the introduction to the edited volume *Alfonso Reyes y los estudios latinoamericanos* (2004) that Reyes, like Pedro Henríquez Ureña, Vasconcelos, Ortega y Gasset, and Erich Auerbach, believed in culture's "redemptive mission," though they advise that today Reyes's position would be "unthinkable in the context of [the methodological mandates of] cultural studies and postmodern discourse's negation of any and all arguments based in origins and certainties" (5). Faber echoes this characterization, affirming that "Alfonso Reyes belonged to a now-extinct species: that of the authentic liberal humanists," and Evodio Escalante makes the counterintuitive (and to my mind, unsuccessful) argument for Reyes as a socialist, concluding that Reyes's apparent Marxism allowed him to "break [. . .] with the 'humanistic' idea and with the [. . .] stereotyped [humanistic] impression we have formed of his thought" (166).[30]

Given the frequency with which Reyes is labeled, celebrated, or targeted as a humanist, as well as the lack of consensus regarding the implications of the above for Reyes scholarship and for literary and cultural studies generally, it may be useful to ask questions such as the following: is Reyes's humanism advisable today, or even possible? If authentic liberal humanists are an "extinct species," as Faber has it, then how can Reyes's broadly liberal, humanistic ideas be applied to current critical paradigms, if at all? In momentarily deferring my discussion of Reyes's understanding of Brazil's place in the Latin American utopia he identifies with *Última Tule*, I will take some time to explore Reyes's attitudes toward humanism, and to describe how these inform his position regarding the intellectual's public role—which importantly, bears directly on his project for building a Latin American utopia in which Brazil would evidently take part. Further, I will contend that far from consigning Reyes's humanistic commitment to the so-called "good old days" of towering, broadly engaged intellectuals such as Auerbach and Walter Benjamin (both of whom, lest we become nostalgic, suffered greatly in their lifetimes), we can identify Reyes as a precursor to the "critical humanism" that has been proposed in recent years by commentators including Edward Said, William Cain, and Julia Kristeva. This provides, I would argue, a broad avenue for Reyes and his ideas to be applied to a range of current problems and debates, beyond my own particular interest in Reyes's utopian vision of Latin America and of Brazil's place in his thought.[31]

Recent proponents of critical humanism, in arguing for the continued relevance of the humanistic tradition, have observed that as a broad disciplinary category, humanism continues to provide a shared cultural vocabulary and serve as a vehicle for denouncing social ills and effecting change. They contend that humanism should not be discarded because *some* scholars who self-identify as humanists have attempted willfully apolitical interpretations or openly reactionary defenses of "our tradition" (Samuel Huntington provides an oft-cited example). In addition, as John Beverley has recently claimed, humanism may face the additional "Trojan horse" of critics who issue their defenses from a declaredly left position, but whose views on literary and cultural production are in fact "neoconservative."[32] Moreover, proponents of critical humanism point out that post-structuralism and some branches of academic Marxism, perhaps due to what for many lay readers amounts to an impractical radicalism advocated via impenetrable vocabulary, have had the unintended effect of further marginalizing socially committed intellectuals working in literary and cultural studies from important public debates. As Said laments in his late volume *Humanism and Democratic Criticism* (2004), the "rightful concern" of the humanities is "the critical investigation of values, history, and freedom," though this has been "effectively detoured" by the current "factory of word-spinning and insouciant specialties, many of them identity-based, that in their jargon and special pleading address only like-minded people, acolytes, and other academics" (14). In short, humanism as an enterprise (whether qualified as "critical" or not) compels intellectuals to *engage* with the world, to address problems of public interest using a shared language and cultural vocabulary that, even if these have been historically closed off to (or at minimum less accessible to) women and racial, religious, and sexual minorities, are nonetheless the birthright of all *because* they are the products of concerted human effort. As Said elegantly puts it, "the humanities concern secular history, the products of human labor, the human capacity for articulate expression [. . .] Humanism is the achievement of form by human will and agency; it is neither system nor impersonal force like the market or the unconscious, however much one may believe in the workings of both" (15).

While it amounts to facile teleology to argue that Reyes somehow anticipated latter-day critical humanism, the picture he paints of the humanist's public role is remarkably similar to those sketched out by Cain, Kristeva, Said, and others, and can in my opinion productively inform the critical humanistic project going forward. In a remarkable passage from the address "Ante la Asociación Cultural de Acción Social" (1939), Reyes, simultaneously echoing Plato and Marx, notes that "not even Marx expels poets from his Republic." Rejecting the idea that writers should be called "intellectual workers," Reyes proposes the following alternative description: "No digamos 'obreros intelectuales,' porque el obrero sólo repite, y el poeta crea y descubre: son funciones distintas." For Reyes, the intellectual's creative function, which grants him the privilege of a distinct title, is closely tied to a compulsory sense of resilient social optimism, which he should transform into action: "Así pues, poetas, *nos incumbe insistir en que los hombres son mejorables*; en que el bien es mayor estímulo que el mal, y las aventuras hacia la concordia más embriagadoras y excitantes que las aventuras de la discordia. Pero si nuestra insistencia ha de ser fecunda, dado lo de prisa que corre el mal en nuestro tiempo, *no basta pensar al hombre mejor, no basta siquiera quererlo: hay que procurar realmente mejorarlo*" (*OC* 11: 233; my emphasis).[33] Reyes reinforces this characterization in "Palabras sobre el humanismo" (1949), arguing here that humanists have by and large been conscious of their intellectual and social responsibilities, and defining contemporary humanism in these words: "Más que como un contenido específico, [el humanismo] se entiende como una orientación. La orientación está en poner al servicio del bien humano todo nuestro saber y todas nuestras actividades." This public-minded "orientation" requires that the humanist properly contextualize his specialized area of study within a broader "topografía general de saber," and compels him to promote intellectual exchange (identified with the value of *libertad*) as a defense against those interests that would dethrone the search for knowledge from a position of authority (*OC* 20: 403). And finally, regarding his own reputation as a humanist, Reyes writes in his posthumous *Anecdotario* (1968), with what must be conscious irony: "No me avergüenzo de que se me llame 'humanista,' porque hoy por hoy humanista casi ha venido a significar persona decente en el orden del pensamiento, *consciente de los fines y de los anhelos humanos*" (qtd. in Alicia Reyes 260; my emphasis). Despite Reyes's playful tone here, we can filter out the following message: the humanist's defining feature is not the extent of his or her textual knowledge (in the previous paragraph Reyes writes that "hasta la heroica ignorancia de las técnicas, de las preceptivas, si ayuda el astro, conduce también al descubrimiento"), but rather a responsiveness to other individuals' "goals" and "yearnings." In other words, to be a true humanist is to be a "representative intellectual" of the sort called for by Said, one who marries the political commitment of the Gramscian organic intellectual with the civic-mindedness of the early-modern Florentine humanist (Said, *Representations* 11; Baron 1: 13).

All this serves to underscore my insistence that Reyes and his *ateneísta* colleagues did *not* practice or advocate a socially disengaged, "ivory tower" version of humanism, despite their self-conscious *arielista* commitment to the defense of high culture and their occasional complaints (particularly apparent in diaries and private correspondence) of lack of time to devote to reading, research, and writing due to cumbersome public obligations. Quite the opposite, Reyes, Pedro Henríquez Ureña, and certainly Vasconcelos recognized "el deber social de las letras," as Reyes affirmed in his "Salutación al P.E.N. Club de México" (1924) (*OC* 4: 436). Here it is instructive to recall that Reyes, despite his privileged background, was not given his humanistic education on a figurative silver platter, at least not as he remembered it. From Reyes's—and also Henríquez Ureña's—writings, one can see that the *ateneístas* understood their education as a series of self-guided, rebellious acts, or as Henríquez Ureña put it, "excursions [that] had the dangerous excitement of forbidden hunts" ("Alfonso Reyes" [1927]; *OC* 2: 161).[34] Consequently, in his own work Reyes celebrated writers and intellectuals who coupled private study with public involvement and made the claim (echoed by numerous Latin American intellectuals and Latin Americanist scholars) for the Latin American writer as a necessarily *public* figure. In his early piece "García Calderón" (1918), Reyes observes that "[e]n la joven América—y éste le es rasgo distintivo—el escritor asume necesariamente, de grado o por la fuerza, responsabilidad de director espiritual: tiene cargo de almas. América adelanta a golpes de entusiasmo por sus *caudillos de la pluma*, y en todas las repúblicas se repite, más o menos, el mito de Cadmo, civilizador y padre del alfabeto" (*OC* 7: 380; my emphasis).[35] Reyes's celebration of Justo Sierra is also significant in this regard. In "Justo Sierra y la historia patria" (1939), Reyes praises Sierra's work and classifies him as one of the "creadores de la tradición hispanoamericana," along with Andrés Bello, Domingo Faustino Sarmiento, Juan Montalvo, Eugenio María de Hostos, Martí, and Rodó. Reyes writes:

> En ellos pensar y escribir fue una forma del bien social, y la belleza una manera de educación para el pueblo [. . .] Tales son los clásicos de América, vates y pastores de gentes, apóstoles y educadores a un tiempo, desbravadores de la selva y padres del Alfabeto [. . .] *No se recluyen y ensimisman en las irritables fascinaciones de lo individual o lo exclusivo.* Antes se fundan en lo general y se confunden con los anhelos de todos. Parecen gritar con el segundo Fausto: "Yo abro espacios a millones de hombres." Su voz es la voz del humano afecto. Pertenecen a todos. En su obra, como en las fuentes públicas todos tienen señorío y regalo. (*OC* 12: 242; my emphasis)

In his "Discurso por Virgilio" (1932–33), Reyes calls for a humanistic education for Mexico's youth of the type he was apparently refused. For Reyes this education would serve not to enshrine the civilizational supremacy of Greco-Roman antiquity, here represented by the Roman poet Virgil, over Mexico's present-day reality, but would provide the vehicle for the spiritual reawakening occasioned by the Mexican Revolution, and would establish Mexicans' collective right to participate in "universal" culture on equal terms. Reyes writes:

> [Q]uiero las Humanidades como el vehículo natural para todo lo autóctono [. . .] En cuanto a decir, con algunos, que el preocuparse del latín es poner a declinar durante años a los chicos del campo—quienes por ahora sólo necesitan arado, alfabeto y jabón—, sería una burda caricatura, un desconocimiento completo de la jerarquización de estudios que exige toda educación nacional, y de la flexibilidad que necesita todo sistema aplicable a un pueblo heterogéneo; [. . .] *Consiste nuestro ideal político en igualar hacia arriba, no hacia abajo.* (*OC* 11: 160–62; my emphasis)

Reyes may fairly be accused of naiveté for his faith in humanistic study's—and more specifically Virgil's—ability to foster rural development, and he seems to anticipate this charge by acknowledging that for "country children" in immediate need of "plows, the alphabet and soap," a copy of the *Aeneid* may seem a useless luxury. He may, moreover, be chided for the implicit snobbery of his vision of a cultural elite (the "caudillos de la pluma," as he put it in 1918) teaching the unwashed peasantry to appreciate the *Georgics* and the *Eclogues*. And Reyes can certainly be taken to task for sharing in a basically Eurocentric position that asserts that the "Mexican spirit" is "bathed" exclusively in a Spanish or broader Latin heritage, with its Mesoamerican inheritance consigned to the status of "archeology" or "absolute past."

However, this does not detract from the strong reformist position Reyes articulates in the piece. In his *discurso*, Reyes defends a nation-building humanism of the kind advanced in the post-revolutionary Mexican educational sphere by, among others, Vasconcelos. As Reyes argues, "decir que todo esto [i.e., las humanidades] no importa al pueblo es tan pueril como querer otra vez que la ciencia sea privilegio de una casta sacerdotal" (*OC* 11: 160). Indeed, Reyes's core idea that "every city is Athens," first articulated in 1918, can be understood as *radical* to the extent that it asserts the potential and right of everyone (no matter how "backward" Europe or North America would judge them) to participate in universal culture. Further, Reyes argues that the national population should be elevated ("igual[ada] hacia arriba") through education in this culture. Despite Reyes's persistent allusions to social levels, he would agree with Said, I think, who argues that "to understand humanism at all [. . .] is to understand it as democratic, open to all classes and backgrounds, and as a process of unending disclosure, discovery, self-criticism, and liberation" (*Humanism* 21–22). Moreover, Reyes's hostility toward excessive disciplinary specialization, which he inherits from Rodó and derides in texts like 1938's "Homilía por la cultura,"[36] points toward a feature of Said's particular vision of critical humanistic practice: the intellectual's assumed "amateur" role, which militates against the intellectual's becoming exclusively or corruptly tied to a particular institution or constituency, and which allows for greater freedom to "raise moral issues" across society and to function as a critical voice who "speak[s] truth to power" (Said, *Representations* 62, 65, 85).

This said, it would be a mistake to assume that Reyes advocated a *completely* engaged, public role for the intellectual—or, for that matter, that latter-day proponents of critical humanism are so naïve as to think that this level of commitment is possible within the confines of the academy. Reyes, again following Rodó, insisted on a classically inspired balance between action and contemplation, between social engagement and intellectual work. In a 1918 review of Max Henríquez Ureña's *Rodó y Rubén Darío* (1918), Reyes celebrated Rodó for striking precisely this balance: "Su optimismo liberal en política—interna e internacional—le lleva a influir en la vida pública de su país (tan necesitado, como todos, del auxilio de sus pensadores), sin descarriarse por eso ni dejar enmohecer los útiles de su oficio de letras" (*OC* 7: 378). Moreover, Reyes reserved the right to judge intellectual work done on the fly, between public commitments, as inferior to that completed during long periods of private study—regardless of the need for the writer in question to maintain a public engagement. For instance, in 1916 Reyes identified Ortega y Gasset's philosophical texts with his "official" life as a politician, and his literary studies with his "personal" or private life, concluding that "[Ortega] [e]s un jefe de partido algo indiferente; es un excelente literato. La filosofía—ayudada por cierta pendiente del temperamento—lo lleva a las inquietudes de la política; la literatura, más desinteresada si cabe, lo emancipa de todo lo que no sea Dios" (*OC* 4: 259). Reyes ultimately recognized that in times of crisis, the intellectual's social responsibility necessarily rules out a life devoted entirely to study. Or as he put it at the end of his appraisal of Ortega, the "confusiones de la furia política" must come before the criterion of "primacía intelectual" (*OC* 4: 261). And as Reyes judged in "En el día americano" (1932), "[l]o mejor para el intelectual absoluto, lo mejor para la inteligencia es conservarse en un término moderado respecto a la acción, y sólo participar en ella lo indispensable, reservándose un sitio de orientación y consejo. Pero, a la hora de los naufragios, también el capitán presta mano al timón, las bombas y las cuerdas" (*OC* 4: 69).

While Reyes identified himself and his fellow *ateneístas* as part of the Mexican Revolution's "generación sacrificada,"[37] as victims of the political tumult they experienced in their youth, he seems to have believed that this "sacrifice," which he identified with his absence from Mexico as a diplomat between 1913 and 1939, was worth the cost. In 1924, he asked the members of Mexico's P.E.N. Club: "[T]odo eso ¿qué importa? ¡Si, por una casualidad que agradezco a mi suerte, pude salvar la continuidad de mi trabajo preferido, la lealtad a mi vocación!" (*OC* 4: 434). As an American intellectual, a designation he implicitly identifies with Latin America, Reyes counted himself especially lucky, writing in "En el día americano" (1932): "[P]or suerte, la inteligencia no ha tenido tiempo entre nosotros [i.e., los americanos o latinoamericanos] de romper con los estímulos de la acción, como acontece en los países agotados por viejas civilizaciones, donde pueden edificarse torres de marfil y teorías estrafalarias conforme a las cuales el hombre de pensamiento que participe en la vida de su siglo viene a ser un 'clérigo traidor.' Que, entre nosotros, los sabios tienen todavía que ser hombres públicos [. . .] esperamos una ventaja" (*OC* 11: 69).[38] In the following section, I will return to this chapter's main argument, elaborating on the utopian vocation Reyes sketched out for the New World and for Latin America (this very much the product of his humanism), before considering in the fifth and final section how Reyes fits Brazil into his vision of Latin America as a geographical, historical, and cultural category.

IV. Latin America's Utopian Vocation: *Última Tule*

Along with his defense of culture and his account of the humanist's public role, one of Alfonso Reyes's major intellectual preoccupations was what he viewed as the utopian vocation or destiny of the American continent, and of Latin America more specifically. The balance of Reyes's reflections on this theme can be found in the volumes *Última Tule* (1942) and *Tentativas y orientaciones* (1944), both of which collect texts written in the 1920s through the early 1940s, as well as in *No Hay Tal Lugar . . . ,* a series of meditations on real and fictional utopias that takes its name from Quevedo's definition of the term *utopia*, and that remained unpublished until it was collected, along with the two previous collections, in volume 11 of Reyes's complete works.[39] Reyes explains the particular way in which he, following in a tradition of New World utopianism that dates from the Spanish and Portuguese chroniclers' first accounts of the New World and from the publication of Sir Thomas More's *Utopia* in 1516, links the ideas of "America" and "utopia," and describes what he considers as the resulting obligation of the people of the New World, and particularly its intellectuals, to incarnate utopia as an ideal for a world standing on the edge of economic crisis and global armed conflict. In the opening pages of "El presagio de América," the first essay of *Última Tule* and a text assembled from a variety of shorter pieces published between 1920 and 1940, Reyes lists a series of literary and mythological utopias located to the west of the columns of Hercules (which were said to have stood at the mouth of the Mediterranean Sea and been inscribed with the words *non plus ultra,* or "there is nothing beyond"), as evidence of the fact that "antes de ser esta firme realidad que unas veces nos entusiasma y otras nos desazona, América fue la invención de los poetas, la charada de los geógrafos, la habladuría de los aventureros, la codicia de las empresas y, en suma, un inexplicable apetito y un impulso por trascender los límites" (*OC* 11: 13–14).[40] In this sense, the early European encounters with the New World would have less to do with the development of maritime technology or with Columbus's decision to sail west to the "Indies" than with an essential human need for and attraction to limit-breaking exploration, which Reyes presents as channeled during the early modern period through the "militant humanism" of writers like More and the "geographical mysticism" of explorers like Columbus, and which to Reyes's mind is closely tied to a broader human need for utopian spaces and visions.[41] As Reyes explains, exploration, humanism, utopia, and poetry were linked together in the European "discovery" of America. He writes, "el descubrimiento de América fue el resultado de algunos errores científicos y algunos aciertos poéticos" (*OC* 11: 44). Notably, Mexican historiographer Edmundo O'Gorman adapted and popularized Reyes's terminology of "invention" over "discovery" in his study *La invención de América* (1958), in which he argues that Columbus's encounter with the New World forced Europeans to "invent" America as a heretofore unknown category, both in terms of its place in world geography and for the retrospective constitution of America's historical "reality" (11–17), an irony noted by Walter Mignolo, whom I quoted in this book's introductory chapter as observing that "[b]efore 1492, the Americas were not on anybody's map" (*Idea* 2).

In terms of utopias, Reyes explains in *No Hay Tal Lugar . . .* that "[o] por larga educación filosófica o por espontánea tendencia al equilibrio entre la esperanza y el recuerdo, los hombres sintieron siempre la necesidad—formulada en el dogma católico, heredero de la sensibilidad de los siglos—de figurarse que proceden de otra era mejor y caminan hacía otra era mejor; que se han dejado a la espalda un paraíso ya perdido y tienen por delante nada menos que la conquista de un cielo, aunque sea un 'cielo terrestre.' Nuestra existencia transcurre entre dos utopías, dos espejismos, dos figuraciones de la ciudad feliz, la que no se encuentra en parte alguna" (*OC* 11: 341). According to Reyes, whose thoughts on the utopian inflections of the Spanish American colonial project, and whose image of the "two figurations of the happy city," no doubt influenced Ángel Rama's account of the same in *La ciudad letrada* (1984), the need for utopias led early modern Europeans to undertake two related efforts: to elaborate literary utopias, which were frequently situated in the Atlantic, if not directly in some version of the "New World" (see More's *Utopia*, Francis Bacon's *New Atlantis*, and Shakespeare's *The Tempest*), and to undertake exploratory efforts to locate these utopias, or spaces like them, in the newly discovered lands across the Atlantic. Reyes interprets these actions as mutually reinforcing, with the literary *utopistas'* descriptions of fantastical "imagined lands" motivating maritime explorers and thus "leading to real discoveries," with these discoveries in turn fueling the demand for more literary utopias.[42] For Reyes, utopian narratives and maritime exploration, in their dialectical interaction, work together as the motor of New World history, propelling it along a given path (*senda*) and toward its ultimate end (*destino*) or meaning (*sentido*), which Reyes describes as a "posible campo donde realizar una justicia más igual, una libertad mejor entendida, una felicidad más completa y mejor repartida entre los hombres, una soñada república, una Utopía" (*OC* 11: 58).[43] Notably, Reyes declares himself elsewhere as averse to historical determinism, whether in terms of fixed scientific "laws" or an ultimate teleological meaning for history, pointing out the power of historical chance or "caprice,"[44] and advocating an eclectic historiographical approach and even the study of possible alternate histories (a practice he amusingly terms *ifismo*).[45] However, Reyes's reading of the dual discovery/invention of America, with its neat bipartite, Hegelian dialectical structure, reveals a degree of providential argumentation; it is as if Reyes believes that America, Hegel's "land of the future," were beckoning European humanists and explorers to locate, map, and describe it, so as to make it legible to Europeans and in this way "real," and to thereby bring about the fulfillment of the continent's utopian vocation. As Reyes writes in a particularly revealing passage of "El presagio de América":

> Antes de ser descubierta, América era ya presentida en los sueños de la poesía y en los atisbos de la ciencia. A la necesidad de completar la figura geográfica, respondía la necesidad de completar la figura política de la tierra. El rey de la fábula poseía la moneda rota: le faltaba el otro fragmento para descifrar la leyenda de sus destinos [. . .] Antes de dejarse sentir por su presencia, América se dejaba sentir por su ausencia.

> En el lenguaje de la filosofía presocrática, digamos que el
> mundo, sin América, era un caso de desequilibrio en los ele-
> mentos de extralimitación, de *hybris*, de injusticia. América,
> por algún tiempo, parecía huir frente a la quilla de los fasci-
> nados exploradores. (*OC* 11: 60–61; author's emphasis)

So what exactly is entailed in Reyes's interpretation of Latin
America's utopian destiny, beyond his rather nebulous calls for
justice, liberty, and happiness as necessary features of an American *Última Tule* he projects into a hazy future? After reading
this chapter's previous two sections, the core features of Reyes's
utopia will be familiar. First, Reyes affirms in various pieces, as
in "Ciencia social y deber social" (1941), the importance of a
broadly cosmopolitan, ethical humanism for the Americas by
speculating that the economic and political crisis confronting
Europe from the 1920s through World War II can be characterized in broad terms as the result of a creeping technocratic
mindset, or "un disparate de la especialización que ha perdido
la norte de la ética" (*OC* 11: 107). As Reyes implies in several
other pieces, such as "Notas sobre la inteligencia americana"
(1936), the difficult condition of the Latin American intellectual
paradoxically allows him to serve as a model for his belea-
guered European counterparts. The Latin American intellectual's public-minded commitment to nation-building compels
him to understand "el trabajo intelectual como servicio público
y como deber civilizador" (*OC* 11: 86). Moreover, Reyes argues that Latin Americans, particularly in the intellectual class,
possess an "internacionalismo connatural" (*OC* 11: 87) which
is likewise the product of their continent's marginal relationship to the centers of Western culture, and which allows them
to broaden their public-minded, nation-building commitment
outward, first to the continent, and eventually to encompass a
global humanistic and cosmopolitan vision; this argument for
the Latin American writer's congenital "internationalism" was
famously defended four years earlier by Jorge Luis Borges in
his 1932 essay "El escritor argentino y la tradición." Reyes explains: "Esto se explica, no sólo porque nuestra América ofrez-
ca condiciones para ser el crisol de aquella futura 'raza cósmica'
que Vasconcelos ha soñado, sino también porque hemos tenido
que ir a buscar nuestros instrumentos culturales en los grandes
centros europeos, acostumbrándonos así a manejar las nociones

extranjeras como si fueran cosa propia. En tanto que el europeo no ha necesitado de asomarse a América para construir su sistema del mundo, el americano estudia, conoce y practica a Europa desde la escuela primaria" (*OC* 11: 87).[46] For Reyes, the Latin American intellectual's need to "study, know, and practice Europe," which is effectively an intellectual byproduct of colonization, should be properly considered in terms of a dynamic of *obligation* and *compensation*. In exchange for Latin America having arrived "tarde al banquete de la civilización europea," as Reyes put it in "Notas sobre la inteligencia americana" (1936), the intellectuals of *nuestra América* are charged with "desempeña[ndo] la más noble función complementaria: la de ir estableciendo síntesis [. . .] la de ir aplicando prontamente los resultados, verificando el valor de la teoría en la carne viva de la acción. Por este camino, si la economía de Europa ya necesita de nosotros, también acabará por necesitarnos la misma inteligencia de Europa" (*OC* 11: 82, 86). In other words, by offering up Latin America—and the Western hemisphere generally—as a possible utopia, Latin American intellectuals are in fact rebalancing their side of a dynamic between America and Europe that was established centuries ago, and which until recently had been predicated on European dominance. With Europe undergoing a difficult, transitional period and America reaching its intellectual maturity, such that it can "toma[r] [. . .] posición" before the rest of the world, Reyes argues that a more equitable transatlantic relationship can now be negotiated ("Posición de América" [1942]; *OC* 11: 255).

Second, Reyes reaffirms the importance of democratic institutions and peaceful coexistence between American nations, complementing his argument on Latin Americans' "innate internationalism" with a presentation of the New World as uniquely suited to achieving continental peace through a common dedication to democracy: Reyes, echoing Rodó's image of the "two eagles" representing Latin and North America, but departing from Rodó's oppositional stance toward the United States, writes that "[l]a cultura americana es la única que podrá ignorar, en principio, las murallas nacionales y étnicas. Entre la homogeneidad del orbe latino y la homogeneidad del orbe sajón—los dos personajes del drama americano—la simpatía democrática oficia de nivelador, rumbo a la *homonoia*" (*OC* 11:

61–62; author's emphasis).[47] Reflecting his belief that democracy requires healthy interpersonal and international relationships, in "En el día americano" (1932) Reyes repeats Rodó and Martí's observation—though without the latter's preoccupation with inevitable US interventionism—that as Americans, "[n]o nos conocemos," and he warns that it is only through mutual understanding and engagement (precisely the opposite of the current "incomunicación") that peace can be maintained (*OC* 11: 64).

And third, having written much of *Última Tule* during the turbulent 1920s and 1930s, Reyes was concerned with the American continent's role as a peaceful, cosmopolitan example and counterpoint to a Europe engulfed by destructive nationalism and war: "[H]oy, ante los desastres del Antiguo Mundo, América cobra el valor de una esperanza" (*OC* 11: 61). In addition, the "locura de Europa" compels America to assume its duty (*deber*) or responsibility (*responsabilidad*) as a "reserva de humanidad" and a "continuadora de civilizaciones" capable of preserving the culture of Europe, and charged with safeguarding exiled European (and particularly Spanish) intellectuals (*OC* 11: 60, 109, 114). In sum, for Reyes, Latin America as *Última Tule* has been granted the capacity and responsibility to show Europe the way toward a form of social organization that, through its dedication to higher ideals, might break with the model of "concentric fatalities" (*fatalidades concéntricas*) Reyes uses to describe the competing claims of exclusivist ethnic, national, and regional affiliations, all of which, according to him, tend to circumscribe one's behavior, foster destructive prejudices, and lead to a provincial, isolationist intellectual stance (*OC* 11: 88–89). As the largest nation in South America, Brazil obviously had a role to play in Reyes's utopian vision for the American continent. Though as I will show in the next section, Reyes's view of Brazil's precise *place* in Latin America as *Última Tule* is ambiguous, with Reyes ultimately falling into established patterns of hispanocentrism and Spanish American identity projection onto Brazil in his attempts to reconcile his pan-Latin and hemispheric project with signs of Brazilian difference.

V. Reyes's Vision of Brazil in America: Language and Utopia

As mentioned earlier, Alfonso Reyes served as Mexico's ambassador to Brazil between 1930 and 1936, living with his wife and family in the Laranjeiras neighborhood of Rio de Janeiro. With six years in Rio, and in accordance with his belief that interpersonal relationships and intellectual exchange form the basis for successful diplomacy, Reyes cultivated friendships with a staggering number of Brazilian intellectuals, the closest of whom were probably the poets Manuel Bandeira (1886–1968) and Ronald de Carvalho (1893–1936) and the Catholic intellectual and critic Alceu Amoroso Lima (1893–1983).[48] Moreover, Reyes made use of the Mexican embassy in Rio to host a series of literary events featuring local intellectuals, actively distributed his work to Brazilian writers, published his own Brazil-themed pieces in local newspapers, and acted to promote Brazil and its literature among his Spanish-speaking peers (Ellison, *Alfonso Reyes e o Brasil* 41–43). Reyes's degree of engagement was such that he could justifiably write the following assessment of his relationship with Brazil, in poetic form, after completing his diplomatic mission:

> Mira, Brasil, que de siempre
> fui tu devoto y fiel;
> mira bien que te he tratado
> en verso y en prosa, y que
> la historia del Rey Candaulos
> en mí se cumple otra vez;
> que tanto de mi tierra dije
> y tus gracias alabé,
> que todos con mucha envidia
> te han querido conocer:
> sólo abandono la plaza
> porque otros piden la vez.
> ("¡Por favor . . . !" [1938]; *OC* 10: 286)[49]

"Don Alfonso" was a popular figure among *carioca* intellectuals, and while in Rio he was received in a number of official and social contexts, including an August 30, 1934 meeting of the Brazilian Academy of Letters, where he gave an address on "México y su historia" (139). As Ellison reports, Reyes's May

21, 1936 *despedida* ("going-away party") at Rio's Jockey Club inspired Bandeira's poem "Rondó dos Cavalinhos" (Rondeau of the Little Horses), which features the lines "Alfonso Reyes partindo, / E tanta gente ficando . . ." ("Alfonso Reyes leaving, / And so many people remaining" . . .). Exactly one month later, Reyes would be the only non-Brazilian to participate in a public *homenagem* ("homage") to Bandeira. Reyes and Bandeira remained friends after 1936, and Ellison, citing Bandeira's repeated requests that Reyes send him books from Mexico, speculates that Reyes played a role in Bandeira's adoption of Spanish American literature as an area of academic specialization ("Alfonso Reyes y Manuel Bandeira" 489–90).[50] The result would be Bandeira's didactic volume *Literatura Hispano-Americana* (Spanish American Literature, 1949), in which the Brazilian poet returned the favor by praising Reyes as an "exemplary humanist," a "pure and delicate poet, an original storyteller, [and] an extremely incisive critic" (209).

Reyes's mode of socialization in Brazil is reflective of his broader philosophical and intellectual program. In an August 6, 1930 letter to his friend, the French novelist and critic Valery Larbaud (1881–1957),[51] Reyes confessed that while Oswald de Andrade, an avant-garde writer from São Paulo and author of a 1928 "Cannibalist Manifesto," had a reputation as a "dangerous man," he found the writer, who "presided, or rather, stirred up" the more radical wing of Brazilian modernism, both "enchanting and brilliant"—a notable feat for Andrade, given Reyes's preference for moderation in public affairs and for inclusive humanism over the subversive, wink-and-nudge radicalism and aesthetic innovation preached by Oswald and his associates.[52] On the other end of the ideological spectrum, after sending him a copy of one of his writings, Reyes became close to Alceu Amoroso Lima, a critic who wrote under the pseudonym "Tristão de Athayde," and who shared Reyes's interest in classical studies and in English writer G. K. Chesterton (1874–1936), two of whose novels Reyes had previously translated to Spanish (Ellison, *Alfonso Reyes e o Brasil* 148).[53] As Francisco de Paula G. de Souza Brazil relates, Reyes "was comfortable with both of the important social groups: [establishment] intellectuals like Ronald de Carvalho, and bohemian intellectuals like Manuel Bandeira" (qtd. in Ellison, *Alfonso Reyes e o Brasil* 130). What is more, Reyes managed the improbable—and telling—feat of sheltering in the Mexican embassy individuals from both sides of Brazil's Revolution of 1930, in which the Old Republic (1889–1930) was overthrown and Getúlio Vargas (President, 1930–45; 1951–54) installed in power (Ellison, *Alfonso Reyes e o Brasil* 59–61; Reyes, *Diario* 327–29). Ellison cites this as an act that endeared Reyes to the *carioca* public, writing that "[f]rom the first days of his stay [in Brazil] and for the four or five following years, Alfonso Reyes would be welcomed in numerous intellectual environments, sometimes playing the important role of mediator" (62). In the years that followed, Reyes maintained his ties with the bohemian left, though he also developed a cordial relationship with President Vargas, who used local radio to commemorate the Mexican ambassador's forty-seventh birthday and his later departure from Brazil (125, 134).

In intellectual terms, Reyes showed himself quite receptive to notions of Brazil as a politically and racially conciliatory society, ideas with a long genealogy in Brazilian thought, and that were developed and popularized by thinkers like Joaquim Nabuco,[54] Oliveira Vianna, Sérgio Buarque de Holanda, and especially Gilberto Freyre, who befriended Reyes and whose *Casa-grande e Senzala* (The Masters and the Slaves, 1933) strongly impacted the Mexican ambassador's thinking on race and culture in Brazil.[55] Indeed, on several occasions Reyes praised Brazil's reputation for political conciliation and for equitable foreign policy (recall Buarque's image of Brazil as a "giant full of bonhomie for all the nations of the world") (*Raízes* 177). Both qualities were amenable to Reyes's moderate and internationalist inclinations.[56] More problematically, from before his arrival in Brazil in 1930, Reyes seems to have subscribed to the idea of Brazilian—and more broadly, Latin American—racial democracy, as he reveals in "Entre España y América: La leyenda americana" (1923). Here he combines a penetrating analysis of European stereotypes of Latin America (a concern that approximates him to Manoel Bomfim and Mário de Andrade, among others) with unfortunate comments regarding the supposed lack of Latin American racial prejudice, and the inevitable, progressive suppression of black "characteristics" in the region through the elevating influence of intermarriage with whites. He writes:

[P]ara la leyenda todos los americanos son negros. Conocido es el fundamento de esta leyenda: los europeos, que
necesitaban muchos esclavos, han importado a América, en
distintas épocas, negros africanos. Algunos hay en la América española; pero muchos más hay en los Estados Unidos.
En la gran República del Norte es fácil medir la población
negra, porque una imperiosa reglamentación la mantiene
alejada del blanco. En cambio, en la América española no
es posible apreciarla, porque [. . .] *no existe allá el prejuicio
de raza, y el negro puro ha desaparecido al cruzarse.* Según
ciertas leyes biológicas, en algunos de los puntos de América
donde se halla esta población mezclada, como en Cuba y en
el Brasil, *los caracteres del blanco tienden a predominar con
sensible rapidez* [. . .] En América se nota un sedimento—en
evanescencia—de mulatos, por algunas zonas limitadas de
Colombia y de Venezuela, Cuba, Santo Domingo y Brasil. Exceptúense las colonias yanquis y europeas—Indias
Occidentales—y los negros de Haití que no son América
española. Donde verdaderamente hay negros, no es, pues, en
la América española. (*OC* 4: 340–41; my emphasis)[57]

Beyond cultivating numerous Brazilian friendships and ab-
sorbing certain locally salient ideas, Reyes wrote some of his
most important essays and speeches while in Brazil, including
"Atenea política" (1932), "Discurso por Virgilio" (1932–33),
and the majority of *Última Tule*. Additionally, during this 1930–
36 period he wrote the creative prose that would constitute
História natural das Laranjeiras (Natural History of Laranjeiras, written in Spanish despite its Portuguese title, and published
1959) and the poems of *Romances del Río de Enero* (1933), as
well as a series of expository prose pieces and speeches that
are broadly "Brazilian" in theme. These include "A Ronald de
Carvalho," "Sobre la tumba de Graça Aranha," "Sobre la reforma de la ortografía portuguesa" (all 1931) as well as "Aduana
lingüística" (1933–41), "Velocidade" (1933), and an open letter
to Renato Almeida published in the Rio de Janeiro daily *A Nação* (to my knowledge the only text Reyes wrote or published
in Portuguese), in addition to the later "Salutación al Brasil"
(1941), and "El Brasil en una castaña" (1942).

Reyes's speech on Carvalho, in which he comments on
Carvalho's intriguing, continentally themed poetry collection
Toda a América (All of America, 1926), merits some discus-
sion. Here Reyes elevates Carvalho's titular poetic figure of

toda a América to the status of a geocultural category more or less synonymous with his utopian-inflected understanding of Martí's *nuestra América*. He describes Carvalho's collection, which features poems set in various Brazilian, Spanish American, Caribbean, and North American locales, in terms of the author's "concepción, robusta y despojada a un tiempo, de esa armonía natural que él supo llamar Toda-la-América. Toda-la-América sea una palabra nueva en nuestros labios y un estímulo igual en nuestros corazones: un santo y seña de acción y de trabajo; un trazo poético de la pirámide que debemos construir entre todos" (*OC* 8: 158). Carvalho's poetic presentation in *Toda a América* of a distinctive "American" civilization requiring authentic, locally generated modes of expression (he writes, "[y]our poets are not of the race of serfs / who dance to the rhythms of the Greeks or Latins") resembles Martí's *nuestra América* paradigm, in that Carvalho admonishes American poets to reject European models in favor of the local. Carvalho also approximates Reyes's adaptation of Rodó's notion of the *magna patria*, in presenting America's glorious future as the product of multiplicity and interpersonal exchange. Carvalho writes of America: "In you there is the creative multiplicity of / the miracle" (110, 132).[58]

Reyes's stint in Brazil would also see him launch *Monterrey* (1930–37), a personal "Correo Literario" named for the city of his birth and which, as he explained in a diary entry for March 6, 1930, he would publish as:

> mi órgano de relación con el mundo literario; me servirá de carta circular a los amigos; allí acusaré recibo de cuantas publicaciones me envían los autores; allí haré "encuestas" por cuenta propia o de mis amigos, no sobre ideas ni posturas intelectuales (que no creo mucho en estas encuestas), sino sobre puntos concretos de investigación literaria y artística. En este orden, será un intermediario erudito entre el que pregunta y el que contesta. La hoja no será del todo una hoja abierta, no [*sic*] tampoco una hoja cerrada. Habrá una selección, y esa selección será mi gusto. Será cosa hospitalaria, pero no cosa pública. No se trata de una colección de artículos o versos, sino de un útil del taller literario [. . .] [L]a conducta de mi pliego literario explicará mejor que todas las definiciones. No tratará de establecer credos, doctrinas ni lanzar manifiestos. Mantendrá la conversación literaria, y

> aunque se venderá en las librerías para comodidad de alguno
> que quiera buscarla, está principalmente destinada a la circu-
> lación privada. (*Diario* 303)

Monterrey was primarily focused on Mexican literature and culture, was written almost exclusively in Spanish, and was penned almost entirely by Reyes, with few outside contributors (Ellison, *Alfonso Reyes e o Brasil* 86–87, 96–97). That said, *Monterrey* certainly reflects the Brazilian and more specifically *carioca* milieu in which all but its final issue was published (No. 14, dated July 1937, was published in Buenos Aires). Reyes himself debuted three Brazil-themed articles in *Monterrey*: the aforementioned "Sobre la tumba de Graça Aranha" (July 1931), along with "Paul Morand en Río" (December 1931) and "Maximiliano descubre el colibrí" (June 1936). In addition, Reyes published Ronald de Carvalho's article, "'Cobardía' de Amado Nervo contra os Traductores Brasileiros" (Amado Nervo's "Cobardía" versus its Brazilian Translators) in the July 1931 issue. Here Carvalho, who like Reyes was interested in promoting Luso-Hispanic intellectual exchange and continental unity, seizes on the challenge of translating a line from the Mexican poet Nervo to Portuguese in order to argue in paradoxical fashion for the ultimate dissimilarity of the Portuguese and Spanish languages, observing that "the two [. . .] are so alike as to be unequal. This instance provides the best demonstration of the theorem of parallels" (*Revistas: Monterrey* 143). Carvalho's interpretation makes a striking contrast to Reyes's own thoughts on the relationship between Spanish and Portuguese, as we shall see in the coming pages.

An additional salient feature of Reyes's editorial activity with *Monterrey* is shown in his reproduction in the March 1932 issue of a letter (dated March 7, 1931) sent to him by the Brazilian writer-diplomat Ribeiro Couto (1898–1963). In the letter, Couto elucidates his idea of the prototypical Brazilian as an *homem cordial* ("cordial man"), a term that would be taken up by Sérgio Buarque de Holanda in his essay "Corpo e Alma do Brasil" (Body and Soul of Brazil, 1935), and given fuller treatment the following year in *Raízes do Brasil*, a text through which the notion of the *homem cordial* would become one of the most successful explicatory metaphors in twentieth-century Brazilian national exegesis. In other words,

Monterrey served as the means by which Buarque learned of Couto's figure of the *homem cordial*; without *Monterrey*, Buarque's *Raízes do Brasil* would, then, lack one of its best-known features. In the following paragraphs we shall return to Reyes's own writing, focusing on his observations on the question of language and on Luso-Hispanic relations. While Reyes would follow Rodó in focusing on issues of language in his characterizations of the Brazilian-Spanish American dynamic, Reyes's particular views on Spanish-Portuguese linguistic interaction would depart to a degree from those of his Uruguayan mentor.

Given language's central function within the Spanish American continentalist project, and its role as a mediating (and complicating) agent of Brazilian-Spanish American relations, it makes sense to begin here in examining Reyes's thinking on the idea of Brazil and its place in America. In his writings that address the Portuguese language directly, Reyes repeatedly makes the case that Portuguese should be understood as related, though not equivalent, to "our" (*nuestro/a*) Spanish language. This use of the possessive pronoun underscores the fact that Reyes understood his audience as implicitly Spanish-speaking, by education if not by birth. For example, in his 1924 piece "Psicología dialectical," which mounts a defense of dialectical variations and differences between historically related languages such as Portuguese, Spanish, and Italian, Reyes describes Portuguese as resembling Spanish and thereby only requiring "partial translation" for Spanish-speakers. He asks: "¿No habéis notado que los italianos nunca logran completamente hablar con pureza en español? Dígase lo mismo del portugués, del brasilero. Como su lengua se parece a *la nuestra*, les salimos a medio campo, para entenderlos, y les basta con traducirse a medias" (*OC* 2: 339; my emphasis).

As in so many other areas, Reyes believed that Spanish and Portuguese could only benefit from exchange, or as he put it in "Aduana lingüística" (1933–41), mutual "fertilization": "El que ama de veras la lengua castellana tiene que amar a la vez la lengua portuguesa. Ambas se fertilizan la una por la otra, y mutuamente se acarician y halagan" (*OC* 14: 166–67). Indeed, Reyes utilizes the occasion of his 1931 tribute to Carvalho to speak of the personal pleasure he takes in "mezcla[ndo] en graciosa naturalidad las dos lenguas de la antigua Romania que siempre han sabido acompañarse y fecundizarse tan bien por el contacto" (*OC* 8: 157). Reyes practiced a form of limited linguistic cross-fertilization in his own writing on Luso-Brazilian topics, making use of *lusitanismos* in the title of his brief prose pieces "Saudade" (published in *Reloj del sol*, 1926), which describes a visit by Portuguese poet Teixeira de Pascoaes to Madrid, in the title of the piece "As Laranjeiras" (1931), and in the following multilingual inventory of the plants and trees he encountered while in Rio:

> De la botánica más a la mano, sin escoger y a lo que acuda solo a la pluma, *y en grata mescolanza de lenguas;* acacia real, árbol del agua o del viajero, árbol del pan, bacurí, bambú, botón de oro, cayú, cabello de urso, cactos, cambará, copo de leite, cravo japonés, esponja vermelha, extremosa, flor de San Juan, pico de papagayo, galán de noche, guayaba, jaboticaba, jazmín del cielo, laranjas, limones, mandioca o yuca, madreselva, magnolia, mamão, mangueira, mimos de Venus, morera, olivos, oreja de burro, oreja de liebre, orquídea, paineira, palma Santa Rita, palmera, rosa, samamboya, tinhorão preto . . . ("Notas varias" [s.d.]; *OC* 9: 495; my emphasis)

Though aside from these *lusitanismos* and *brasileirismos*, when Reyes addressed Brazilian topics or spoke to a Brazilian audience, whether in person or in print, he invariably did so in Spanish as opposed to Portuguese—his open letter to Renato Almeida constitutes a notable exception.[59] One wonders how much importance Reyes placed on learning Portuguese, or if perhaps he assumed, as in "Psicología dialectical," that Brazilians, if they could understand him in Spanish, were sufficiently approximate to him in cultural terms as to be considered part of the Spanish American *nosotros* ("we/us"), that is, the sense of fraternal fellow-feeling that as we have seen, was key to the continentalist projects of Bolívar, Martí, Rodó—and now Reyes.

Reyes seems aware, however, of the fact that the Portuguese language's (tenuous) degree of distinctness from Spanish has certain consequences, both interpersonal and theoretical. Early on during his stay in Brazil, Reyes wrote a May 9, 1930 letter to Valery Larbaud in which he described Portuguese—and his inability to speak it—as contributing to both his sense of loneliness and Brazil's apparent intellectual isolation: "Estoy en los términos del mundo conocido; parece mentira que tan leve divergencia lingüística baste para poner un trozo del planeta en bloqueo perpetuo con respecto a los demás! Nunca he estado tan solo" (Larbaud and Reyes 85).

In a later text, the 1941 article "De poesía hispanoamericana," which Reyes wrote for *The Nation* and which was designed to give a US audience an overview of Latin American poetry, Reyes is again forced to confront the question of the Portuguese language's identity or difference vis-à-vis Spanish, and must also address a perennially vexing dilemma for analysts and anthologists of Latin American literature: whether to include Brazilian texts in his article, which would call into question the assumption of "Latin American" literature's assumed Spanish origin and heritage, or to exclude Brazil and thereby undermine the possibility that the scope of his analysis might apply to the whole of "Latin America." In this instance Reyes takes the exclusionary path, offering this carefully worded and ultimately ambiguous explanation for his exclusion of Brazilian literature: "Por ser nación de lengua lusitana, dejamos fuera de esta reseña al Brasil, que sigue *camino aparte, aunque no divergente*" (*OC* 12: 256; my emphasis).[60] We might ask if these "distinct though not divergent" paths run parallel, as per Ronald de Carvalho's 1931 article on Amado Nervo, with its mention of the "theorem of parallels." While it is tempting to argue that Reyes's hand is forced in this instance by editorial concerns (though passing mention of one or two Brazilian names would not have lengthened the article by any appreciable degree), there is reason to believe that for Reyes, the issue of linguistic difference runs deeper, complicating his scheme of "separate but not divergent paths" for Portuguese and Spanish. We should recall that for Reyes, language was more than a vehicle for expressing ideas. Rather, Reyes considered language, and the particular history of a given language, as *formative* of a speaker's ideas and broader worldview: Reyes wrote in 1943's "Discurso por la lengua" that "[u]na civilización muda es inconcebible. Sólo a través de la lengua tomamos posesión de nuestra parte del mundo" (*OC* 11: 313). At the level of discrete ideas, a Spanish-speaker may incorporate foreign words into her speech in order to convey particular meanings unavailable in her native language, as Reyes and many other non-Lusophone writers have done with the Portuguese term *saudade*, a word that has sometimes been described as untranslatable.[61] However, in terms of one's essential worldview, this linguistic border crossing is not as readily available.[62] We are inevitably raised and educated in a given language (or languages, in the case of bilingual speakers), which Reyes believed to condition the contours of one's thought. As he wrote in his 1924 "Discurso académico," "[e]n las palabras—leve signo, ráfaga apenas—está impreso nuestro destino: *hablamos, sentimos, en lengua castellana*" (*OC* 4: 438; my emphasis). Reyes elaborated on these thoughts in his "Discurso por la lengua" (1943). Even as he cites Jacob Burckhardt in arguing that "el principio de la historia es la libertad del bastardeo," and argues that "[u]na lengua pura es un paradigma, una abstracción," Reyes also contends in typically Romantic fashion that for each nation or group, "[e]l alma, el patrimonio espiritual se conserva en el vehículo de la lengua." Moreover, Reyes explains that he considers it a privilege as a Mexican and Latin American writer to "hablar en español y entender el mundo en español" (*OC* 11: 312–13, 315). Following Reyes's logic, Mexicans and Brazilians necessarily understand the world with a certain degree of difference simply because they are educated in and speak different (albeit closely related) tongues, and reproduce distinct cultural and intellectual traditions *through* these languages.[63] While Reyes viewed these linguistic-historical traditions as equally valid (note his rejection of Castilian as the prestige form of Spanish in "Psicología dialectical"), and while he believed that they could benefit in verbal and conceptual terms from mutual exchange, for Reyes they remained nonetheless distinct—a conclusion at odds with Rodó's stated view of Spanish and Portuguese's overriding equivalence. And while Reyes, as a proponent of intellectual and cultural *bastardeo*, rejected on principle notions of linguistic purity and isolation, he was nonetheless invested in the affirmation of certain overriding distinctions between languages, ideas, genres, periods, and peoples, as Faber has noted.[64]

In addressing the complex relationship between Portuguese and Spanish, Reyes frequently employs the revealing metaphor of the *telaraña* (spider web), which underscores his interest in linguistic cross-fertilization even as he insists that he speaks *as* a Spanish speaker, *to* other Spanish speakers (or to Brazilians who can hopefully understand his Spanish). In "Sobre la reforma de la ortografía portuguesa" (1931), Reyes writes:

> La red invisible de la lengua—una lengua, sin embargo, tan cercana y tan parecida a *la nuestra*—ha resultado una telaraña de acero lo bastante resistente para contribuir con eficacia a mantener la unidad de este inmenso continente metido dentro de otro: la nación brasileña. Acabada ya la formación del pueblo, la primera evolución nacional, la red se afloja ahora lo bastante para volverse permeable. Permeable hasta cierto punto, claro está. (*OC* 9: 59; my emphasis)[65]

Having astutely judged the "steel" spider web of language a factor in Brazil's political and intellectual autonomy, Reyes tacitly admits a degree of linguistic and intellectual non-communication between Spanish America and Brazil, describing the latter as an "immense continent placed within another."[66] However, Reyes remains hopeful that linguistic exchange is possible, since after all, Portuguese is a language that is "so close and so much like *our own*." With such a premium placed on exchange, Reyes reacted with a comprehensible level of frustration at what he occasionally saw as Brazil's intellectual isolationism, commenting in an uncharacteristically critical passage of his diary for 1933 on the "estado de aislamiento en que vive la mente brasileña" (qtd. in Ellison, *Alfonso Reyes e o Brasil* 145). Once again on the offensive regarding the need for dialogue, in "Posición de América" (1942) Reyes prescribes intellectual exchange (presented elsewhere as a solution for war, academic overspecialization, and numerous other ills) as a remedy to the problem of historical, cultural, and simple linguistic non-communication between Portuguese- and Spanish-speakers. He addresses the question of linguistic difference by asserting that for Spanish-speakers (again identified as *nosotros*), Portuguese represents a "permeable spider web." He explains:

> Es innegable que las diferencias de lengua establecen hiatos; innegable que cada lengua se funda en una metafísica o representación del mundo. Pero este hiato camina a la evanescencia práctica dentro de las comunidades culturales de la humanidad presente, en que las minorías creadoras de normas sociales se educan y piensan en varias lenguas. La

transmisión establece puentes y vados, camino del mínimo de unidad indispensable. *Entre las lenguas latinas del continente, el portugués es una telaraña permeable para el español, aunque haya contribuido a sostener la unidad moral del noble pueblo brasileño;* [. . .] Las grandes inspiraciones morales y políticas, el libre viento de la democracia que va y viene por el continente, operan como niveladores, rumbo a la *homónoia* o armonía internacional. Por todos los argumentos llegamos, pues, a una conclusión positiva. La toma de posición de América ante la cultura tiene el camino libre. (*OC* 11: 268–69; my emphasis on all except "homónoia")[67]

As in his defense of culture, Reyes praises those Latin American intellectuals willing to work toward greater linguistic and cultural contact between Brazil and Spanish America. In his 1931 tribute to Ronald de Carvalho, Reyes returns to the "parallel" vocabulary he and Carvalho share, describing a state of inter-American non-communication that, given the speech's Brazilian setting and subject, seems to refer particularly to Luso-Hispanic relations. Employing metaphors that evoke the Iberian maritime voyages, and approximating Rodó's image in "Iberoamérica" (1910) of Brazil and Spanish America as two rivers originating in the same region (but not quite from the same spot), Reyes notes that "[s]iguiendo rutas paralelas, nunca se encontraban nuestros barcos. No sabíamos que éramos unos, y los pueblos americanos vivíamos tan alejados unos de otros como tal vez de nosotros mismos—porque la ignorancia de lo semejante supone siempre, en mucho, el desconocimiento de lo propio." Predictably, Reyes charges the Latin American poet (whom he views as "en nuestros pueblos, el organizador de la esperanza") with restoring to its lost unity a region he alternately identifies with the figures of Martí's *nuestra América* and Carvalho's *toda a América* (*OC* 8: 158–59). In my view, the relevant question to ask is, what were Reyes's intentions in attempting to reconcile Brazil's political, cultural, and linguistic difference with the utopian unity he advocated for the region? At this point it becomes necessary to address Brazil's *specific* role in Reyes's utopian vision for America.

In terms of the notion of Latin America as an *Última Tule*, it is significant that Reyes on at least two occasions in his writing identifies the term specifically with Brazil. In the first instance, from a 1931 letter written to his friend and government supervisor Genaro Estrada, the reference is not complimentary. Reyes, evidently unhappy during the first days of his residency in Rio as ambassador, writes: "Yo estoy muy lejos del mundo, en la Ultima Tule: esto es la luna" (qtd. in Zaïtzeff 161). Here Rio de Janeiro—or Brazil in general—is presented as a kind of Brigadoon or Hurtado (a legendary Spanish town occasionally mentioned by Reyes) and is identified with intellectual isolation and provincialism, qualities that as we have seen are antithetical to Reyes's desired state of affairs.[68] Yet Reyes makes a much more positive characterization in his poem "A Río" (1931), which dates from the same year as his letter, and in which he praises the city as a lost tropical paradise: "[Y]o no sabía que eras Última Tule, / sola entre tus angélicas aguas, verdes y azules" (OC 10: 266). Reyes presents Rio de Janeiro in this second, more positive light on several other occasions, both in prose and in verse. In the prose piece "Ubérrima Urbe" (written 1931, first published 1933–34), Reyes offers a description of Rio de Janeiro that is rich in references to classical, Judeo-Christian, and the New World chroniclers' accounts of paradise, describing the city in mythical tones as a site for the harmonious fusion of man and beast and of city and nature. In doing so, Reyes uses the same noun (*mescolanza*) to describe the wondrous encounter of the human and the telluric as he employs in 1931's "As Laranjeiras" (OC 11: 495) to describe the intermixing of the Spanish and Portuguese languages:

> En otra parte, habría el riesgo de que el suelo y el cielo fueran marchitándose poco a poco: no aquí. La misma vitalidad del ambiente, las auras y los juegos, han de mantener el buen equilibrio. Triunfo hasta hoy de todos, y de todo seguirá triunfando en Río Janeiro la virtud terrestre, la Deidad Ctónica, haciendo entre el árbol, la piedra y el hombre una *mescolanza* generosa. Las casas echarán raíces: las ventanas engendrarán yerbas trepadoras; el hombre y el animal se frecuentarán con cierto respeto, y con más atenuada envidia la mujer y la rosa; el niño se confundirá con la fruta; la penca, con el soldado en armas. Entre el velar y el dormir correrá un cordón de manso fuego. Aquel hortelano podrá volverse un antiguo Término en lo que hasta para imaginarlo y contarlo; como en Ovidio. Y Pan, tronco que acaba en hombre, será el símbolo acomodado para la ciudad todavía plástica,

aún no desprendida de la mano de Dios. El Paraíso—decía
Vespucio—no puede estar lejos de aquí. (*OC* 9: 472; my
emphasis)

Reyes expands on this pantheistic and paradisiacal description
in a number of poems written during his time in Rio. In "Río
de Olvido," published in *Romances del Río de Enero* (1933),
Reyes writes of a miraculous encounter of land and sea, of
"[l]a tierra en el agua [que] juega / y el campo con la ciudad," add-
ing in "Guanabara" (1933) to this description. In this second
poem, Reyes describes Guanabara Bay, "donde el mar y la tierra
se mordían" as the product of an originary sexual encounter
between an "Adán marino" and an earthly Eve (*OC* 10: 148,
385).

So which "Última Tule" is Brazil to be for Reyes, the inhospitable Brigadoon of his letter to Estrada, or the tropical Eden
of his poems and of "Ubérrima Urbe"? Reyes's ambivalence on
the question of Brazil as *Última Tule* is mirrored by a broader
ambivalence with regard to Brazil's place in Latin America. In
texts like the essays that comprise *Última Tule*, and in "Posición
de América" (1942), Reyes wrestles, as have so many other
Spanish American writers, critics, and exegetes, with the question of how to fit Brazil into a vision of Latin America grounded
in notions of a common Spanish-origin language, history, and
identity. In these pieces, Reyes on several occasions projects a
Spanish American identity onto Brazil, persistently addressing
himself to fellow Spanish-speakers as his audience, and com-
mitting numerous semantic slippages between the categories of
Spain and *Iberia* and *Spanish America* and *Latin America*. For
instance, in "El presagio de América," even as he cites numerous episodes from Portuguese maritime history in describing
the Iberian encounter with the New World, Reyes makes the
following characterization:

> Obra de colonización deficiente, media España se traslada a
> América y empieza a vivir según su leal saber y entender. De
> aquí nuestras repúblicas; de aquí que el orbe hispano desbor-
> de con mucho de los límites *del Estado peninsular.* Tal es el
> sentido profundo de la creación ibérica, creación del pueblo,
> creación del soldado desconocido que se llama, lisa y llana-
> mente, *Juan español.* (*OC* 11: 51; my emphasis)

In this narrative of colonization, *João português* is evidently absent, either ignored all together or implied as a variation of the prototypical *Juan español*, who journeys from an apparently singular "peninsular State" to the New World. While Reyes of course understood that Portuguese sailors and colonizers also made such transatlantic crossings, it is nonetheless significant that the idea of Latin America as a region grounded in a specifically *Spanish* origin resonated so strongly for Reyes that he would (perhaps unconsciously) distort the historical record. Reyes offers another example of identity projection in his much-anthologized "Notas sobre la inteligencia americana" (1936), which he introduces as a series of observations on "that which is called Latin America." After he acknowledges that he speaks as a Mexican, he notes that "lo que digo de México [. . .] podría decirse en mayor o menor grado del resto de nuestra América." He then offers a reading of nineteenth-century Latin American (read as "Spanish American") history that is characterized by violent quarrels between pro- and anti-Spanish factions, and between political conservatives and liberals. Nowhere is Brazil's distinct historical trajectory (which he acknowledges in other texts) mentioned, though Reyes does provide anecdotal references to two important figures in early colonial Brazil, João Ramalho and Caramuru (*OC* 11: 82, 84–85).[69] The closest Reyes comes to acknowledging the limited applicability of this reading of Latin American history to Brazil comes in "Capricho de América" (1933), in which he cites the fact that Spanish American independence leaders would refer to their audiences as *americanos* as evidence of "un espíritu continental." He qualifies his statement with the proviso that "[n]aturalmente, este fenómeno sólo es apreciable en los países hispanoamericanos, únicos para los cuales tiene sentido." Though significantly, in writing of "[s]ajones e iberos," Reyes places his analysis within the tradition of Hegel, Ranke, and Chevalier, by dividing the Western hemisphere in dialectical fashion into two halves, one "Anglo" and the other "Latin" (*OC* 11: 76–77)—a practice that, as we saw in this book's first chapter, may obscure other possible binaries, as between Brazil and Spanish America, and may work to conceal tensions and inconsistencies that are internal to Latin America as a geo-cultural category. This is consistent with Reyes's vision of the essentially homogeneous character of "our

America," which he presents in "Posición de América" (1942) as the outgrowth of cultural, religious, and linguistic "commonalities," but most importantly as the product of a common history closely identified with Bolivarian federalism:

> De un modo general y *sin entrar en odiosos distingos,* los pueblos de América, por el impulso de su formación histórica semejante, son menos extranjeros entre sí que las naciones del viejo mundo. Hay comunidad de bases culturales, de religión y lengua. Y por su captación étnica, están singularmente preparados para no exagerar el pequeñísimo valor de las diferencias de raza, concepto estático sin fundamento científico ni consecuencia ninguna sobre la dignidad o la inteligencia humanas, uniformes en principio cuando se les ofrecen iguales posibilidades; cosa transitoria cuya exacta nivelación nuestra América entiende como uno de sus deberes sociales inapelables e indiscutibles.
>
> [. . .]
>
> De esta grande homogeneidad en las mayorías nacionales de América, ha resultado que nuestros pueblos hayan podido, *según el sueño de Bolívar,* desarrollar cierta labor armoniosa y continuada de conversación internacional, sostenida por más de medio siglo [. . .] y sorprendente si se considera la magnitud del territorio que cubre y el semillero de pueblos que abarca. (*OC* 11: 265–66; my emphasis)

Though the Bolivarian paradigm is clearly inapplicable to Brazil (as Reyes acknowledges in "Capricho de América"), and has had little intellectual resonance in Brazil beyond isolated figures such as Sílvio Júlio, it functions in the above-cited portion of "Posición de América," as well as in certain moments of *Última Tule*, as the lynchpin for the Latin American solidarity Reyes seeks to promote. Reyes's continentalist agenda, as with Rodó, leads him to run the risk of historical inaccuracy on several occasions, as when he effectively implies Brazil's participation in the early nineteenth-century Spanish American independence struggle. Reyes asks: "¿[N]o recordamos todos que *los países sudamericanos,* gesto repetido en nuestros días, se prestaban tropas, caudillos y héroes, para ayudarse en las campañas de la independencia y en la defensa continental, entendida como interés común? Las mismas proclamas de los primeros insurgentes se dirigían, con profundo instinto, a *los americanos en general*, y no a los nacionales de este o aquel país recortado por los accidentes de la geografía, la historia o la administración jurisdiccional de las antiguas colonias" (*OC* 11: 267; my emphasis). While Reyes almost certainly did not mean to suggest that Brazil participated in this effort, his continentalist rhetoric, deployed in defense of a familiar, distinctly Spanish American form of group identity grounded in a mutually reinforcing interplay of national and supranational identities, forces him to do so.

***

In his otherwise incisive piece "Down with Tordesillas!" (1993), Jorge Schwartz judges Alfonso Reyes to have "scarcely benefited from his experience as a diplomat in Brazil in terms of a closer exchange with Brazilian literary culture" (186). This characterization is far from accurate. As we have seen, Reyes gave over a significant portion of his intellectual production between 1930 and 1936 to Brazilian themes, and his feverish activity as a cultural and diplomatic ambassador went far beyond the level of the merely "anecdotal or personal." While Reyes *did* almost invariably address his Brazilian audience in Spanish—a point to which Schwartz seems to object—the depth of Reyes's work in mediating between the Hispanic and Lusophone spheres at the levels of literature, culture, and history militates against the conclusion that his choice to speak and work in Spanish while in Brazil was based in a sense of ethno-linguistic arrogance, or due to disinterest in the Portuguese language or in Luso-Brazilian literature. Regardless, examination of Reyes's thoughts on language, and particularly his conception of an apparently unproblematic relationship between Spanish and Portuguese as constituting a mutually permeable *telaraña* (spider web), which he couples with the familiar moves of folding Brazil into a Spanish-origin historical narrative and narrating *from* a declaredly Spanish-speaking speaking position and *to* other assumed "Spanish-speakers" (even if his interlocutors are Brazilian), point to the lingering hispanocentrism that informs Reyes's vision of Brazil and its place in his American utopia. In this sense we may understand Reyes as carrying forward a certain continentalist-utopian rhetoric favored by Bolívar,

Francisco Bilbao, José María Torres Caicedo, and Rodó, and as ultimately falling prey to the same inconsistencies as these writers on the question of Brazil's place in Latin America.

Nonetheless, Reyes's treatment of Brazil's Latin American location and of Luso-Hispanic relations presents certain advantages to the contemporary observer: the centrality in Reyes's worldview of interpersonal, international, and cross-disciplinary exchange and his acknowledgement of some degree of Brazilian cultural and linguistic difference *within* Latin America, along with his vigorous defense of humanism, give us at least some of the tools for undertaking a new kind of comparative Luso-Hispanic analysis. This approach would acknowledge the contingency and historical situatedness of terms like "Latin America," and would respond with a certain skepticism to the essentializing nationalism that often underlies Spanish American identity projection onto Brazil, as well as Brazilian selective approximation to Spanish America. Before closing this study, we must return to the other side of the Luso-Hispanic frontier, in order to examine the work of Brazilian critic and historian Sérgio Buarque de Holanda (1902–82). In looking to the thematic continuities between Buarque's early criticism and his best-known text, the interpretive essay *Raízes do Brasil*, we will consider a final context in which Luso-Hispanic "disconsonance" has been manifested: in the *evasion* of acknowledged cross-border influence, here pertaining to the obscured "roots" of José Enrique Rodó in Buarque's thought.

Sérgio Buarque de Holanda

Obscured Roots of Rodó
in *Raízes do Brasil*

A tentativa de implantação da cultura européia em
extenso território, dotado de condições naturais, se
não adversas, largamente estranhas à sua tradição
milenar, é, nas origens da sociedade brasileira, o fato
dominante e mais rico em conseqüências. Trazendo
de países distantes nossas formas de convívio, nossas
instituições, nossas idéias [. . .], somos ainda hoje
uns desterrados em nossa terra. [17]
—Sérgio Buarque de Holanda
Raízes do Brasil (Roots of Brazil, 1936)

O Brasil, entre todos os países do Novo Mundo, é
talvez, ainda que, o menos compenetrado de sua
posição continental. A circunstância de sermos uma
nação americana parece afetar-nos como um fato
acidental, cujas conseqüências podemos transformar
à vontade. O próprio nome de América é hoje,
entre nós, uma palavra comemorativa, boa para
discursos e formalidades. Bem diversa é a atitude
dos nossos vizinhos hispânicos, para os quais ela
representa, em primeiro plano e acima de tudo, uma
realidade hispano-americana, apenas admitindo-se
que homens de outra estirpe, que anglo-saxões, por
exemplo, pretendam partilhar dessa mesma realidade.
"Americano," para um argentino, é em primeiro lugar
um indivíduo de língua espanhola. [18]
—Sérgio Buarque de Holanda
"Considerações sobre o americanismo"
(Considerations on Americanism, 1941)

In the May 1920 edition of the São Paulo-based *Revista do Brasil*, Sérgio Buarque de Holanda (1902–82), a *paulistano* literary critic only eighteen years of age and a member of one of Brazil's oldest and most storied families, published the short piece "Ariel," the second article of his very young career.[1] Buarque, shortly to affiliate with the modernist movement that was to make its debut in São Paulo during the Semana de Arte Moderna (Week of Modern Art) in 1922, and later to be canonized as one of Brazil's great *intérpretes* ("interpreters") for his classic *Raízes do Brasil* (Roots of Brazil, 1936) and confirmed as a respected historian as the author of such studies as *Visão do Paraiso* (Vision of Paradise, 1959), gave little sign of the celebrated figure, the "referential eminence in Brazilian social thought," he was to become (Guimarães, in Monteiro and Eugênio 37). A well-educated young man and an "irreverent and somewhat eccentric reader" who was prone in his criticism to excessive displays of erudition, the monocle-wearing Buarque of the 1920s cut an odd figure in São Paulo and Rio de Janeiro intellectual circles.[2] He enrolled in Rio's Faculdade de Direito (Law School) in 1921, though he was much more interested in literary bohemia than the legal profession. The writing Buarque produced during this first phase of his career (running from 1920 up to his formative 1929–30 stay in Germany), during which he served as the "representative" in Rio de Janeiro of the short-lived but highly influential São Paulo modernist journal *Klaxon* (1922–23) and co-founded the even shorter-lived *Estética* (1924), consisted almost entirely of criticism, though he also tried his hand, rather less successfully, at short fiction and aphoristic writing.[3] Buarque's early critical-journalistic texts were partially collected by Francisco de Assis Barbosa in the volume *Raízes de Sérgio Buarque de Holanda* (Roots of Sérgio Buarque de Holanda, 1988) and were studiously compiled by Antonio Arnoni Prado in the two-volume *O Espírito e a Letra: Estudos de Crítica Literária* (The Spirit and the Letter: Studies in Literary Criticism, 1996). Buarque's early criticism, which addressed a broad range of literary topics, is marked at times by an overwrought irony and a preciousness of tone, by a certain lack of stylistic coherence, and by an eclectic (not to say scattershot) choice of theme—all in sharp contrast to the clear style, focused approach, intellectual rigor, and careful documentation of Buarque's later, more precisely historiographical work.[4] While as a mature writer Buarque would become "horrified" by what he had published as a younger man, judging the criticism and journalism written between 1920 and the 1936 publication of *Raízes do Brasil* to be "irrelevant" (Barbosa 11), various critics have noted a significant degree of thematic coherence between Buarque's early and supposedly more "mature" later work.[5] As João Kennedy Eugênio writes:

> Though these articles vary in character and circumstance, their internal coherence as a whole is [nonetheless] surprising. The distinction between Portuguese and Spanish, between Iberian and Anglo-Saxon tradition, the valorization of cultural singularity, the critique of the rationalization of life and of cultural imitation [. . .] all of these themes can be seen, repeatedly, in the young Sérgio's articles. Some would reappear in *Raízes do Brasil*. (Monteiro and Eugênio 426)[6]

This chapter will look directly at these thematic connections, focusing specifically on the links between Buarque's early critical pieces like "Ariel" (1920) and *Raízes do Brasil,* a seven-chapter "essay" on Brazil's historical "roots," and in the words of one commentator, an "interpretation of the formation of Brazilian society as a singular process, distinct from the other Latin American nations."[7] A classic interpretation of Brazilian history and culture, *Raízes do Brasil,* now in its thirty-first reprinting in Brazil, is unquestionably Buarque's best-known and most influential work. Specifically, I will focus in this chapter on what I consider the pervasive influence on Buarque of Uruguayan writer-critic José Enrique Rodó (1871–1917), author of *Ariel* (1900), and I will argue that Buarque's effective obscuring of Rodó's influence—and of his broader engagement with Spanish American literature and intellectual paradigms—in both his early writing and in *Raízes* is symptomatic of an ongoing tendency in Brazilian literary and essayistic discourse toward selective, limited approximation to Spanish America. Arguing against those—including the mature author himself—who dismiss Buarque's early writing as unrepresentative juvenilia, in this chapter's first section I link Buarque's curious, partial acknowledgement of Rodó in "Ariel" to a broader, Rodó-inherited preoccupation

185

with the opposition between a congenital "Latin" idealism and an "Anglo-Saxon," United States-identified utilitarianism. In the second section I demonstrate how Buarque moves these concerns into his "mature" work, exploring how *Raízes do Brasil* began its life as an aborted *Teoria da América* (Theory of America), and offering a reading of *Raízes* that illustrates the appreciable but seldom-commented *arielista* influence to be seen in that text.[8] Moving into the chapter's third and final section, I will describe how contemporary Brazilian cultural critic Silviano Santiago (b. 1936) unwittingly reproduces Buarque's obscuring of Rodó in his *As Raízes e o Labirinto da América Latina* (The Roots and the Labyrinth of Latin America, 2006), a recent comparative study of Buarque and Mexican poet and essayist Octavio Paz (1914–88), and an important contribution to the emergent Luso-Hispanic comparativism I champion in this book. My overall argument in this chapter is aimed first at demonstrating how the eminently comparative structure of *Raízes do Brasil*, a study Antonio Candido memorably describes as "built using an admirable methodology of opposites,"[9] can be traced to Buarque's early period of Rodó-inspired continentalist reflection. And second, I present Buarque's gradual de-emphasis of Rodó and of *arielismo* (an erasure mimicked by Santiago) as symptomatic of a lingering tendency in Brazilian national exegetic discourse toward the obscuring of literary, cultural, and fraternal ties to Spanish America.

I. Buarque, a Lost Child of Ariel?

Buarque's "Ariel" is, at minimum, a curious article. As João Kennedy Eugênio explains, Buarque's argument in the text "revolves around the key notion of authenticity and its opposite, imitation [. . .] Iberian and Anglo-Saxon America are presented as irreconcilable variations of Western culture" (qtd. in Monteiro and Eugênio 431).[10] Departing from an essentially bifurcated view of North and South American civilization that in the first instance is grounded in Romantic notions of divergent racial or civilizational "geniuses," and then folded into a more basic opposition between Latin and Anglo-Saxon/Teutonic cultures (which Buarque inherits most immediately from Rodó, though this notion remits further to Michel Chevalier, Leopold von Ranke, and Hegel), Buarque begins the article with a general observation concerning the costs of imitating another nation's "characteristic" qualities: "É caso digno de nota que quando uma nação, atraída pela grandeza ou pelos progressos de outra pertencente a raça diversa da sua, é levada a imitar sem peias seus traços característicos e nacionais, procura especialmente as qualidades nocivas e as menos compatíveis com a sua índole" ("it is worth noting that when a nation, attracted by the greatness or progress of another, racially distinct nation, is compelled toward uncritical imitation of its characteristic national qualities, it tends to imitate noxious qualities, those that are least compatible with its way of being"). Buarque then narrows his focus to criticize what he views as a specifically Brazilian tendency to "macaquear tudo quanto é estrangeiro" ("imitate everything foreign"), and observes the corresponding problem of uncritical Brazilian adoption of US culture and values, which he presents as having been exacerbated by the advent of republican government in 1889 (*Espírito* 1: 42).[11] Buarque seems particularly concerned in "Ariel" with the perceived threat of "Yankee utilitarianism," a form of social organization he warns cannot be effectively applied to Brazil, a country whose racial or civilizational character mark it, in his opinion, as fundamentally distinct from the United States. Responding to those Brazilians (presumably republican political actors and positivist intellectuals) who would seek to emulate the material success of the United States via uncritical importation of a Yankee *ethos*, Buarque warns: "[A] índole de um povo não se modifica tão facilmente à simples ação de agentes externos" (*Espírito* 1: 42–45; "A people's way of being cannot be changed so easily under the simple influence of foreign agents"). Despite the opposition he demarcates between the opposing ideals of "Yankee" utilitarianism and "Latin" idealism, Buarque makes the curious move of identifying his critique of the former not with Rodó's *Ariel* (1900)—which having been written a mere twenty years earlier would seem the idea's immediate source—but with German philosopher Arthur Schopenhauer (1788–1860):

Nos Estados Unidos há [. . .] um ar infecto de corrupção que exala das classes que governam, difícil de ser encontrado na

> Europa. O utilitarismo e a preocupação de ganhar dinheiro,
> a *auri sacra fames*, conquistaram os norte-americanos em
> detrimento do espírito intelectual, da moralidade políti-
> ca e da própria liberdade individual. Isso deu azo a que
> Schopenhauer os qualificasse de proletários da humanidade.
> (*Espírito* 1: 43; author's emphasis)[12] [19]

Indeed, Buarque does not refer to Rodó by name until the text's
final paragraphs. And when he *does* mention Rodó, he somewhat misleadingly describes the "notable Uruguayan thinker"
as "recently deceased" (Rodó had died in Sicily three years
earlier), and never mentions Rodó's *Ariel* by name:

> Ariel, o gênio do ar, em *The tempest* de Shakespeare, re-
> presenta a espiritualidade em contraposição a Caliban, sím-
> bolo do utilitarismo, e que além do mais é um *savage and
> deformed slave.*
>
> Ariel, diz Clarín, no estudo publicado como Prólogo à
> magnífica obra do notável pensador uruguaio José Enrique
> Rodó, recentemente falecido, Ariel "ama a inteligência por
> si mesma, a beleza, a graça e os puros mistérios do infinito."
> (*Espírito* 1: 45–46; author's emphasis) [20]

Despite Buarque's curiously partial attribution, in which Rodó
is presented more as an afterthought than as the argument's
intellectual point of origin, and in which an idea famously associated with Rodó is implicitly credited to Schopenhauer (a
thinker for whom the menace to South America of US utilitarianism could hardly have qualified as a pressing concern),
those familiar with Rodó will have a clear sense of the degree
of his influence on Buarque. At this point we should consider
other sources on which Buarque might plausibly have drawn in
"Ariel," beyond Rodó and Schopenhauer, as a means to resolve
the question of Rodó's primacy vis-à-vis these other thinkers.

Putting aside for a moment the shadow cast by Rodó over
Buarque's article, which is evident in both its title as well
as in Buarque's (by all appearances reluctant) acknowledgement of the Uruguayan writer at its conclusion, it should be
admitted that numerous antecedents to Buarque's position in
"Ariel" can be found in earlier Brazilian reflections on national
identity. Indeed, as the critic Roberto Schwarz notes in his
brilliant essay "Nacional por Subtração" (National by Subtrac-

tion, 1987), the preoccupation with affirming an authentically *national* consciousness, and the concomitant worry that one's national culture is inauthentic due to excessive foreign influence, have been prominent features of Brazilian criticism from the early nineteenth century to the present.[13] Buarque's use in "Ariel" of terms on the order of "nosso temperamento" ("our temperament") and "índole" ("way of being/manner") remits to Romantic-era thinking on national "genius," as does his concern with affirming the country's unique "caráter nacional" ("national character") through the location, collection, and deployment of "authentic" literary and historical materials, a problem he addresses in his earliest published piece, "Originalidade literária" (Literary Originality), which appeared in the April 22, 1920 edition of the *Correio Paulistano*, shortly before the publication of "Ariel." Here Buarque asserts that "[a] emancipação intelectual não é, nem podia ser, um corolário fatal da emancipação política. Esta é um fator secundário [. . .] na evolução do espírito de um povo" ("Intellectual emancipation is not, nor can it be, a necessary corollary of political emancipation. It is a secondary factor [. . .] in the evolution of a people's spirit"). Further, Buarque predicts that "[o] Brasil há de ter uma literatura nacional, há de atingir, mais cedo ou mais tarde, a originalidade literária. A inspiração em assuntos nacionais, o respeito das nossas tradições e a submissão às vozes profundas da raça acelerarão esse resultado final" (*Espírito* 1: 35, 41; "Brazil will have a national literature, it will achieve, sooner or later, literary originality. Inspiration taken from national topics, respect for our traditions, and submission to the deep voices of the race will hasten this final result"). The Brazilian novelist, journalist, and politician José de Alencar (1829–77) expressed precisely this concern decades earlier, in his inaugural 1856 public letter on Gonçalves de Magalhães's epic poem *A Confederação dos Tamoios* (The Confederation of the Tamoios). Here the future author of the classic *indianista* novels *O Guarani* (The Guarani Indian, 1857) and *Iracema* (1865) criticizes Magalhães for failing to make effective use of the "Brazilian *Nibelungen*," and in judging *A Confederação* a failed Brazilian national epic, elucidates his own vision for what would constitute the bases for a successful, truly *national* Brazilian literature (865–66).[14] Nearly twenty years later, a young Machado de Assis (1839–

1908), later to become arguably Brazil's most important novelist, qualified Alencar's call for "authentic" national literature in his essay "Instinto de Nacionalidade" (Instinct of Nationality, 1873). Here Machado distinguishes between a "superficial" literary nationalism identified with the overlaying of local motifs onto essentially foreign models, and a more substantial, "interior" national feeling that would compel the writer to approach a full range of literary topics *as a Brazilian*, such that he would become "a man of his time and of his country even when he addresses subjects that are remote in time or space" (804).[15] Moving forward, Buarque's concern with national literary and cultural authenticity was shared by his colleagues in the Brazilian modernist movement, such as Oswald de Andrade, who in his "Manifesto Antropófago" (Cannibalist Manifesto, 1928) advocated the reconstitution of an "authentic" Brazilian culture through the "cannibalization," rather than imitation, of European and North American ideas.[16]

As with his argument for cultural authenticity, Buarque's critique of utilitarianism in "Ariel," even if it draws primarily on Rodó, also borrows from earlier Brazilian thinkers. Buarque clearly looks, for example, to the warnings of monarchists like Joaquim Nabuco and Eduardo Prado, as voiced in *Balmaceda* (1895) and *A Ilusão Americana* (The American Illusion, 1893), that US-style republican institutions are antithetical to the Brazilian character.[17] Indeed, the shortcomings and dangers of utilitarianism constituted one of the recurring themes of the young Buarque's criticism. In the article "O Homem-Máquina" (The Man-Machine, 1921)—a sort of dystopian inversion of Rodó's prophetic *El que vendrá* (1896)—Buarque writes of the "lie" of utilitarianism, tying it specifically to the United States and describing its progeny, the "man-machine" of the future, as "um instrumento de segunda ordem ao lado dos aparelhos mecânicos que lhe encarem, um meio auxiliar de importância secundária; não será mais a criatura ideal, inteligente, o criador genial e criterioso" (Monteiro and Eugênio 561; "a second-order instrument, alongside the mechanical apparatuses that contain him, an auxiliary tool of secondary importance; he will no longer be an ideal, intelligent creature, a genial and discerning creator").[18]

All this said, the dominant intellectual influence to be seen in Buarque's "Ariel" remains that of Rodó.[19] In arguing for

Buarque's article as an implicit "endorsement" of *arielismo*, as João Kennedy Eugênio contends, we should first look at the young Buarque's broader engagement with Rodó and with Spanish American literature and ideas (Eugênio and Monteiro 431). As a young critic, Buarque displayed an intense interest in Spanish and Spanish American literature that, if we trust both the progression of his writing and what we know of the evolution of his private library, tapered off over time—though it certainly left its mark on the comparative Luso-Hispanic structure of *Raízes do Brasil*, as we shall see.[20] Buarque's early criticism is littered with references to the Spanish *Siglo de Oro*, to Cervantes, and to picaresque literature as features of his discussion of a panoply of Latin American writers, both canonical (Rubén Darío, Pablo Neruda) and more obscure (José María Vargas Vila, José Santos Chocano, Alberto Nin Frías). In his 1920 article "Santos Chocano," Buarque notes the peculiarity of his hispanophilia among Brazilians, and alluding to the mutual intelligibility of the Portuguese and Spanish languages, writes: "A despeito dessa opinião [. . .] releva dizer que muito tesouro desconhecido, mormente no terreno das letras, existe aí, à matroca, pelos países da América Espanhola" (*Espírito* 1: 54; "In spite of this opinion [. . .] it is worth affirming that there is much hidden treasure there, particularly in the area of letters, to be had at little cost [i.e., without great linguistic effort], in the Spanish American countries"). Colombian writer Vargas Vila (1860–1933) and Peruvian poet and journalist Santos Chocano (1875–1934) each merit short critical profiles from Buarque, who presents them as "exceptional" Latin American writers.[21] It is tempting to speculate that Buarque might have complemented these profiles with others, and that his projected but never completed volume *Os novecentistas* (Twentieth-Century Men), which he was planning during this period, would have thereby served as an update or companion piece to Darío's collection of authorial profiles, *Los raros* (1896).[22]

Turning to Rodó specifically, Buarque makes several references in his shorter work that show him to have been broadly familiar with the Uruguayan critic. In addition to "Ariel," Buarque makes passing mention of Rodó's travel volume, *El Camino de Paros* (1918) in a 1921 article entitled "Plágios e Plagiários" (Plagiarisms and Plagiarizers), later reprising

Rodó's oppositions between Latin America/North America, idealism/utilitarianism, and Ariel/Caliban in his article "Considerações sobre o americanismo" (Considerations on Americanism, 1941), and giving a 1952 review of Jorge de Lima's volume *Invenção de Orfeu* (Invention of Orpheus) the title "Motivos de Proteu" (Motives of Proteus)—a clear reference to Rodó's own *Motivos de Proteo* (1909) (*Espírito* 1: 116–30; 2: 567–71; *Cobra* 22–27). Though curiously, Buarque fails to refer to Rodó by name in either his 1941 or 1952 piece—just as he failed to directly refer to Rodó's *Ariel* in his own "Ariel." While traces of Rodó are to be found in Buarque's work, it is remarkable how faintly they are inscribed.

However, we need not rely entirely on biographical details and textual references in establishing that Rodó's *Ariel* constituted the primary influence for Buarque's "Ariel," and that more broadly, Rodó represents an important point of reference for understanding Buarque's early criticism. Several thematic and linguistic parallels can be observed between the two Ariels. Perhaps most obviously, Buarque's distinction in his "Ariel" between admiration and imitation of the United States, "[n]ão há quem, intimamente, deixe de admirá-lo, embora poucos sejam os que podem estimá-lo" ("there is no one who, deep down, does not admire [the US], though few hold it in esteem"), is clearly derived from Rodó's oft-quoted statement in *Ariel* concerning the people of the United States: "[A]unque no les amo, les admiro" (*Espírito* 1: 44; Rodó 235). And on the subject of "Yankee utilitarianism," we may compare Buarque's statement, "[o] utilitarismo e a preocupação de ganhar dinheiro, a *auri sacra fames*, conquistaram os norte-americanos em detrimento do espírito intelectual, da moralidade política e da própria liberdade individual" ("Utilitarianism and the desire to make money, *auri sacra fames,* have conquered the North Americans to the detriment of the intellectual spirit, of political morality, and even of individual liberty"), with the following quotation from Rodó's *Ariel*: "[S]i [. . .] se pregunta cuál es en ella [i.e., la vida norteamericana] el principio dirigente, cuál su *substratum* ideal, [. . .] sólo se encontrará, como fórmula de ideal definitivo, la misma absoluta preocupación del triunfo material." Moreover, Rodó observes: "Pródigo de sus riquezas [. . .], el norteamericano ha logrado adquirir con ellas, plenamente, la satisfacción y la vanidad de la magnificencia suntuaria; pero no ha logrado adquirir la nota escogida del buen gusto" (*Espíritu* 1: 43, 45; Rodó 236–37; author's emphasis).

Buarque further betrays Rodó's influence in his contention that US civilization, which both writers describe as fundamentally utilitarian, runs counter to certain allegedly Latin American and Brazilian characteristics—namely, a congenital idealism. In a statement that foreshadows the language of *Raízes do Brasil*, Buarque advises that "[o] nosso caminho a seguir deverá ser *o mais conforme a nosso temperamento*. Não possuímos a atividade, a disposição a certos trabalhos, de modo tão acentuado, como os habitantes das terras frias" (*Espírito* 1: 44; my emphasis; "the path we are to follow should be *the most in keeping with our temperament*. We do not possess the activity, the disposition for certain tasks to the same extent as do the inhabitants of cold lands").[23] Similarly, Rodó observes that "[l]a civilización de un pueblo adquiere su carácter, no de las manifestaciones de su prosperidad o de su grandeza material, sino de las superiores maneras de pensar y de sentir *que dentro de ella son posibles*," and makes the following judgment: "[N]o veo la gloria [. . .] en el propósito de desnaturalizar el carácter de los pueblos—su genio *personal*—para imponerles la identificación con un modelo extraño al que ellos sacrifiquen la originalidad irreemplazable de su espíritu" (225; my emphasis; 232; author's emphasis). Further, both writers warn of the consequences of indiscriminately mixing together elements of the two civilizations. Rodó argues in *Ariel* for maintaining the "dualidad original de [. . .] constitución" of Anglo and Latin America, and writes of "[e]se irreflexivo traslado de lo que es natural y espontáneo en una sociedad al seno de otra, donde no tenga *raíces* ni en la naturaleza ni en la historia" (Rodó 232–33; my emphasis)—note Rodó's terminology here, and his caution against attempts to remodel a society in ways not consonant with its historical "roots." Meanwhile, Buarque warns of "o pandemônio que nasceria do entrelaçamento de duas civilizações completamente diferentes" (*Espírito* 1: 44; "the pandemonium that would result from the intertwining of two completely different civilizations"). Finally, the influence of

Rodó on Buarque can be seen in other pieces written around the time "Ariel" was published in the *Revista do Brasil*. In the article "A Cidade Verde" (The Green City, 1920), Buarque makes a plea for Brazilians to preserve traditional street names (and by extension, an authentically national urban culture) that strongly resembles Rodó's argument in "Ciudades con alma" (1917), a piece written a mere three years earlier. Here Rodó argues that a city represents "un valor espiritual, una fisonomía colectiva, un carácter persistente y creador," and laments the fact that "[e]l patriotismo de ciudad, energía tan vital y creadora como puede serlo el patriotismo de nación, es un sentimiento que aún no encuentra en nuestra América condiciones que le den el arraigo hondo y pertinaz que requiere para ser fecundo" (*OC* 1294–95).

If we have established Rodó as the primary influence for Buarque's "Ariel" and as a strong presence in Buarque's other early texts (such as "A Cidade Verde"), a question nonetheless remains: in an article named "Ariel," a text that like Rodó's *Ariel* is deeply concerned with the problem of North American utilitarianism, why would Buarque not credit Rodó up front, and why would he attribute the critique of US utilitarianism to Schopenhauer (drawing on one of the philosopher's minor essays to boot) and not to Rodó, who wrote on this precise subject a mere twenty years earlier in one of the most widely read essayistic texts in all of Latin American literature? Buarque's motive remains unclear. However, and at the risk of deepening the mystery, we can establish that Rodó's influence, far from being confined to Buarque's early criticism, can also be perceived in later works such as *Raízes do Brasil*, this despite the fact that Rodó is *never once* referenced in that text. In tracing the continuity of Rodó's largely uncredited influence on Buarque from "Ariel" through *Raízes*, and in accompanying the transformation of *Raízes* from a panoramic, projected *Teoria da América* to a more circumscribed and properly national study of Brazil's historical "roots," I will argue that—despite Buarque's reputation for deep engagement with Spanish America, particularly at the level of historiography—we can observe a progressive de-emphasis on Buarque's part of the Spanish American dimension of his work, one that correlates with an ongoing "hispano-skeptical" tendency in Brazilian national and exegetic discourse.

II. From a Theory of America
to the Roots of Brazil

Buarque's career as a literary critic took a sharp turn in June 1929, when he accepted an offer to travel to Germany, Poland, and Russia as a correspondent for the *Jornal do Brasil*. While Buarque was unable to enter Russia, and stayed in Poland for only a short time, he spent a productive period of months in late Weimar-era Berlin, writing for the *Jornal,* working for the Brazilian embassy, translating film scripts to Portuguese (including Joseph von Sternberg's *The Blue Angel*, 1930), meeting German intellectual luminaries such as the novelist Thomas Mann,[24] and intermittently attending university classes in history and the social sciences. Through these intellectual encounters, Buarque came into contact with the work of sociologist Max Weber (1864–1920), whose *The Protestant Ethic and the Spirit of Capitalism* (1905) was to exert a powerful influence on *Raízes do Brasil*, and of Friedrich Meinecke (1862–1954), by then the dean of Germany's historians.[25] Brazil's Revolution of 1930, which brought Getúlio Vargas (President, 1930–45, 1951–54) to power, compelled Buarque to end his German sojourn and return home in December of that year.

Importantly, the genesis of Buarque's *Teoria da América* project seems to have predated his Berlin period, and indeed, he appears to have brought the project with him to Europe and to have continued to develop it while there. According to Buarque, he settled on the idea to write an interpretive study called *Teoria da América* as early as the mid-1920s, recalling many years later in the introduction to his volume *Tentativas de Mitologia* (Attempts at Mythology, 1979) that while his responsibilities as a journalist and law student in Rio de Janeiro were causing him to lose interest in literature, "d[o] que não me livraria depressa era do projeto de *Teoria da América,* pois justamente durante a estada no [. . .] estrangeiro naqueles meu *Wanderjahre* alemães, ela principiará a ganhar forma definitiva. O contato de terras, gentes, costumes, em tudo diferentes dos que até então conhecia, pareceu favorável à revisão de idéias velhas e a busca de novos conhecimentos que me ajudassem a abandoná-las, ou a depurá-las" (29; author's emphasis; "what I would not free myself of so quickly was the *Theory of America* project, and it was precisely during my time abroad, during my German 'wandering year,' that it began to gain definitive form. Contact with lands, peoples, and customs that were entirely different from those I had known until then seemed favorable for my revision of old ideas and for the search for new knowledge that would help me abandon or purify these ideas").[26] Buarque reports that he returned to Brazil in December 1930 with a "notebook of some 400 pages for a book I intended should be called *Teoria da América.*" From this he "tir[ou] o essencial" (*Tentativas* 30; "removed the essential content"), publishing this in March 1935 in the journal *Espelho* as "Corpo e Alma do Brasil: Ensaio de Psicologia Social" (Body and Soul of Brazil: An Essay in Social Psychology). In developing the project further, Buarque apparently abandoned the title of his article in order to avoid confusion with Thomaz Lopes's travel volume *Corpo e Alma de Paris* (1909), though the text Buarque published in 1935 would nonetheless provide the basis for two chapters of *Raízes do Brasil*, which was published the following year as an expansion of "Corpo e Alma do Brasil," Buarque having by then rewritten "todo o restante [. . .] de novo sem nada que lembrasse a antiga 'Teoria'" (Buarque and Graham 6; authors' emphasis; "all the rest [. . .] again so that nothing remained of the old 'Theory'").

While I cannot definitively say what factor or factors prompted Buarque's shift between 1930 and 1936 from a proposed continental or even hemispheric study (*Teoria da América*) to a more or less national (albeit comparative) published essay (*Raízes do Brasil*), possible causes can be found in Buarque's shifting sense of his profession from bohemian critic to historian-in-training, and in his readings from German historiography. Indeed, in making this shift to historiography, Buarque seems to adhere to Meinecke's admonition, contained in the opening of his *Cosmopolitanism and the National State* (1907), for the "true historian" to focus on national as opposed to broader histories: "[U]nder [. . .] scrutiny every nation proves to have its unique individual aspects. If the social sciences try to penetrate as deeply as possible into the general characteristics of nations, the true historian will concentrate more on observing the particular features of an individual nation as faithfully and precisely as possible" (9–10).[27] In addition, it may be that the irredentist tendencies of the fascist movements on the rise in Europe during Buarque's 1929–30 German period made less palatable continentalism on the order of Rodó's *magna patria*, which the Uruguayan conceived as a fundamentally ideal union, though which could perhaps imply future movement toward political confederation.[28] And then there is the force of the Brazilian exegetic tradition, of which *Raízes do Brasil* is part. As Pedro Meira Monteiro reminds us, *Raízes*, like Gilberto Freyre's roughly contemporaneous *Casa-grande e Senzala* (The Masters and the Slaves, 1933), is the "inheritor of an essayistic tradition that was fundamental in the formation of a Brazilian national consciousness," one which, as we have seen over the course of this book, has quite unlike Spanish American essayistic discourse been persistently skeptical of the sweeping, continentalist gestures implied by a title like *Teoria da América* (*Queda* 39). In this sense, in narrowing his focus from *América* or *América Latina* to Brazil's specific historical "roots," Buarque traces a pattern of evasion similar to that followed by Manoel Bomfim in the progression from his *A América Latina: Males de Origem* (Latin America: Originary ills, 1905) to his later *O Brasil na América* (Brazil in America, 1929), and falls in line with the "hispano-skeptical" tendency exemplified by fellow Brazilian writers like José Bonifácio, Prado, Euclides da Cunha, and Nabuco.

What, if anything, remains of Buarque's abandoned *Teoria da América* in *Raízes do Brasil*? In what respects does *Raízes* depart from the earlier text, and in what respects does it resemble what the *Teoria* might have looked like if it had been published in its early form? Tragically, Buarque at a later date lost the notebook that contained his *Teoria*, which precludes us from anything like an adequate reconstruction of the changing contours of the project as it evolved from the mid-1920s through the first half of the 1930s.[29] Nonetheless, we may speculate as to some of the main features that would have distinguished Buarque's *Teoria da América* from *Raízes*. First and foremost, the title of the *Teoria* implies that Buarque originally envisioned that his argument would have been continental or hemispheric in sweep.[30] Indeed, Evaldo Cabral de Mello speculates in his "Posfácio" to *Raízes do Brasil* that while "the [*Teoria da América*] project did not go forward [. . .] it would not be excessive to suppose that it would have consisted of a Weberian reading in the comparative sociology of the colonization of Portuguese, Spanish, and Anglo-America" (190). In contrast, *Raízes do Brasil*, though it retains a comparative architecture that must be seen as inherited from the original *Teoria*, is ultimately *national* in focus, and is concerned with determining through comparison and differentiation "to what extent we [Brazilians] represent, in an American context, 'the ways of life, the institutions, and the worldview we inherit'" (Brasil Pinheiro Machado, in Monteiro and Eugênio 167).[31] This implies that Buarque *significantly narrowed* the focus of his study somewhere between the mid-1920s and the 1935 publication of "Corpo e Alma do Brasil," and probably more precisely at some point between 1930, the year he returned to Brazil, and 1935.

The tension between the narrower national focus of *Raízes do Brasil* and the wide-screen ambitions of the aborted *Teoria da América* project are apparent in several moments in *Raízes*, beginning in the study's opening chapter, which sets out to trace Brazil's Iberian origins but whose title, "Fronteiras da Europa," with its curious use of the plural, suggests that Brazil (or is it Latin America at large?) may find its "roots" in *two* "frontier" European nations. That is, it presents Portugal *and* Spain as the "frontiers of Europe."[32] This national/supranational tension is apparent in the chapter's opening sentences, which counterpose "Brazilian society" as the essay's subject with an implied reference to the whole of Latin America as the progeny of those "distant countries" (again note Buarque's use of the plural) located at the "frontiers of Europe." Buarque writes, from the first edition of *Raízes*: "Todo estudo comprehensivo da *sociedade brasileira* ha de destacar o facto verdadeiramente fundamental de constituirmos o unico esforço bem succedido, e em larga escala, de transplantação da cultura européa para a zona de clima tropical e sub-tropical [. . .] Trazendo de *paizes distantes* as nossas formas de vida, nossas instituições e nossa visão do mundo [. . .] somos ainda uns desterrados em nossa terra" (*Raízes 1ª edição* 3; my emphasis; "Any comprehensive study of *Brazilian society* must emphasize the truly fundamental fact that we represent the only successful large-scale effort to transplant European culture onto a tropical or sub-tropical climate [. . .] Having brought from *distant countries* our ways of life, institutions, and worldview [. . .] we are even today exiles in our own land").[33]

Does Buarque mean to say of Brazilians exclusively that they are "exiles in [their] own land," or might this exilic status apply to Spanish Americans as well? The tensions that run through Buarque's argument preclude us from definitively answering this question. Similar national/continental ambiguities may be observed elsewhere in *Raízes do Brasil*, as in its famous fourth chapter, "O Semeador e o Ladrilhador," in which Buarque counterposes the figures of the Luso-Brazilian *semeador* ("sower") and the Spanish American *ladrilhador* ("harvester, cultivator"), and in the final chapter, "Nossa Revolução" (Our Revolution), in which the possessive *nossa* seems suspended between the Brazilian nation and the broader span of *nossa América*.[34]

Notwithstanding Buarque's statement from 1979 regarding the total obliteration of the *Teoria da América* during his final rewrite, we may detect numerous traces of the earlier *Teoria* in *Raízes do Brasil* as the text has come down to us today. Buarque's lost notebook can be said to haunt *Raízes*, in a sense, as a sort of disruptive specter, much as Spanish America has perennially haunted Brazilian reflections on national identity, with the figure of José Enrique Rodó, the implied (though unstated) subject of Buarque's earlier "Ariel" (1920), representing another such spectral presence.[35] In the remainder of this section, I will enumerate some of the ways in which *Raízes do Brasil*, though it never once references Rodó or his *Ariel*, is a text that is nonetheless indebted to Rodó, and one that carries forward key thematic elements of the *arielista* program as elucidated by Rodó, and as discussed by Buarque in his early criticism.

If Buarque tempers the optimism displayed in "Ariel" regarding the eventual triumph of "Latin" idealism over "Yankee utilitarianism" between 1920 and 1936, as Pedro Meira Monteiro notes, he nonetheless maintains at the structural level of *Raízes do Brasil* Rodó's conceptual opposition between North American utilitarianism and Latin American idealism. In the text's second chapter, "Trabalho & Aventura" (Work and Adventure), for example, Buarque presents two ethics at play in the historical development of Brazil, and of national communities generally—that of the *trabalhador* ("worker") and that of the *aventureiro* ("adventurer"). Buarque's worker, though ennobled by his Weberian associations, resembles in certain respects the utilitarian "Yankee" lampooned by Rodó in *Ariel* or the "man-machine" chained to "mechanical apparatuses" of Buarque's 1921 article "O Homem-Máquina." Buarque's *trabalhador* operates in an instrumental, rationalized fashion, through "esforço lento, pouco compensador e persistente" ("steady, persistent effort, with little compensation"), and while he "sabe tirar o máximo proveito do insignificante" ("knows how to extract maximum profit from the [seemingly] insignificant"), his understanding is limited, and "[s]eu campo visual é naturalmente restrito" (*Raízes* 44; "his field of vision is naturally restricted"). The worker fails to comprehend or value the adventurer's seemingly unproductive impetuousness, unpredictability, and non-rationalized, profoundly interior need to explore uncharted physical and intellectual territory, a "spirit" that earns the adventurer, and not the worker, the title of Brazilian national *paterfamilias*: "Na obra da conquista e colonização dos novos mundos coube ao 'trabalhador' [. . .] papel muito limitado, quase nulo. A época predispunha aos gestos e façanhas audaciosos" (45; "The 'worker' played a very limited, almost nonexistent role in the work of conquest and colonization. The period was predisposed toward audacious gestures and deeds"). While Buarque is careful to note that the *aventureiro* and *trabalhador* are dialectically opposed archetypes, and that both necessarily exist in varying degrees in *any* national reality,[36] he presents Brazil and the Spanish American republics as particularly marked by the adventurer's "ethic" or "spirit," writing, "[e]ssa ânsia de prosperidade sem custo, de títulos honoríficos, de posições e riquezas fáceis, tão notoriamente características da gente de nossa terra, não é bem uma das manifestações mais cruas do espírito de aventura?" (46; "this concern with prosperity without effort, with honorific titles, with easy wealth, all notoriously characteristic of the people of our land, are these not the most naked manifestations of the spirit of adventure?").[37] For Buarque, the distinction between a prototypical Ibero-American predominantly impelled by an idealistic "ethic of adventure" and his North American counterpart, for the most part guided by a utilitarian "ethic of labor," has profound consequences in differentiating Brazil—and Latin America generally—from the United States, though the difference between Buarque's argument in "Ariel" and that which he sustains in *Raízes do Brasil* is that in his 1936 text, the implications are not presented as categorically positive or negative, but are understood as the necessary consequences of a given *Weltanschauung*, representing a sort of "mixed bag" of positives and negatives. On the positive side, we have the prototypical Luso-Brazilian's "adventurous" audacity, which leads him to the New World, along with his apparent lack of racial prejudice, while on the negative side, we find his resistance to productive agriculture and to bureaucratic efficiency, and a tendency toward superficial, legalistic humanism, or *bacharelismo*.[38]

The question confronting Buarque when he moves in his final two chapters, "Novos Tempos" (New Times) and "Nossa Revolução" (Our Revolution), from a reconstruction of Brazil's historical "roots" to a diagnosis of how this history conditions Brazil's present-day challenges and future prospects, is whether character traits that are presented as *essentially* Luso-Brazilian (and collected in an "ethic" of adventure) can in the final analysis be disregarded or abandoned if found to negatively impact the nation's outlook for future political and economic development. In other words, if Luso-Brazilian "indolence" has led to agricultural inefficiency and underinvestment, can this interior quality be rejected and replaced in the name of higher agricultural yields? Put another way, Buarque must answer the question of whether Brazil's "roots" can be cut, or must be preserved in some form. Let us examine this issue via two corollaries to Rodó and Buarque's distinction between North American utilitarianism and Latin American idealism, the first a new typological opposition drawn by Buarque, between *iberismo* (Iberianism) and *americanismo* (Americanism), and the second a renewed argument on Buarque's part for national *authenticity*, and for a corresponding commitment to reconciling "imported" or "foreign" ideas and models to local conditions.

Buarque presents *iberismo* and *americanismo* as two possible development paths for twentieth-century Brazil, introducing them in the notoriously enigmatic final chapter of *Raízes*.[39] For Buarque *iberismo* refers to the nation's Iberian heritage or "roots," and to the rural, agrarian society the Portuguese implanted in the New World, as discussed in the essay's third chapter, "Herança Rural" (Rural Inheritance). Further, *iberismo* is closely tied to the idea of *sobrancería*, a quality of self-sufficiency and self-focus that predisposes an individual to impose his will on others, which Buarque borrows from the Spanish language and views as characteristic of the Iberian character, and which Silviano Santiago interprets as the key to Buarque's reading of Ibero-American civilization.[40] By contrast, Buarque identifies *americanismo* with the urban, bureaucratic, and utilitarian social model represented in Brazil by cities like São Paulo, and more distantly, by the United States. Buarque's Weberian arguments elsewhere in *Raízes* in favor of urbanization and bureaucratic efficiency and impartiality would seem to predispose him to embrace *americanismo*, and indeed, he identifies this path as guiding Brazil's future. He writes of "a inauguração de um estilo novo, que crismamos talvez ilusoriamente de americano, porque seus traços se acentuam com maior rapidez no nosso hemisfério" (172; "the inauguration of a new style, which I perhaps illusorily term 'American,' since its features are more quickly accentuated in our hemisphere"). However, Buarque's concern for Brazil's historical development *within the boundaries* of its people's essential "character"—a preoccupation he shares with Rodó—causes him to take a more cautious stance. In a frequently misinterpreted passage from "Nossa Revolução," Buarque calls not for *immediate* substitution of the new "American" social order for the outmoded "Iberian" ways of Brazil's past, but rather for *steady displacement* of the latter by the former: "Ainda testemunhamos presentemente, e por certo continuaremos a testemunhar durante largo tempo, as ressonâncias últimas do lento cataclismo, cujo sentido parece ser o do aniquilamento das raízes ibéricas da nossa cultura para a inauguração de um estilo novo" (172; "We now witness, and we will certainly continue to witness for a great deal longer, the latest effects of the slow cataclysm, which seems to amount to the liquidation of the Iberian roots of our culture and the inauguration of a new style").

While readers of "Nossa Revolução" tend to focus on the "cataclysm" forecast by Buarque as opposed to its modifier *lento* ("slow"), and on his use of the term *aniquilamento* ("annihilation"), Buarque more than tempers the notion of violent annihilation of *iberismo* and of quick, forceful implantation of *americanismo* in his reference to the long duration of this process of change; in subsequent paragraphs Buarque speaks in similarly incremental terms of "nossa evolução histórica" ("our historical evolution"), and of the "desaparecimento progres-sivo [de] formas tradicionais" ("progressive disappearance of traditional forms"). These suggest, as does the adjective *lento*, that Buarque envisioned a transformative *process* that would allow for successful adaptation of foreign ideas to the Brazil-ian milieu, in keeping with the concern he aired sixteen years earlier in his critique of the republican leadership's misguided attempt to uncritically graft features of "*yankee* utilitarianism" onto Brazil's national body (*Espírito* 1: 43; author's emphasis). In *Raízes*, Buarque clearly advocates change—Candido is cor-rect in judging the text fundamentally anti-*saudosista*—but he does so with an awareness of the need to adapt *americanismo* to Brazil's specific conditions, a view he makes plain in his criti-cism of earlier generations' failures to do the same.[41] Zeroing in on the leadership of the Old Republic (1889–1930), here identi-fied collectively as "positivists," Buarque describes their attempt to impose US-style democracy on a country with no republican tradition as "[trazendo] de terras estranhas um sistema complexo e acabado de preceitos, sem saber até que ponto se ajustam às condições da vida brasileira e sem cogitar das mudanças que tais condições lhe imporiam" (160; "taking from foreign lands a complex system loaded down with precepts, without knowing to what extent these would apply to the conditions of Brazilian life and without considering the changes these conditions would impose [on the republican model]"). The last part of this sentence is key, as it affirms once again that, far from being a case of easy reproduction in the tropics of Anglo-European ideas, it is the *lo-cal conditions themselves* that impose certain changes and limits on imported "foreign" ideas, and compel a more gradual adoption than is implied in the notion of "annihilating" Brazil's historical "roots." This suggests in turn that the Brazilian body politic (or at least the nation's governing elite) must take care in adapting "foreign" ideas and organizational models (such as liberal de-mocracy, modern agriculture, or modern bureaucracy) to local conditions. Or to employ the horticultural metaphor proposed by the title of *Raízes*, foreign elements must be successfully grafted onto the national body or roots, thereby making these elements *authentically* Brazilian. The alternative (rather suicidal from the perspective of the nation *qua* plant) would be to destroy the nation's "roots," to "annihilate the past," as Candido has it, and to somehow start over with a new, modern set of national ideas and tendencies.[42] As stated earlier, most critics seem to believe that Buarque advocates the latter course in the closing pages of *Raízes do Brasil*, though I hold that despite the ambiguities and contradictions that mark "Nossa Revolução," he does not. Rather, I subscribe to the position eloquently advanced by José Ortiz Monasterio that "Buarque's central argument seems to be that a new society can't be created from nothing, as an abstraction or by mere force of will: rather, it is our *roots* that retrospectively teach us what we have been and what our possible future might be" (Monteiro and Eugênio 301; my emphasis).

Let us explore the closing paragraphs of "Nossa Revolução" in a bit more detail. Buarque's argument here is indeed ambiguous, as perhaps befits the conclusion of a text built on a series of reversible typological oppositions, though as I hope to have shown, his argument certainly does not amount to a univocal call for the "aniquilamento das raízes ibéricas de nossa cultura" (172; "annihilation of the Iberian roots of our culture"). Indeed, it is more sensible to analyze Buarque's position (barring the possibility that his argument is poorly articulated or simply confused) with reference to its dialectical structure, and to the series of dialectical oppositions (*aventureiro/trabalhador, idealismo/utilitarismo, semeador/ladrilhador* and *iberismo/ americanismo*) that structure the text. If we view dialectic in classically Hegelian terms, as entailing the confrontation of mutually exclusive (and paradoxically, mutually dependent) alternatives and the overcoming (*Aufhebung*) or "sublation" of the one by the other, it should be clear that a simple or total "liquidation of Brazil's Iberian roots" is impossible: to the extent that the victorious thesis (here *americanismo*) negates and thereby incorporates its antithesis (*iberismo*), the antithesis survives, as an *americanismo* adapted to local conditions, appropriate for application in an environment strongly conditioned by the *iberismo* of the past. Moreover, Buarque's concern with promoting those progressive changes "that are possible within a given [civilization]" (Rodó's phrase)—that is, his desire to advance changes that are reconciled with Brazil's essential "character" or "temperament"—precludes a simple, quick adoption of an "Americanist" and utilitarian "ethic of labor" at the expense of Brazil's enduring past.[43] Far from abandoning Brazil's essential "reality," Buarque loftily speculates in the concluding paragraph of *Raízes do Brasil* on the possibility that "nos encontraremos um dia com a nossa realidade" (31; "one day we will find ourselves confronted by our reality"). This gesture, whose language of encounter and recognition again suggests Hegel, closes the circle of national self-alienation opened in the text's first paragraph, in which Buarque declares that "somos ainda hoje uns desterrados em nossa terra" (187–88; "we are even today exiles in our own land"). In pursuing "[a]s formas superiores de sociedade" ("the superior forms of society"), a statement that recalls Rodó's reference in *Ariel* to "superiores maneras de pensar y de sentir," Buarque cautions that Brazilians must not renounce the ideal, here "nosso próprio ritmo espontâneo" ("our own spontaneous rhythm"), in favor of "um compasso mecânico e uma harmonia falsa" ("a mechanical compass and a false harmony") that are no doubt the products of utilitarianism, and are most likely manufactured in the United States (*Raízes* 188; Rodó 225). Having hopefully illustrated the strong *arielista* streak that runs through *Raízes do Brasil*, to which, as mentioned earlier, Buarque responds with not one reference to Rodó in the text, we will now move to Silviano Santiago's analysis of Buarque in his study *As Raízes e o Labirinto da América Latina* (2006), where one notices a similar evasion of Rodó, and a further obscuring of the extent of his influence on Buarque.

III. Rodó, Entangled in Buarque's Roots, Lost in Paz's Labyrinth

As with Sérgio Buarque in *Raízes do Brasil*, Silviano Santiago does not once mention Rodó by name in *As Raízes e o Labirinto da América Latina*, though as is arguably the case with Buarque's 1936 essay, there are numerous moments in Santiago's study that seem to compel that he acknowledge the author of *Ariel*. Santiago cites Buarque's "Ariel" early in his first chapter, characterizing the young Buarque's argument somewhat simplistically as calling for a Eurocentric as opposed to pro-United States orientation for Brazil, and writing that "as Buarque positions himself as in favor of Eurocentrism, the essay ends by singing the praises of Ariel, to the detriment of Caliban" (17n5).[44] This reference correlates the Shakespearean

figures of Ariel and Caliban with notions of European civilization versus US utilitarianism, as had Rubén Darío (in his 1896
profile of Edgar Allen Poe) and Rodó before Buarque. This
suggests that Santiago is familiar with Rodó's reading of *The
Tempest*, as would be expected of a scholar of Latin American
literature of Santiago's stature. It is curious, then, that Santiago
does not take the opportunity to credit Rodó here, though this
ultimately works to benefit Santiago's argument, which presents
Buarque's *Raízes do Brasil* and Octavio Paz's *El laberinto de la
soledad* (1950) as texts authored at a specific historical moment,
at the culmination of a discursive tradition in which "literary
knowledge [constituted the] basis for the great interpretations
of Latin America" (15). Situating these texts chronologically at
the end of one historical period and at the beginning of a new
phase marked by US neo-colonial domination of Latin America
and by the displacement of literary or humanistic knowledge
by the rhetoric of the social sciences, Santiago argues on the
page following his initial reference to Ariel and Caliban that
"until [the Second World War], the Monroe Doctrine [. . .] was
presented more as working to prevent possible interventions by
Spain and Portugal in their colonies than as the basis for new,
profound neo-colonial violations which would become manifest
from the 1940s" (18). Santiago's is an interpretation of United
States interventionism that appears to take little account of
nineteenth-century US expansionist actions in the Caribbean,
which culminated in the 1898 American intervention in the Cuban independence war, and which in turn provided a good deal
of the impetus for José Martí to write "Nuestra América" (1891)
and for Rodó to write *Ariel* (1900). In overlooking these events,
Santiago excludes from his analysis any possibility of situating
texts like Paz's *El laberinto de la soledad* (1950) or, perhaps
less obviously, Buarque's *Raízes do Brasil,* within *arielismo* or
nuestra-americanismo as Latin American discursive/interpre-
tive traditions. Indeed, Santiago's lack of focus on key late nineteenth-century texts like "Nuestra América" and *Ariel* becomes
obvious in his later statement, in which he characterizes Paz
as responding in *El laberinto* to "the enigma of the emptiness
[. . .], of the lamentable state in which the question of South
American identity, in contrast to North American hegemony,
found itself [in 1950]" (40). This implication that Paz's text is

an isolated, late instance of literature-inspired Latin American interpretation disregards both the fact that in the first chapter of *El laberinto*, Paz implicitly engages the *nuestra América/la otra América* binary in counterposing Mexico and the United States in his discussion of the figure of the *pachuco,* and that in his later chapter on "La 'inteligencia' mexicana," Paz situates himself within a constellation of contemporary Mexican *intérpretes*, many of whom (Alfonso Reyes, José Vasconcelos, Leopoldo Zea) explicitly drew on Rodó and Martí's formulations.[45]

While Santiago's failure to mention Rodó may be understandable in the case of his first allusion to Shakespeare's Ariel and Caliban, Santiago commits a more glaring omission at the close of his second chapter, in which he makes a glowing reference to Richard Morse's study *O Espelho de Próspero* (Prospero's Mirror, 1988). And though I wholeheartedly concur with Santiago's evaluation of Morse's study as an exemplary account of "the weight and value of Latin American culture in the context of U.S. economic hegemony," I cannot but fault his failure to mention that Morse deliberately paraphrases Rodó's *El mirador de Próspero* (1913) in the title of his study (Santiago 50; Morse 13). Instead, Santiago offers the following explanation of Morse's title: "It is clear from the title of his work and his choice of an interpretive methodology that does not reject literature that Morse, similarly to the Cuban essayist and poet Roberto Fernández Retamar in *Calibán* (1971), is indebted to (*é devedor da*) Shakespeare's play *The Tempest*" (51). Santiago's statement is technically correct, though it overlooks the obvious fact that Morse and Retamar, in dialoguing with Shakespeare, both make prominent use of Rodó's interpretation of Shakespeare's play in *Ariel*—Morse via his titular reference to Rodó's *El mirador de Próspero* and Fernández Retamar by way of his inversion of Rodó's preference for Ariel as a privileged symbol of Latin American idealism in favor of Caliban as a representation of Third World resistance. I cannot say exactly what causes Santiago to fail to mention Rodó here. While outright ignorance of Rodó and his *Ariel* represents a theoretical possibility, this seems extremely improbable. What seems a more likely but more prosaic explanation is that Santiago, despite his considerable erudition and sensitivity to the nuances of Paz's text, is simply less knowledgeable about Spanish American literature

and intellectual history than he is about the literature and intellectual history of his own country; revealingly, Santiago's
analysis of Buarque is grounded to a much greater extent in
contextual references to Buarque's peers and his place in the
canon than is his analysis of Paz, which is much more in the style
of a "close reading."

My aim in raising the issue of Rodó's obscured influence in
Buarque's "Ariel" and in his later *Raízes do Brasil*, along with
the Uruguayan essayist's outright exclusion from Santiago's
As Raízes e o Labirinto da América Latina, is not to suggest
hostile intent or deliberate obscurantism on the part of Buarque
or Santiago. Rather, I believe that Rodó's omission from these
texts is symptomatic of a long-standing lack of dialogue between the Brazilian and Spanish American literary and intellectual traditions—and between academic Luso-Brazilianists
and Hispanists. Even in the case of thinkers as widely read and
open to comparative approaches as are Buarque and Santiago,
I would argue that a lingering Luso-Hispanic "disconsonance"
(David William Foster's term) results in moves such as the
young Buarque's crediting of the idea of "Yankee utilitarianism" to a prestigious German philosopher (Schopenhauer) as
opposed to a Uruguayan essayist (Rodó) who, though largely
unread in Brazil, nonetheless represents the idea's more immediate source. Further, this "disconsonance" seems to inform
Santiago's reading of Buarque and Octavio Paz, manifesting itself in his apparent lack of awareness of Rodó's centrality to the
Spanish American essayistic canon and his inevitable influence
on Paz's *El laberinto de la soledad*, along with Rodó's status
as *the* key figure in Spanish American *Tempest* interpretation
and an obvious point of reference for both Richard Morse and
Roberto Fernández Retamar.

***

Over the previous chapter I have presented Sérgio Buarque de
Holanda's very particular intertextual relationship with José
Enrique Rodó as an example of the sort of challenge that faces
those working toward a truly comparative Luso-Hispanic studies. By way of conclusion, responding to this challenge seems
to me to require something beyond archival work aimed at

elucidating forgotten instances of Luso-Hispanic dialogue, and close reading undertaken to discover the inner mechanics and rhetoric of key texts, though these are both necessary activities. We must of course dedicate time and energy to analysis of topics such as José Enrique Rodó's misreading of Almeida Garrett in "Iberoamérica" (1910), Joaquim Nabuco's reference to a semi-invented Chile in his critique of Brazil's republican leadership in *Balmaceda* (1895), and Alfonso Reyes's ambiguous identification of Brazil with the idea of *Última Tule*, to cite three issues I have addressed in this book. But more fundamentally, we must in my view direct a critical eye toward the geo-cultural categories—Latin America, Hispano- or Ibero-America, Iberia, and so on—that structure the conceptual terrain within which disciplines such as Latin American, Luso-Brazilian, and peninsular studies operate. As Barbara Fuchs reminds us:

> National and literary classifications are enabling fictions [. . .] with varying degrees of success in framing particular texts or subjects. While we might assign texts to conceptual categories or match subjects with national identities retrospectively, it behooves us to recover the intricacy of the textual and political landscape [. . .] In some cases, this might require a creative or [. . .] *perverse* departure from subsequently codified categories, a critical turn (trope) of reframing that releases the text from established ways of reading, all while attending to historical context. (66; author's emphasis)

Achieving the objective of entangling (or re-entangling) the Brazilian and Spanish American intellectual traditions is no doubt an overly ambitious goal, though it nonetheless represents the motive that led me to write this book. Indeed, the scale of the comparative Luso-Hispanic project is enormous, and requires a diversity of participants working in a plethora of focus areas, textual genres, and periods, and applying a range of interpretive models. My hope in writing *Nossa and Nuestra América* has been to provide one individual contribution to this much larger project. It is my sincere wish that with the growth of Luso-Hispanic studies—whether predominantly due to political and economic integration, the rise of Brazil as a regional and global power, facilitated cross-border communication, or the efforts of individual scholars and academics—we will in the decades that follow come to speak more of Brazilian and Spanish American literary and cultural *exchange* than we will of "disconsonance," mutual lack of knowledge, or non-communication, such that it will no longer be accurate to speak of *Nossa* and *Nuestra América* as counterposed.

Appendix
English Translations

The following are English translations of the longer passages quoted in the original Portuguese in the text. The numbers in brackets in the text correspond to the numbers below. All translations are mine.

Introduction
This Our Disunion

1   We Brazilians have little interest in Spanish American things. Our gazes, our thoughts, our tastes are almost always directed toward the Old World [. . .] Those given to long journeys almost always prefer to take pleasure in the serene civility of London's streets or in the pleasant apathy of Paris rather than feel the imposing majesty of the Andes or the awe-inspiring magnificence of the Amazonian rainforest.

Chapter One
Counterposing *Nossa* and *Nuestra América*

2   The birds that sing here, / Do not sing as they do there.

3   Fearless man-monsters disembark; / And after the banner they run, they fly, / What Fanaticism, what greed were loosed. / Peaceful peoples, innocent Indians! / The armed Spaniard shows his rage. / The Tigers believed God made the world / To be their prey. On all sides / American blood, still steaming, / The earth wets and softens the footfalls / Of the prideful Andalusian riders.

Chapter Two
José Enrique Rodó: "Iberoamérica," the *Magna Patria*, and the Question of Brazil

4   Not once will you find in use among our writers the word "Spanish," to exclusively designate a non-Portuguese inhabitant of the Peninsula. Before Castile united with Aragon, and long after it had joined with Leon, etc. we and the other nations of the Spains—Aragonese, Grenadines, Castilians, Portuguese and everyone, were called Spaniards by countrymen and foreigners alike; just as today we still indistinctly refer to Prussians, Saxons, Hanoverians, and Austrians as Germans; just as Neapolitans, Milanese, Venetians and Piedmontese all receive the name of Italians. The fatal loss of our political independence after the battle of Alcácer-Quibir gave to the kings of Castile and Aragon the title of kings of the Spains, which they retained even after the glorious restoration [of Portuguese independence] of 1640. But Spaniards we are, and Spaniards we should be proud to be.

Chapter Three
Joaquim Nabuco: Monarchy's End and the "South Americanization" of Brazil

5   We are in America's republican whirlwind. We are a dead body spinning around in anarchy's tornado. In this state should we, those who have children, abandon society to its destiny or found another country elsewhere? If nothing can save the nation, we must fight to raise up the minority, the moral part of society [. . .] We must, then, remain Brazilians, seeing Brazil become a Venezuela, a Mexico, an Argentina, a Chile; the property of the despot of the day.

6   Chile had the sort of strong government we never had [. . .] To destroy a government that has had the most admirable results in order to replace it with a mere theory amounts to a lack of common sense.

7   "We are experiencing a crisis" is what is said in Brazil. A
     mistake! We are in America's republican whirlwind. We
     are a dead body spinning around in anarchy's tornado. In
     this state should we, those who have children, abandon
     society to its destiny or found another country elsewhere?
     If nothing can save the nation, we must fight to raise up
     the minority, the moral part of society [. . .] We must, then,
     remain Brazilians, seeing Brazil become a Venezuela, a
     Mexico, an Argentina, a Chile; the property of the despot
     of the day. It is as if the world has reverted to a state of
     fetishism or cannibalism! But for precisely this reason it
     was our destiny to be born during this period. In future
     centuries Latin America will have to be *civilized* or not
     be Latin; our duty consists in making sure that the minor-
     ity's moral level is greater than its political level, and to
     dissociate moral development from incurable political
     stagnation.

8   How Brazil has so quickly "south-americanized," and with
     such fury! [. . .] Now we have civil wars of all sorts! And
     who will save himself from this flood? [. . .] These people,
     who wouldn't sacrifice themselves for a Pedro II, are sac-
     rificing themselves for fanaticism, those who aren't being
     paid or coerced by a Floriano! How South American this
     is, how one sees the typical degradation of this unhappy
     hemisphere—along with the bestial despotism, the imbe-
     cile republicanism of the Paraguayan!

9   I am increasingly convinced that civilization in Brazil end-
     ed with the monarchy. What we now have are the remains
     of it. What one sees is extraordinary. Principle is no longer
     capable of reining anyone in, nor can social pressure pre-
     vent the worst crimes. What does it matter if the country
     falls to pieces and after falling to pieces each piece is in
     the most complete state of misery and abjection? [. . .] The
     class of men who govern is unbelievable, the processes
     used by the government are obscene, undignified, or ri-
     diculous. They copy the decrees of the South American
     collection, of the besieged states of Uruguay, Argentina,

Bolivia, how should I know? The newspapers' adulation of the dictator is as grotesque as that of the Guaranis in Paraguay.

10   In the Republic there is no notion of national honor, nor are there international traditions, nor a feeling for the homeland [. . .] A Republic, whatever it might be, one or many, independent or tributary, prosperous or failed, with Brazilians or with *chins* [i.e., Chinese immigrants], as long as it's a Republic. This is the morality of the roulette-player in action. Brazil has become a gambling den, and the so-called republicans are nothing more than the domino-playing rat-catchers [. . .] of this political hole.

11   Our parents knew how to create and preserve, while we only learned how to destroy and tear apart. We have thrown everything away, even their memory. In what respect does this civil war differ from other American civil wars? Those who fight each other all believe they fight for a just cause, that they have right on their side, exactly as occurs in all South American wars. Each side is sure of being right, that it is dying for a noble cause, a national cause par excellence, and so the generations come and go, bleeding themselves dry for a series of national causes, each of which prevents the country from coming together enough to take one step forward. Our republicans seem to believe that these wars do not repeat themselves, just as before they were impossible, given our habits and our docility. Events prove them wrong every day, and the more they are proven wrong, the more assertive they become. One needs a young man's indignation and an old man's experience in order to speak the truth to this despicable republic.

12   It can be affirmed that in the Revolution of 1891, the old Chilean spirit, of the Portales and the Montts, would have been resolutely with society and against Balmaceda. The task of finding antecedents for Balmaceda may tempt the learned men of his party, but it is entirely in vain. Balmaceda erupts onto the scene of Chilean history like an unexpected apparition; he evokes, one might say,

and in the context of the Chilean presidency, the South American dictatorial genius that had until then never before penetrated that institution. To justify Balmaceda as part of a line running through the country beginning in 1833 amounts to an act of cynicism. His defense can be radical, democratic, scientific if one wishes, but it cannot be historical, conservative, or constitutional, and certainly not one that interprets the Constitution as the sum of those tacit conquests made by the spirit of institutions over the letter of the document.

13 In *our countries*, where the nation remains in a state of permanent immaturity, liberties, the rights of each man, the common patrimony, are protected only by certain principles, by certain traditions and customs, that are no more than moral barriers that could easily fall before the weakest blow. In these countries, where liberty lacks the protection of power, where the law is weak, institutions cannot thrive that can only survive in a nation like the United States, whose opinion is a force that can topple any government, and whose [political] parties are armies that within hours can rise up, armed, under the command of their chiefs, and that for this reason respect each other as would two great powers.

14 I have always felt great admiration toward Chile. There is more national energy, it seems to me, in that narrow strip of land between the mountains and the Pacific than there is in all the rest of South America. With no ill-feeling toward our neighbor on the River Plate [i.e., Argentina], who has for political reasons compelled us to cultivate friendly relations with Chile, we have the most noble reasons for seeking friendship with that country. I'm not sure which man of spirit said, years ago, that he had only found two organized and free nations in Latin America: *the Empire of Chile and the Republic of Brazil* . . . Though we are, without exception, the most egalitarian society in the world (history will judge whether despite the monarchy, or because of it), and though Chile is, on the contrary, ruled by a political aristocracy, we both experienced the same

continuity of order, of parliamentary government, of civil liberty, of administrative transparency, of seriousness, of decorum, and of official dignity. Both governments were exceptions in South America, pieces of solid ground surrounded by turbulent, bloody waves.

15   If we enjoyed liberty during the monarchy, this was only because power contained itself. This was due to the elevated national consciousness *that almost all modern sovereigns have*, due to inheritance, education, and historical selection. Respect for the dignity of the nation and a desire for it to be highly esteemed in the world were natural for the monarchy, which governed through moral force alone.

16   Many are saying that I will be [. . .] a minister. That would truly be an earthquake! "Poor country!" is all I can say. How our luck is like that of Spain, of Peru, of Uruguay! What destiny is reserved for us? Don't you feel, speaking amongst ourselves, that we smell like an animal waiting to be caught, that we are a dead body that the waves cast upon the shore, where the birds of prey wait for it? Why do I write to you in this way?

Chapter Five
Sérgio Buarque de Holanda: Obscured Roots of Rodó in *Raízes do Brasil*

17   The attempt to implant a European culture over an extensive sweep of land, one whose natural conditions were, if not adverse, then largely unfamiliar to the millennial tradition [of the Europeans], is the dominant and most consequential fact concerning the origins of Brazilian society. Having brought from distant countries our ways of being, institutions, and ideas [. . .], we are even today exiles in our own land.

18   Brazil, of all the countries of the New World, is perhaps the least aware of its continental position. The fact of our being an American nation seems to us an accidental fact,

whose consequences we can transform at will. Today the term "America" is for us a commemorative word, useful for speeches and formalities. The attitude of our Hispanic neighbors is quite diverse. For them "America" represents, first of all, and above all, a Spanish American reality. They only admit to themselves that men of another lineage, Anglo-Saxons, for example, would think of identifying themselves with this same reality. An "American," for an Argentine, is in the first place a Spanish-speaking person.

19   In the United States there is [. . .] a sickening air of corruption exhaled by the governing classes, which is difficult to find in Europe. Utilitarianism and the desire to make money, *auri sacra fames*, have conquered the North Americans to the detriment of the intellectual spirit, political morality, and even individual liberty. This inspired Schopenhauer to describe [the North Americans] as the proletarians of humanity.

20   Ariel, the airy spirit of Shakespeare's *The Tempest*, represents spirituality, in contrast to Caliban, the symbol of utilitarianism, and further, a *savage and deformed slave*.

   Ariel, says Clarín in the study published as a prologue to the magnificent work by the notable Uruguayan thinker José Enrique Rodó, who is recently deceased, "loves intelligence as an end in itself, along with beauty, grace, and the pure mysteries of the infinite."

Notes

Introduction: This Our Disunion

1. See Foster, "Spanish American and Brazilian Literature: A History of Disconsonance" (1992); Costigan and Bernucci; and Fitz.

2. See Saraiva on the effect of political conflict for Luso-Hispanic intellectual exchange, particularly his descriptive phrase *complexo de Aljubarrota* ("Aljubarrota complex") (203).

3. See Unamuno, "Español-Portugués" (1914) (*OC* 4: 527). See also Neil Larsen's more recent anecdote of a 1995 seminar he taught at the University of São Paulo, and his Brazilian students' unfamiliarity with key Spanish American cultural theorists. Larsen notes, similarly to Unamuno, that those non-Brazilian theorists who have managed to surmount the "walls dividing Brazil from the rest of Latin America" are those consecrated first by the "Euro-North American metropolis" (75).

4. See Niemeyer interview in *Nossa América* (21).

5. See *Revista Iberoamericana* 64.182–83 (Jan.–June 1998); *Chasqui* Special Issue No. 1 (2004); *A América Hispânica no Imaginário Literário Brasileiro/Brasil en el imaginario literario hispanoamericano* (2007); Raúl Antelo's *Na Ilha de Marapatá* (1987); Leopoldo M. Bernucci's *Historia de un malentendido* (1989); Eduardo Lourenço's *O Outro Lado da Lua* (The Other Side of the Moon, 2005); Silviano Santiago's *As Raízes e o Labirinto da América Latina* (The Roots and the Labyrinth of Latin America, 2006); Bruce Dean Willis's *Aesthetics of Equilibrium* (2006); and Richard A. Gordon's *Cannibalizing the Colony* (2009).

6. Throughout this book I refer to the Southern Common Market as MERCOSUR/L, in recognition of its two acronyms—MERCOSUR in Spanish and MERCOSUL in Portuguese.

7. Special recognition is due to Brazilian anthropologist Darcy Ribeiro (1922–97), who was instrumental in establishing the Memorial da América Latina, and to Portuguese public intellectual Eduardo Lourenço (b. 1923), whose efforts led to the creation of the Centro de Estudos Ibéricos.

Chapter One
Counterposing *Nossa* and *Nuestra América*

1. See Rodó's "Rumbos Nuevos" (1910), Oswald de Andrade's "Manifesto Antropófago" (Cannibalist Manifesto, 1928), Borges's "El escritor argentino y la tradición" (1932), and Reyes's "Notas sobre la inteligencia americana" (1936).

2. See, for example, Antero de Quental's *Causas da Decadência dos Povos Peninsulares* (Causes of the Decline of the Peninsular Peoples, 1871) and Oliveira Martins's *História da Civilização Ibérica* (History of Iberian Civilization, 1879).

3. See also Juderías's discussion of Chevalier (267).

4. See Mignolo, *Idea* 2.

5. For the term "sub-Américas," see Ardao, *Génesis* 15.

6. Rodó's misreading of Almeida Garrett will be discussed in Chapter 2.

7. See Ardao, *Génesis* 82; and Guerra and Maldonado 32.

8. See Leopoldo Zea's *Dialéctica de la conciencia americana* (1976), for example.

9. See also Ardao, *Génesis* 9.

10. On this issue, Emília Viotti da Costa perceptively notes: "Brazilian history has gone two ways: either it has become an exercise in identifying the similarities between what has happened elsewhere and what happens in Brazil, or it has become a desperate search for the 'Brazilian specificity'" (172).

11. Mignolo argues that designations like *Anáhuac* function as alternative frameworks through which many Latin Americans (particularly in areas with a strong indigenous heritage) organize dissenting mental pictures of the hemisphere (*Idea* 2).

12. See Stavans, Introduction 11.

13. See Mignolo, "The Movable Center"; Smith, *Nations* 116.

14. See Ardao, *Génesis* 66; Smith, *Nations* 119–20; and Smith, *Ethnic Origins* 131, 134–38.

15. For a comparison, see Heater on dual allegiance in federations (95–97).

16. See Bolívar, "Jamaica" 169, 171.

17. That said, parallels can be drawn. In terms of Spanish American nationalism's dependence on the incorporation of liminal or extra-national territories such as Brazil, see the example of Russia's seventeenth- to nineteenth-century expansion toward the former Constantinople as part of its self-imagining as a "Third Rome." See also Austria and Prussia's competing eighteenth- and nineteenth-century claims to authority over the ancient Holy Roman Empire. In contrast to these examples, the Spanish American case is notable for its almost entirely rhetorical character. Spanish America need not conquer Brazil, but merely assume a sort of intellectual authority that would allow its intellectuals to "speak" for it. For discussion of extra-territorial claims and collective identity, see Smith, *Ethnic Origins* 222.

18. See Guerra and Maldonado on the importance of the Spanish American independence struggle in creating a sense of shared identity (20).

19. On nineteenth-century regional conferences, see Guerra and Maldonado. The sharing of diplomatic personnel strikes me as a particularly illustrative example of Spanish America's two-tiered nationalism.

20. See Veríssimo, *América Latina*.

21. Notions of projection, identity projection, and projective identification have specific connotations in psychology and psychoanalysis. I use "identity projection" in a rather more colloquial sense throughout this book, and in the specific context of essayistic discourse and discussion of geo-cultural categories.

22. On Brazil and the idea of "rounding out," see Buarque and Graham 14.

23. Incidentally, the "Centro de Estudos Latino-Americanos" at the Universidade de São Paulo is named for Rama.

24. For an example of inclusion, see the following: "Though it is in Brazil where this conflict [regionalism vs. cosmopolitanism] has been rigorously theorized, within renovated and, above all, modernized perspectives, this did not fail to [also] take place in the other Spanish American countries" (Rama, *Transculturación narrativa* 23–24). And of exclusion: "Mediation allowed for this cultural conformation that had been achieved through centuries' worth of effort at accumulation and re-elaboration: in the case of Brazil, an organic national culture; in the case of Spanish America, the development of fruitful intercommunication among its various areas" (55).

25. There have been exceptions to this rule, as with Manuel de Oliveira Lima (1867–1928), a Brazilian writer, historian, and diplomat. See his articles "As repúblicas irmãs" (The Sister Republics, 1905) and "O sentimento monarquista" (The Monarchists' Feeling, 1905). Oliveira Lima does, however, admit to "exaggerated fraternization in [republican] discourse" in Latin America (53, 74, 81).

26. Stavans links the Brazilian tradition of essayistic national exegesis to Brazil's liminal position with regard to Latin America, writing that "[t]his ambivalence is often at the heart of Brazilian essays dealing with collective and particular identities. They ask questions such as 'Where do we fit in?' with considerably more vehemence that [*sic*] do other Latin Americans" (Introduction 11).

27. In the essay "Literature and the Rise of Brazilian National Self-Identity," Antonio Candido notes a "desire for complete differentiation" in nineteenth-century Brazil, and terms "exaggerated nativism" a "constant theme in Brazilian literature almost up to our days" (33, 38). Also note that Candido himself took up the *pícaro* vs. *malandro* question in his essay "Dialética de Malandragem" (Dialectic of Malandroism, 1970).

28. The phrase "purity of customs" is taken from Mário de Andrade's "Amérique Latine" (1934), qtd. in Antelo 192.

29. See also Prado, 18–19, 24, 31, 110–13; and Candido, *Recortes* 132.

30. See the article "Contrastes e Confrontos" (Contrasts and Confrontations) in da Cunha 111–16.

31. See also Candido, *Recortes* 133–34.

32. Veríssimo also labels some degree of "exaggerated appreciation and expression" as a "racial defect" of Spanish Americans (*América Latina* 23).

33. For a brief, enlightening interpretation of Bomfim's *A América Latina*, see Candido, *Recortes* 137–39.

34. To be fair, Bomfim describes a variety of peoples—not just Spanish Americans—in a language that is strongly racialist—this despite his stated opposition to racial determinism.

35. Note the providential tone of this statement.

36. As Rodó remarked in "Bolívar" (1912), America was "more his country than [Gran] Colombia" (550).

37. Masur contends that by 1815 Bolívar "was not thinking in terms of creating a great South American state," but rather an alliance of independent states (266).

38. Bolívar expands this argument in his address to the Congress of Angostura (1819), arguing that America's mixed heritage and colonial experience serve to nullify race prejudice, as well as condition the sort of republican government it should adopt—a conservative presidential democracy, in Bolívar's opinion (*Writings* 39). I am grateful to Geoff Shullenberger for his observation on providential miscegenation.

39. As Madariaga writes concerning Bolívar's intentions for the 1826 Congress of Panama: "As to membership, he was at bottom for a purely Spanish-American Congress, and therefore without either the United States, Haiti, or Brazil" (533).

40. See letters to Santander from May 30 and October 10, 1825, and a letter to J. Hipólito Unanué, also from May 30, 1825 (Bolívar, *Cartas* 4: 342–55; 5: 107–13).

41. For a related declaration, see Bolívar's 1826 address to Bolivia's Constituent Congress (*Writings* 58).

42. Viana Filho illustrates this point by analyzing several of Bonifácio's documents from this period (*José Bonifácio* 34).

43. On Bonifácio's close relationship with D. Pedro I during this period, see Cavalcante 76–77.

44. Nabuco inherited this position, as will be shown in Chapter 3.

45. The phrase *Fanatismo férreo* ("iron fanaticism") features in Bonifácio's "Ode à Poesia" (Ode to Poetry) (42), and *Fanatismo* is likewise mentioned in his poem "A Criação" (Creation) (*José Bonifácio* 42, 60).

46. Bonifácio's "Ode aos Gregos" (Ode to the Greeks), which opens with an invocation to the "Muse of Brazil," is particularly interesting in this regard (*José Bonifácio* 69).

Chapter Two
José Enrique Rodó: "Iberoamérica," the *Magna Patria*, and The Question of Brazil

1. For biographical information on Rodó, see Benedetti; Gómez-Gil; Pérez Petit; and Rodríguez Monegal's "Introducción General" to Rodó's *OC*.

2. See Zum Felde on Rénan's influence on Rodó (2: 77). See also Pereda 90; and Rodríguez Monegal, "Metamorphoses" 81. Darío's comments on Caliban "reign[ing] on the island of Manhattan," from his 1894 profile of Poe, are an obvious precursor to Rodó's discussion in *Ariel* (*Los raros* 16).

3. See Rodó's October 12, 1900 letter to Unamuno regarding his French influences (*OC* 1379).

4. See Hale in Bethell's *Ideas and Ideologies in Twentieth Century Latin America* (1996) for discussion of the "new continent-wide idealism" and of Rodó's reception in Spanish America (181). See also Bollo's *Sobre José Enrique Rodó* (1951) for discussion of Rodó's intellectual impact.

5. See Sánchez 107–29.

6. See also Benedetti on Rodó's twentieth-century influence (94, 103).

7. *Ariel* achieved an "exceptional" nine printings in Spain and Spanish America between 1900 and 1911 and was even pirated (Benedetti 46; Rodríguez Monegal, in *Rodó* 30). See also Miller 209n59.

8. See Reyes's reference to Rodó as "el Maestro" in a November 1909 letter (qtd. in Rodó, *OC* 1464). Max Henríquez Ureña also refers to Rodó using this term (9).

9. Vaz Ferreira discusses this list in his *Moral para intelectuales* (1908) (202–03).

10. Letter to Antonio Rubió y Lluch, April 14, 1889 (Rodó, *OC* 1329; author's emphasis).

11. In Havana, Max Henríquez Ureña reprinted *Ariel* in numbers 29–44 (Jan. 12–Apr. 28, 1905) of *Cuba Literaria*, while his brother Pedro published a study on Rodó in numbers 29–30. On November 6, 1910, Rodó and Max's mutual friend Jesús Castellanos gave the speech "Rodó y su *Proteo*" at the Sociedad de Conferencias de Habana (Rodó, *OC* 1442–43). In Mexico, the state government of Nuevo León reprinted *Ariel* for free distribution—for details, see Rodó's November 28, 1908 letter to Pedro Henríquez Ureña (*OC* 1445–46) and Alfonso Reyes's November 1909 letter to Rodó (*OC* 1464–65). Finally, Pedro gave the speech "La obra de José Enrique Rodó" at the Ateneo de México in 1910.

12. For more on Rodó's influence, see Benedetti 46.

13. See Miller for a summary of Rodó's fame in the decades following the publication of Ariel, the downward revision of his reputation beginning in the 1940s, and recent reappraisals, of which Miller's own reading of Rodó is an important example (24–25).

14. For an overview of critical responses to Morse's thesis, see Roberto Ventura, "Calibanismo de Americano Atrai Críticas" (An American's Calibanism Draws Criticism).

15. The most recent translation of Rodó's *Ariel* that I know of is by Denise Bottman (Campinas, SP: UNICAMP, 1991).

16. Bandeira included a brief entry on Rodó in his *Literatura Hispano-Americana* (Spanish American Literature, 1949). His discussion borrows heavily from Alberto Zum Felde's *Proceso intelectual del Uruguay* (1930) (Bandeira 182; Zum Felde 100–04, 113). Cardoso published three essays on Rodó between 1920 and 1925.

17. Etcheverry cites Rodó as mentioning Emperor D. Pedro II and Euclides da Cunha in an unpublished 1910 speech, though I cannot confirm the accuracy or extent of these discussions (10). Rodó also briefly mentions seventeenth-century Portuguese writer Francisco de Melo in *Motivos* (Rodó, *OC* 387).

18. For a representative example, see Chapter 54 of *Motivos* (Rodó, *OC* 367). For other references, see Rodó, *OC* 439, 719, 797, 805.

19. Rodó's correspondence as collected in his 1967 *Obras completas* shows at least eight occasions on which he sent unsolicited copies of his work to writers like Darío, Leopoldo Alas (aka Clarín), and Unamuno (1319–1476). See also Miller 35.

20. For a discussion of Rodó's use of the term *magna patria*, see Max Henríquez Ureña 9, 41–47.

21. I discuss Bolívar's view of imperial Brazil as "Portuguese" in Chapter 1.

22. For the Rodó-Fichte connection, see Brading.

23. See the digitized document "El Te-Deum," page 3, which shows a photo of "the Bolivian, Uruguayan, Spanish, Japanese, and Brazilian ministers."

24. See also Rodó's call in "La enseñanza de la literatura" (1908) for a history of Spanish American literature that "atendiese debidamente a la relación de la actividad literaria con los caracteres de raza, de país, de sociabilidad, de instituciones, que concurren a imprimir el sello en la literatura de cada nación y cada época," as well as his mention in "Juan Montalvo" (1913) of language as the "instrumento verbal de la raza, que compon[e] lo que llamamos el *genio* del idioma," and his stress on "[e]l vínculo del idioma común" between Spain and Spanish America in a letter to the Academia Española (*OC* 533, 611, 1194; author's emphasis).

25. Joaquim Nabuco also entertained the possibility of a "delatinized" Latin America, warning in a February 28, 1891 diary entry that "in the coming centuries Latin America must either be *civilized* or not be Latin" (*Diários* 2: 34–35; author's emphasis).

26. This speech, to the best of my knowledge, remains unpublished. See Rodríguez Monegal, in Rodó, *OC* 48–49; Etcheverry 17.

27. Rodó's description of Guanabara Bay in "Cielo y agua," anticipates José Vasconcelos and Reyes's descriptions of Brazil as a utopian space, as I discuss in Chapter 4.

28. Rodó's rhetoric of fraternal ties is reproduced in a November 1909 telegram to Rio Branco. Here Rodó writes of an agreement that "ha venido a estrechar más las viejas amistades de estos pueblos hermanos." Rio Branco's response is notably free of this fraternal language, and is framed in terms of Brazilian interests (qtd. in Etcheverry 7n6).

29. Iberianism reached a peak of popularity in Portugal and Spain in the mid- to late nineteenth century, when successive crises made iberianists' calls for radical reorganization of the peninsula (as a united monarchy, a decentralized federal republic, a pan-Iberian customs union, etc.) more palatable and less far-fetched. For an overview, see Campos Matos; Rocamora.

30. Interestingly, Joaquim Nabuco in a April 23, 1909 lecture on Camões given at Cornell University acknowledges the valence of *España/Espanha* as equivalent to *Hispania*, though he insists on the ultimate linguistic difference of Spanish and Portuguese (*OC* 10: 407).

31. This was the sort of argument Darío advanced in his 1896 appraisal of Portuguese poet Eugénio de Castro, in which he chastised his fellow Spanish Americans for their ignorance of Luso-Brazilian literature (*Los raros* 230–31; my emphasis).

32. From Herder: "The climate, it is true, may imprint on each its peculiar stamp, or it may spread over it a slight veil, without destroying, however, its original national character" (284). See Miller for Rodó's familiarity with Herder (42).

33. Some descriptions of Portuguese that I have heard include Miguel de Unamuno's misattribution to Cervantes of the idea that Portuguese is a "castellano sin huesos." Others include descriptions of Portuguese as a kind of underwater Spanish, as Spanish crossed with French, and less kindly, as a generic sort of "bizarre" Spanish. For Unamuno, see *OC* 1: 194.

34. On Rodó as a reader of Valera, see Pereda 166n284. Rodó also mentions Valera a number of times in his work, as in "Menéndez Pelayo y nuestros poetas" (1896).

35. I would like to thank Sérgio Campos Matos for helping me to locate this reference. Given Rodó's passing familiarity with Garrett and his repeated references to *Camões*, it is almost certain that he was quoting from *Camões* in "Iberoamérica," or was repeating another writer's (probably Valera's) interpretation of this passage.

Chapter Three
Joaquim Nabuco: Monarchy's End and the "South Americanization" of Brazil

1. For Nabuco's encounter with Darío, see Darío's 1905 article "Graça Aranha" (*Escritos dispersos* 2: 243).

2. See, for instance, Silveira; Dennison, *Joaquim Nabuco*; Dennison, *From Monarchism*; Souza Andrade, *Joaquim Nabuco e o Brasil*; Souza Andrade, *Joaquim Nabuco e o Pan-Americanismo*; and Costa.

3. The term *liberal utilitarianism* refers to the utilitarian as opposed to rights-based argument for individual liberty. For Mill as a liberal utilitarian, see Skorupski, "John Stuart Mill" 373–74, and Introduction 23.

4. Eduardo Prado (1860–1901) was a journalist and editor of the *Comércio de São Paulo*. A monarchist, Prado's publications include *A Ilusão Americana* (The American Illusion, 1893). Manoel Bomfim (1868–1932) penned various essayistic texts, including *A América Latina: Males de Origem* (Latin America: Originary Ills, 1905) and *O Brasil na América* (Brazil in America, 1929).

5. Nabuco held to this nostalgic view until months before his death. See his February 12, 1909 speech, "Lincoln's Centenary," given in Washington, DC (2).

6. Exceptions include Argentine writer Martín García Mérou, who launched an early critique of Nabuco's position in *Balmaceda* in his *El Brasil intelectual* (1900), and much more recently, Stephanie Dennison, who devotes a short section of her 2006 study of Nabuco to the text.

7. This is much to the consternation of Faoro, who describes *Um Estadista do Império* as a text that solidified an elitist interpretation of the Second Empire (124).

8. According to Carolina Nabuco, the episode ended with "the purchase of the runaway slave in Joaquim's name, as a gift from his godmother" (8).

9. For Machado's review, see Carolina Nabuco 11.

10. For a later example of Nabuco's criticism of Dom Pedro II, see the pamphlet "O Erro do Imperador" (The Emperor's Error, 1886), which criticizes the Emperor's decision to call for a new government after the liberal Dantas government lost a no-confidence motion by one vote (*OC* 12: 243). See also Nabuco's comment that it was during his years in São Paulo that he read Alencar's "Letters" (*Minha Formação* 33).

11. For evidence of Nabuco's enthusiasm for Bagehot and English cabinet government, see his reference to Bagehot's vision of the monarch's power as one of "funções meramente latentes" ("merely latent functions") in an April 29, 1879 parliamentary speech. Nabuco also references Mill here (*OC* 11: 34, 42).

12. See also Nabuco's characterization (*Minha Formação* 45; author's emphasis), as well as Dennison, *Joaquim Nabuco* 23–24, 49, 67.

13. For Bagehot, "constitutional royalty acts as a *disguise*. It enables our real rulers [i.e., the cabinet and Parliament] to change without heedless people knowing it" (97; author's emphasis). In other words, the efficient/dignified distinction allows a privileged minority to govern while the majority is safely distracted by royal weddings, ceremonies, and so on.

14. See also Williams's discussion in *Marxism and Literature* (1977) on the trappings of the British monarchy as "residual" to modern British capitalist democracy as the day's "dominant" social form (122–23).

15. Nabuco anticipates this discussion of Bagehot in the article "A Rainha Vitória" (Queen Victoria, 1897) (*OC* 9: 159).

16. Nabuco references this idea of the Constitution as a "grande mecanismo liberal" ("great liberal machine") in a November 16, 1884 campaign speech in Recife (*OC* 7: 300).

17. Nabuco returned to this idea in a 1901 diary entry (*OC* 2: 221; my emphasis).

18. Nabuco met Thiers on January 10, 1874, as he notes in his diary (*OC* 1: 30). See also Nabuco's account of Thiers and the Commune in *A Intervenção Estrangeira Durante a Revolta de 1893* (Foreign Intervention during the Revolt of 1893, 1895) (*OC* 2: 257).

19. For evidence, see Nabuco's June 16, 1874 diary entry (*OC* 1: 62).

20. See Nabuco's diary entries for March 1, 2, 5, and 8, May 13, and June 13, 1877 (*OC* 1: 123–26, 151, 166).

21. On Nabuco's broader program, see Needell 166.

22. In this context Paraguay is more or less interchangeable with any other "barbaric" territory, though its proximity and conflicted role in Brazilian history give it special relevance. Later Nabuco warns that slavery threatens Brazil with becoming the "Java da América" ("Java of America") (*OC* 7: 187).

23. The term *mongolização* is taken from a November 16, 1884 campaign speech (Nabuco, *OC* 7: 307). See also Nabuco's speeches for September 3, October 8, and March 22, 1879 (*OC* 11: 25) and his October 12, 1884 campaign speech in Recife (*OC* 7: 253–54).

24. See also Nabuco's comparison between the damage caused by Brazil's prior "africanization," and the "mongolization" that would necessarily follow from large-scale Chinese immigration (*OC* 7: 118–19).

25. Nabuco, perhaps attempting to reach the largest possible number of readers, appeals in *O Abolicionismo* to anti-Argentine nationalism (traditionally identified with Brazilian monarchism), *and* to the continental rhetoric employed in the 1870 republican manifesto. For an example of the latter, see *OC* 7: 218.

26. The same concern for national unity motivated Nabuco's contemporaneous effort to restructure the Empire along federal lines. In 1885 and 1888 he unsuccessfully introduced bills to the Chamber of Deputies to transform Brazil into a federal monarchy (Carolina Nabuco 143–45, 170–80; Viotti da Costa 221).

27. In the first of these pamphlets Nabuco makes this bold declaration: "I was a Monarchist because logic told me that it was not right for any national group to take advantage of the resentment that slavery had aroused; *because I could foresee that the revolutionary successor of the parliamentary monarchy could only be military dictatorship, while its legitimate evolutionary successor was civil democracy; because I felt that the Republic in Brazil would be the same pseudo-republic to be found in all Latin America*" (qtd. in Carolina Nabuco 198; my emphasis).

28. For Bagehot's thoughts on monarchy transitioning to republican government, see Ford 315. On Nabuco's belief in development toward a republic, see Salles 137–45.

29. See also Nabuco's characterization of Spanish history from his "Terceira Conferência no Teatro Santa Isabel" (Third Conference at the Saint Isabel Theatre, November 16, 1884), which reads as if it were a laundry list of commonly ascribed "Spanish" traits (*OC* 7: 323; my emphasis).

30. See Nabuco's comment on Spain's maintenance of fellow-feeling with its ex-colonies (*OC* 11: 43).

31. See also Dennison, *Joaquim Nabuco* 132. This argument for Brazil's political unity in the face of Spanish America's failure to achieve the same has became commonplace in Brazilian historiography, as in Bomfim's *O Brasil na América* (1929) and Buarque's *Raízes do Brasil* (1936).

32. On the issue of how 1889 worked to approximate Brazil to Spanish America, see José Murilo de Carvalho (*A Construção/O Teatro* 235–36).

33. For Nabuco's characterization of the Regency, see *OC* 3: 35.

34. Dennison observes: "As a known monarchist, Nabuco had been fortunate to escape the fate of many of his monarchist colleagues: house arrest, imprisonment and even physical violence. His letters reveal an overriding sense of uncertainty as to his future, particularly during and after the naval revolt" (*Joaquim Nabuco* 101).

35. The Baron of Rio Branco (born José Maria da Silva Paranhos Júnior, 1845–1912), is best known as a diplomat, though he was also a parliamentarian and journalist. As Brazil's Minister of Foreign Relations (1902–12), Rio Branco worked to define Brazil's territorial limits through negotiation. He favored multilateralism, and attempted to foster good relations with Europe, the US, and Brazil's neighbors.

36. For a similar evaluation, see Nabuco's December 7, 1889 letter to Rio Branco (*OC* 13: 184).

37. See Alan S. Kahan's *Aristocratic Liberalism* (1992), which analyzes Mill, Jacob Burckhardt, and Alexis de Tocqueville.

38. As Salles puts it, in *Um Estadista,* Nabuco "sought to defend the value of a period of Brazilian history that, at least in terms of its statesmen and its good society [*boa sociedade*], was equal to the civilizational parameters of Europe" (177–78). See also Faoro's less generous assessment (127).

39. For another Paraguay comparison, see Nabuco's October 19, 1893 diary entry (*OC* 2: 71).

40. Nabuco's fears were no doubt stoked by visual representations of Brazil and Argentina's new-found republican ties—for example, Pereira Neto's December 14, 1889 allegory in the *Revista Ilustrada* of the two countries, both represented as women wearing Phrygian caps, their right arms joined around a scepter on which rests another cap (qtd. in José Murilo de Carvalho, *A Formação* 82).

41. As Clodoaldo Bueno describes, many leaders of the incipient Republic were anxious to foster closer relations with Spanish America—particularly Argentina (25).

42. Here I use the term "South American" not as a geographical designation, but in reference to a series of unfavorable qualities Nabuco ascribed to the continent, and particularly to the Spanish American republics.

43. See Carolina Nabuco's assessment that in *Balmaceda* her father "reached his full vigor" as a writer and that his articles on Chile were "of a burning timeliness for Brazil" (209, 220).

44. For another text in the tradition of Montesquieu's *Lettres persanes,* see Spanish writer José de Cadalso's *Cartas marruecas* (1793).

45. See specifically the following episodes depicted in Gonzaga's *Cartas*: Minésio's disdain for members of the governing assembly (42–43), Gonzaga's description of the people as "flies" (53) and Minésio's rejection of noble customs (89–90). See also the seventh letter generally for the governor's rejection of law and established precedent (110–22).

46. See Blakemore's summary of Nabuco's position (397), as well as Dennison, *Joaquim Nabuco* 87.

47. Dennison notes: "What ideologically separated the figures of Nabuco and Balmaceda was the question of dictatorship [. . .] [H]is [i.e., Balmaceda's] [l]iberalism did not exclude the use of dictatorial authority and certainly on this point he was at odds with Nabuco the parliamentarian" (*Joaquim Nabuco* 86).

48. See also Sérgio Buarque de Holanda's assessment in "Elementos Básicos da Nacionalidade: O Homem" (Basic Elements of Nationality: Man, 1967) (Monteiro and Eugênio 625).

49. See Nabuco, *OC* 2: 245.

50. Recall Mill's belief in a two-way relationship between a people's character and its government, with "good" or "bad" traits resulting in good or bad government, respectively. For a critique of Nabuco's sarcastic comments on republicanism as a "cosmic force," see Veríssimo's 1895 review of *Balmaceda* ("A Revolução Chilena" 45).

51. García Mérou takes particular exception to Nabuco's characterization of Chile in his "Post-Scriptum" (284–85).

52. See also Nabuco's April 18, 1894 diary entry (*Diários* 2: 99).

53. Here I intentionally reference the civilization/barbarism distinction famously invoked by Domingo Faustino Sarmiento in *Facundo* (1845).

54. On Nabuco's later view of the importance of Latin American alliances, see his March 3, 1904 letter to Rio Branco (*OC* 14: 157–58).

55. Brazil's 1904 rebuffing in its border dispute with Britain may have contributed to Nabuco's adoption of Pan-Americanism. For evidence, see Nabuco's 1905 letter to Graça Aranha (qtd. in Carolina Nabuco 307).

56. See from Nabuco's December 19, 1905 letter to Rio Branco: "[S]ou francamente monroista [. . .] Note você que eu não acompanho as idéias de Mr. Roosevelt sôbre ocupação norte-americana, ou outra, de alfândegas, etc., de países sul-americanos. O meu monroismo é mais largo e não me prende a êsses expedientes que êle imagina para 'justificar' [. . .] a doutrina de Monroe perante a Europa [. . .] Para mim o que eu quero é uma espécie de aliança tácita, subentendida, entre os nossos dois países" (*OC* 14: 238; "I am frankly a Monroist [. . .] Note that I do not share Mr. Roosevelt's ideas on North American and foreign occupation of the customs offices, etc. of South American countries. My Monroism is broader and does not tie me to these expedients, which he has imagined to 'justify' [. . .] the Monroe Doctrine before Europe [. . .] What I want is a sort of tacit, understood alliance between our two countries").

57. Further, Dennison notes: "The threat of militarism still loomed in Brazil in 1905, and thus it is understandable that Nabuco might well have been convinced of the potential of the United States to defend the civilian government in Brazil via its flexible interpretation of the Monroe Doctrine" (*Joaquim Nabuco* 150).

Chapter Four
Alfonso Reyes: Culture, Humanism, and
Brazil's Place in the American Utopia

1. See Monsiváis paraphrased and quoted in Rose Corral's "Alfonso Reyes y la cuestión del americanismo," in Pineda Franco and Sánchez Prado 171, 184n1. Select scholars continue to work on Reyes, notably Ignacio M. Sánchez Prado, author of *Naciones intelectuales: Las fundaciones de la modernidad literaria mexicana* (1917–1959) (2009) and co-editor of several volumes, including *Alfonso Reyes y los estudios latinoamericanos* (w/ Adela Pineda Franco, 2004).

2. Reyes's notion of *Última Tule* borrows from Seneca's play *Medea* (213).

3. A "many-tentacled octopus" is my translation of Alicia Reyes's descriptive term for her grandfather (Alicia Reyes 170). Much of the biographical information on Reyes is taken from her biography and from Salinas's chronology (18–19).

4. See Reyes's account in "Pasado inmediato" (1939) (*OC* 12: 195).

5. For this and more details on the Ateneo group, see García Morales 84.

6. For an early description by Reyes of Caso, Vasconcelos, and Pedro Henríquez Ureña, see "Rubén Darío en México" (1916) (*OC* 4: 305).

7. This phrase is extracted from the *Estatutos del Ateneo de México* (qtd. in Alicia Reyes 44).

8. The group convinced Bernardo Reyes, Alfonso's father and then the governor of Nuevo León, to print 500 copies of *Ariel*—without Rodó's consent—for free distribution "to the youth of the country" (García Morales 123).

9. The *Generación del 98* comparison is fairly canonical, but the connection to Portugal's Generation of 1870 merits explanation for those unfamiliar with Luso-Brazilian literary and intellectual history. Both the *ateneístas* and the Portuguese group, whose members included Antero de Quental, Eça de Queiroz, and Oliveira Martins, organized themselves around the ideal of democratic dialogue through public conferences (the *Sociedad de Conferencias* in Mexico, and the *Conferências do Cassino* in Portugal in 1871), and both rejected right-leaning orthodoxy (moribund Romantic poetics and authoritarian university administration in Portugal, Porfirian positivism in Mexico).

10. Miller notes that Reyes "is often dismissed today—just as Rodó is—as a conservative Hellenist and Hispanist" (110), though her interpretation of Reyes (like my own) is evidently at odds with this characterization.

11. Pedro Henríquez Ureña wrote the following of Rodó in his posthumous *Historia de la cultura en la América hispánica* (1947): "If Rubén Darío was considered the greatest poet of his time, José Enrique Rodó was considered the greatest prose writer. Like Darío, Rodó has been the victim of the reactions of later generations; like him, he preserves a lofty stature, regardless of his detractors" (qtd. in Rodó, *OC* 1448, 1466).

12. See Reyes's account in his diary (32).

13. See particularly "Rumbo al Sur" (1918), in which Reyes describes the Spanish American diplomats' 1913 removal from Paris by train to the Spanish border (*OC* 2: 141–50).

14. The invocation of Athens and ancient Greece also served to make the case for Mexico's spiritual unity with the rest of Latin America, even as it remained politically distinct. According to this argument, the ancient Greek city-states represented a cultural unity, though they were separate, rival political entities. As Pedro Henríquez Ureña wrote, "if we conserve that childish audacity with which our ancestors described every American city as 'Athens,' I would not hesitate to compare us to the politically distinct but spiritually united peoples of classical Greece and Renaissance Italy" (*La utopía* 5).

15. On the topic of language, its ability to shape thought, and the speaker or writer's consequent obligation to use it responsibly, see Reyes's enlightening 1949 historiographical synthesis, "Mi idea de la Historia" (*OC* 22: 214).

16. See Reyes's "Ciencia social y deber social" (1941) (*OC* 11: 118) and "Discurso por Virgilio" (1932) (11: 170, 174).

17. See also Zamora 225–26.

18. As Reyes explained in a September 20, 1954 letter to Jorge Mañach, his father's death may have inclined him toward a more conciliatory approach to politics (*Cartas* 147–50).

19. Miller notes: "Like Rodó, Reyes resisted extremes" (112).

20. See also Paz's extended discussion of Reyes in *El laberinto de la soledad* (1950) (176–79).

21. See also Faber's generally satisfying description of Reyes's liberalism as "moderately left-wing, institutional, and anti-revolutionary" (Pineda Franco and Sánchez Prado 34).

22. See also Reyes's comment from the same speech regarding the "zona intermedia" between individualism and socialism (*OC* 11: 251).

23. See Miller for Reyes's admiration of Burckhardt (122).

24. This is my translation from the longer, revealing definition of culture Reyes presents in "Posición de América" (*OC* 11: 257). Reyes's position on transmission of culture approximates Nietzsche's views on history as spelled out in "On the Utility and Liability of History for Life" (1874), in which he argues that history is only valuable to the extent that it can ground present and future projects. See also Miller, who argues that for Reyes, culture "was process rather than product" (129).

25. This is my translation from "Atenea política" (1932) (*OC* 11: 194).

26. See Reyes, "Por la asociación de escritores," from *Los dos caminos: Cuarta serie de Simpatías y diferencias* (1923) (*OC* 4: 354).

27. For an example of this criticism, see Zamora, who casts Reyes along with Pedro Henríquez Ureña and Paz "in a liberal ideological tradition, or within an immemorial philosophical custom of privileging the word to the point of idolatry" (234).

28. See also Reyes's "En memoria de Antonio Caso" (1946) (*OC* 12: 155).

29. I am grateful to Marimar Patrón Vázquez for her valuable insights on the issues discussed in this section.

30. Reyes was clearly uncomfortable with the totalitarian character of certain rightist and leftist regimes, as he makes clear in "Ante la Asociación Cultural de Acción Social" (1939). While it may be defensible to classify Reyes as a democratic socialist (in the mold of Eduard Bernstein), this does not annul his commitment to humanism, as Escalante suggests, or to democratic institutions.

31. For a more skeptical view, see Bové.

32. See also Kristeva, whose characterization of a renewed humanism bridging the gap between neoliberal "technological management" and right-leaning "obscurantism" approximates Reyes's call in "Esta hora del mundo" (1939) for humanists to split the difference between fascist "exaltación nacional" and the "exacerbación capitalista" plaguing so-called left-leaning democracies (Kristeva 17; Reyes, *OC* 11: 242).

33. See also "Esta hora del mundo" (1939), in which Reyes mentions the "trabajador intelectual—el creador de todos los provechos sociales, de que el trabajador manual es el mero repetidor" (*OC* 11: 252).

34. See also Pedro Henríquez Ureña's praise in "Utopía de América" for the "magisterial men" who are "creators or saviors of peoples" (*La utopía* 6).

35. This recalls Rodó's description in "Rumbos nuevos" (1910) of the ideal American writer as a "cura de almas" (Rodó, *OC* 523).

36. See Reyes, *OC* 11: 204.

37. This phrase is taken from Reyes's "Pasado inmediato" (1939) (*OC* 12: 215).

38. Note Reyes's reference to Julien Benda's *The Treason of the Intellectuals* (1927). See also Pedro Henríquez Ureña, who writes the following in *Utopía de América:* "It is our custom to require magisterial ability of even the part-time writer [*escritor de gabinete*]: because he had this, José Enrique Rodó was [a] representative [writer]" (6).

39. Given the extent of José Enrique Rodó's influence on Reyes, it is quite possible that Reyes referenced the idea of *Ultima Thule* via Rodó's parable of the Eastern king in *Ariel* (216).

40. Put another way, "el Continente americano, antes de ser una región geográfica reconocida, era ya un anhelo apremiante y casi una necesidad poética de las gentes [. . .] Siempre fue algún sitio quimérico y atrayente donde fundar los cimientos de alguna república perfecta." See "En la VII Conferencia Internacional Americana" (1933), in Reyes, *OC* 11: 73. See also Reyes's use of Charles V's motto *Plus Ultra* in "Ante la Asociación Cultural de Acción Social" (1939) (*OC* 11: 231–32).

41. These terms are borrowed from section titles of Reyes's "El presagio de América" (*OC* 11: 17, 29).

42. "Estas tierras imaginadas suelen dar origen a verdaderos descubrimientos. Buscando los países míticos, se da con América" (Reyes, *OC* 11: 346). See also Reyes's observation: "[E]s bien sabido que precisamente el descubrimiento de América provocó el auge de la literatura utópica en la Europa renacentista" (*OC* 11: 364).

43. The preceding three terms are all from *Última Tule* (*OC* 11: 57, 62, 73, 79).

44. This is a reference to Reyes's "Capricho de América" (1933), first published in the Brazilian periodicals *A Nação* and *Jornal do Brasil*, and later collected in *Última Tule* (*OC* 11: 75–78).

45. See 1949's "Mi idea de la historia" (Reyes, *OC* 22: 211). In "El héroe y la historia" (1943), Reyes credits the term *ifismo* to Franklin D. Roosevelt (*OC* 9: 352).

46. On the Latin American writer's internationalism, see also "Posición de América" (1942) (Reyes, *OC* 11: 264).

47. Escalante defines *homonoia* for Reyes as "unification of ideas and the idea of unification, the key to and premise for [. . .] a new international harmony that would be impossible unless it begins in America and within the [. . .] leveling conditions provided by democracy" (Pineda Franco and Sánchez Prado 158). See also Reyes's description of a Spanish American impulse toward mutual approximation in "Atenea política" (1932) (Reyes, *OC* 11: 192).

48. For a more complete list of Reyes's Brazilian friends and associates, see Ellison, *Alfonso Reyes e o Brasil,* especially 42–43, 47–49, and 254.

49. On Reyes's campaign to triumph socially in Rio, see Zaïtzeff 158. For an exhaustive list of texts Reyes received from Brazilian writers, see the "Publicaciones recibidas" column in any issue of *Monterrey*.

50. Reyes was also involved in selecting titles for a series of Brazilian texts to be published in Spanish translation by Mexico's Fondo de Cultura Económica (Ellison, *Alfonso Reyes e o Brasil* 238).

51. Valery Larbaud's work, which includes the novel *Fermina Marquez* (1911), often focused on Spanish American themes.

52. See Larboud and Reyes 91; and Reyes's July 29, 1930 diary entry (*Diario* 323).

53. Reyes translated Chesterton's *The Innocence of Father Brown* (1911) and *The Man Who Was Thursday* (1908) into Spanish in 1921 and 1922, respectively. Lima invited Reyes to give a talk on the English writer at the Centro Dom Vital in 1932 (Ellison, *Alfonso Reyes e o Brasil* 156–57; Salinas 18–19).

54. On Nabuco and the idea of Brazilian racial democracy, see his rather *saudosista* reflections on his plantation childhood, discussed in Chapter 3.

55. Reyes reports in the June 1936 issue of *Monterrey* that he had recently received a copy of the 2nd edition of *Casa-grande e Senzala* (240). On Freyre's friendship with and influence on Reyes, see Ellison, *Alfonso*

Reyes e o Brasil 52, 72–73. See also Freyre's essay "Don Alfonso," first published in *O Cruzeiro* (Rio de Janeiro) on March 25, 1961 (*A Americanidade e Latinidade* 125).

56. For examples of Reyes's praise for Brazilians as "natural negotiators," see "La constelación americana" (1936) and "El Brasil en una castaña" (1941) (qtd. in Ellison, *Alfonso Reyes e o Brasil* 228, 230).

57. See also Reyes's rather detached description of Spanish colonialism in Africa in his review of J. Bravo Carbonel's *Fernando Póo y el Muni, sus misterios y riquezas, su colonización* (1917) (*OC* 4: 36–42).

58. Certain elements of *Toda a América*, however, would likely not have appealed to Reyes, particularly Ronald de Carvalho's celebration of technology and of destructive, creative force. See particularly Carvalho 120, 145–46.

59. Ellison has interpreted Reyes's Brazil-themed short fiction and poetry as an allegorical and amorous reading of his desire for linguistic and cultural cross-fertilization between Brazil and Spanish America. Moreover, he notes that Reyes incorporates several *lusitanismos* into the poems of his *Romances del Río de Enero* (*Alfonso Reyes e o Brasil* 75, 190, 197).

60. Miguel de Unamuno used the same "parallel" phraseology for Spain and Portugal in a 1914 speech given in Figueira da Foz (*Escritos* 225).

61. See Almeida Garrett's *Camões* (1825) (Note A to Canto I, 173), and Nabuco's April 23, 1909 lecture at Cornell University (*OC* 10: 407–08). Freyre makes a similar observation in his volume *O Brasileiro entre os Outros Hispanos* (The Brazilian among the Other Hispanics, 1975), linking *saudade* to a specifically Portuguese cultural context (124).

62. For two examples of Reyes's use of *saudade*, see "Saudade," which describes Teixeira de Pasocaes's visit to Spain, from *Reloj de sol: Quinta serie de Simpatías y diferencias* (published 1926) (*OC* 4: 385) and "Atenea política" (1932) (*OC* 11: 191).

63. See Reyes's description of the Portuguese language in "Aduana lingüística" (1933–41) as "[i]lustre por ser la expresión de una grande epopeya histórica que dejó sus huellas en todo el mundo conocido, y todavía supo abrir al esfuerzo humano nuevos caminos" (*OC* 14: 166).

64. See Pineda Franco and Sánchez Prado 26, 39.

65. Note the similarity between Reyes's discussion of the relationship between Spanish and Portuguese as metaphorically structured by a *telaraña de acero* and Rodó's position, as discussed in this book's second chapter, which has Portuguese and Spanish as two tones, or *matices*, of the same language.

66. Note the implications of Reyes's curious geographical image for Brazil's liminal relationship to "Latin America": Brazil is both its own continent, and therefore distinct, and one placed within the South American landmass, and thus a component part of the larger whole.

67. See similar references to the Portuguese language as a *telaraña* in "Salutación al Brasil (En la Hora Nacional de Radio)" (1941) and "El Brasil en una castaña" (1942) (Reyes, *OC* 9: 185, 191).

68. See also from Reyes's description of Rio in an April 10, 1930 diary entry: "Mundo demasiado colonial donde todavía la gente no sabe vivir y las cosas son malas. Desconcertante soledad en que me encuentro" (*Diario* 312). Finally, see "Aguja de las playas" (1936), in which Reyes described his feeling of disorientation shortly after arriving in Rio, "aquella laberintosa ciudad" (*OC* 9: 486).

69. João Ramalho was an early Portuguese colonist shipwrecked off the Brazilian coast between 1510 and 1512 and later found with the Tupiniquins in the São Paulo highlands. He played an important role in the later Portuguese colonization of the region. Caramuru (Diogo Álvares Correia), another Portuguese shipwreck victim, lived among the Brazilian Amerindians in the early to mid-sixteenth century. He used his intermediate position between the Portuguese and the local peoples to facilitate colonization. He died in 1557.

Chapter Five
Sérgio Buarque de Holanda: Obscured Roots of Rodó in *Raizes do Brasil*

1. Beloved Brazilian musician Chico Buarque is Sérgio Buarque de Holanda's son. The elder Buarque's first article, "Originalidade Literária" (Literary Originality), was published in the April 22, 1920 edition of the *Correio Paulistano*, days before the publication of "Ariel" in the *Revista do Brasil*. For the most part, biographical information on Sérgio Buarque in this chapter is taken from the "Apontamentos para a Cronologia de Sérgio" (Notes for a Chronology of Sérgio) compiled by Buarque's widow, Maria Amélia Buarque de Holanda, accessible online at <http://www. unicamp.br/siarq/sbh/biografia_indice.html>. On Buarque's youth, see Eduardo Henrique de Lima Guimarães (Monteiro and Eugênio 37–41).

2. This description is borrowed from Antonio Arnoni Prado's introduction to Buarque's *O Espírito e a Letra* (21).

3. A set of Buarque's aphorisms was published in the journal *Fon-Fon!* in October 1921. For his early short fiction, see "Uma Viagem a Nápoles," published in the *Revista Nova* in December 1931 (Monteiro and Eugênio 563–82).

4. Eduardo Henrique de Lima Guimarães writes of Buarque's literary style circa 1920 as "somewhat precious" ("um tanto rebuscado") (Monteiro and Eugênio 41).

5. See, for example, João Ricardo de Castro Caldeira (*Perfis Buarqeanos* 61) and João Kennedy Eugênio (Monteiro and Eugênio 430–31). Indeed, this thematic carryover is confirmed in reviewing Buarque's publishing debut, the article "Originalidade Literária" (Literary Originality, 1920), which contains a comparative judgment of the Portuguese as "less idealistic" and "more practical" than the Spanish. Buarque would repeat this comparison in *Raízes do Brasil* and *Visão do Paraíso*. Eugênio also refers to Buarque's displeasure at efforts to compile his early work (Monteiro and Eugênio 426).

6. On this theme see also Antonio Arnoni Prado (Buarque, *Espírito* 1: 22).

7. See Maria Odila de Leite da Silva Dias (Monteiro and Eugênio 326).

8. Edgar Salvadori de Decca's is the only argument I have read that contends that Rodó is a meaningful influence on Buarque in *Raízes* (Monteiro and Eugênio 220).

9. See Candido's "O Significado de Raízes do Brasil" (The Meaning of Raízes do Brasil, 1967) (*Raízes* 12).

10. An equally satisfying descriptive opposition for Buarque's analysis would be tradition/innovation, as Eduardo Henrique de Lima Guimarães offers (Monteiro and Eugênio 41).

11. For analysis of this aspect of Buarque's anti-utilitarian argument, see João Kennedy Eugênio (Monteiro and Eugênio 425–59). Note the proximity between Buarque's statement on Brazilians' propensity for imitation and novelist Mário de Andrade's declaration that he wrote the novel *Macunaíma* (1928) because, "[t]he Brazilian does not have a character [. . .] He does not have a character because he possesses neither his own civilization nor a traditional consciousness" (169).

12. In referencing Schopenhauer, Buarque seems to draw on the philosopher's critique of US republicanism in the essay "On Jurisprudence and Politics," collected in the *Parerga and Paralipomena* (1851) (2: 253).

13. By extension, Roberto Schwarz points out the impossibility of disentangling local and global elements, thereby challenging the notion that a "deep genuine national [culture]" can be found free of foreign influence, that is, "unadulterated." Nonetheless, his observation on the consistency of this preoccupation stands (32).

14. See also Alencar's "O Nosso Cancioneiro" (Our *Cancioneiro*, 1874) (962). For an echo of Alencar's concern for proper respect for national traditions, see Buarque's article "A Cidade Verde" (The Green City, 1920), in which Buarque laments the apparent tendency in Brazil to "dar cabo do que temos de mais precioso—as tradições" (*Espírito* 1: 69; "kill off the most previous thing that we have—[our] traditions").

15. Machado writes: "A poet is not national merely because he inserts the names of many of the country's flowers and birds into his verses, which can result in a nationalism of vocabulary and nothing more" ("Instinto" 807).

16. For Buarque's account of his relationship to Brazilian modernism, see Buarque and Graham 4, 13–14. See also Santiago 101–05, 127, 245.

17. Buarque writes: "Um outro fator que influiu sobremodo para o desenvolvimento do utilitarismo no povo brasileiro e dessa nossa tendência natural para imitar tudo que é estrangeiro, foi a importação do regime republicano" (*Espírito* 1: 43; "Another factor that has greatly contributed to the development of utilitarianism in the Brazilian people and of our tendency to imitate everything foreign was the importation of the republican regime"). For analysis of the young Buarque's debt to earlier Brazilian monarchism, see João Kennedy Eugênio, in Monteiro and Eugênio 425–59.

18. Further explorations of the connection between a dangerous utilitarianism and the US example can be seen in "A Cidade Verde" (The Green City, 1920) and "A Decadência do Romance" (The Decline of the Novel, 1921) (*Espírito* 1: 69–71, 105–07).

19. Commentators on Buarque seem to agree, with Pedro Meira Monteiro and Edgar Salvadori de Decca both contending that the article can be read as a "review" of Rodó's *Ariel* ("As Raízes do Brasil" 166). See also Decca in Monteiro and Eugênio 220.

20. Santiago notes that Buarque's interest in Spanish American literature and culture was a rarity in the Brazilian literary milieu of the 1920s (101). Buarque's diminished literary (though not historiographical) interest in Spanish America is evident in his private library, held at the Universidade Estadual de Campinas. This contains a scant number of Spanish American literary texts, only one of which could plausibly have been acquired before the author's reported purge of his collection in 1927—Julián Martel's *La bolsa* (Buenos Aires: Estrada, s.d.). This leads me to conclude that if Buarque ever possessed copies of the Spanish American writers he reviewed in his early criticism (Rodó, Darío, Vargas Vila, Santos Chocano, etc.), he gave these away, as he reports in the introduction to the volume *Tentativas de Mitologia* (Attempts at Mythology, 1979) (29). See also Maria Amélia Buarque de Holanda's chronology.

21. See the articles "Vargas Vila," published in the June 4, 1920 edition of the *Correio Paulistano*, and "Santos Chocano," published in the June 1920 edition of *A Cigarra* (*Espírito* 1: 47–56). For references to these writers as exceptional, see Buarque, *Espírito* 1: 48, 55–56.

22. Antonio Arnoni Prado refers in his introduction to *O Espírito e a Letra* to the early 1920s as "the moment in which [Buarque] plans *Os novecentistas*, which he would never publish; in which he alludes to the need to define new tasks for the Latin American intellectual" (1: 23; author's emphasis). As for the possibility that *Os novecentistas* would have been modeled on *Los raros*, it should be noted that Buarque was familiar with Darío's 1896 portrait of Portuguese poet Eugénio de Castro, one of the writers profiled in *Los raros*. See Buarque's "Os Poetas e a Felicidade—II" (Poets and Happiness—II, 1921) (*Espírito* 1: 95).

23. See also Buarque's humorous piece "Rabugices de Velho" (An Old Man's Rabies, 1920), and his reference to "nossa civilização técnica, utilitária" ("our technical, utilitarian civilization") in contrast to indigenous traditions in "O Mito de Macunaíma" (The Myth of Macunaíma, 1935) (*Espírito* 1: 63–65, 260).

24. See "Thomas Mann e o Brasil" (Thomas Mann and Brazil, 1930) (*Espírito* 1: 251–56).

25. See Richard Graham's interview with Buarque (5). Much has been written on the Weber-Buarque comparison. Monteiro's *A Queda do Aventureiro* (The Fall of the Adventurer, 1999) is useful in this regard.

26. The term *ambitious* is borrowed from Monteiro's *A Queda do Aventureiro* (24).

27. For an extended discussion by Buarque of Meinecke, though not of *Cosmopolitanism and the National State* in particular, see Buarque's "O Atual e o Inatual na Obra de Leopold von Ranke" (The Current and the Passé in the Work of Leopold von Ranke, 1974) (*Prefácios* 162–218).

28. See Buarque's critique of both Brazil's fascistic *integrationalistas* and of Brazilian communists at the close of *Raízes* (187–88). For a summary of Buarque's social-democratic politics, see Candido (Monteiro and Eugênio 30–36).

29. Eduardo Henriques de Lima Guimarães reports the manuscript lost (Monteiro and Eugênio 57n18). Numerous other sources confirm this, including Pedro Meira Monteiro, who has undertaken extensive research at the Sérgio Buarque de Holanda Archive at the Universidade Estadual de Campinas.

30. Curiously, in *Raízes do Brasil* Buarque occasionally employs the terms *nossa América* and *nossa América do Sul,* though without reference to Rodó or Martí (*Raízes* 39, 43).

31. Here Brasil Pinheiro Machado quotes from the first page of *Raízes do Brasil* (31).

32. Indeed, if Buarque were concerned exclusively with Portugal, he presumably would have titled the chapter "Fronteira da Europa," as in "Portugal, frontier of Europe."

33. Compare with the language ultimately settled on by Buarque: "A tentativa de implantação da cultura européia em extenso território, dotado de condições naturais, se não adversas, largamente estranhas à sua tradição milenar, é, nas origens da *sociedade brasileira,* o fato dominante e mais rico em conseqüências. Trazendo de *países distantes* nossas formas de convívio, nossas instituições, nossas idéias [. . .] somos ainda hoje uns desterrados em nossa terra" (*Raízes* 31; my emphasis; "The attempt to implant a European culture over an extensive sweep of land, one whose natural conditions were, if not adverse, then largely unfamiliar to the millennial tradition [of the Europeans], is the dominant and most consequential fact concerning the origins of *Brazilian society.* Having brought from *distant countries* our ways of being, institutions, and ideas [. . .] we are even today exiles in our own land").

34. This final chapter provides numerous examples of tension between a national and continental frame of reference. See, for instance, Buarque's observations that "[n]o Brasil, *e não só no Brasil,* iberismo e agrarismo confundem-se" ("in Brazil, *and not just in Brazil,* iberianism and agrarianism are confused with one another"), and that "[s]e a forma de *nossa cultura* ainda permanece largamente ibérica e lusitana, deve atribuir-se tal fato sobretudo às insuficiências do 'americanismo' [. . .], O americano ainda é interiormente inexistente" (*Raízes,* 172; "if *our culture* remains largely Iberian and Lusitanian, this should be attributed to the insufficiencies of "Americanism" [as it has been practiced or applied locally]

[. . .], On the inside, [the prototypical Brazilian or Latin American] is not American").

35. See Jacques Derrida's *Specters of Marx* (1994).

36. Buarque explains: "Ambos participam, em maior ou menor grau, de múltiplas combinações e é claro que [. . .] nem o aventureiro, nem o trabalhador possuem existência real fora do mundo das idéias. Mas também não há dúvida que os dois conceitos nos ajudam a melhor ordenar nosso conhecimento dos homens e dos conjuntos sociais" (*Raízes* 44–45; "The two appear combined, in varying degrees, and clearly [. . .] neither the adventurer nor the worker has any real existence outside the world of ideas. But it is likewise doubtless that the two concepts help us to better order our understanding of men and of social groupings").

37. See also the following, from the same chapter: "O que o português vinha buscar era, sem dúvida, a riqueza, mas riqueza que custa ousadia, não riqueza que custa trabalho" (Buarque, *Raízes* 49; "What the Portuguese came [to Brazil] looking for was wealth, but wealth earned through daring, not wealth earned through work").

38. On the Luso-Brazilian adventurer's lack of racial pride and his social plasticity, see Buarque's (in retrospect quite indefensible) statement: "[C]umpre acrescentar outra face bem típica de sua extraordinária plasticidade social: a ausência completa, ou praticamente completa [. . .] de qualquer orgulho de raça. Ao menos do orgulho obstinado e inimigo de compromissos, que caracteriza os povos do Norte" (*Raízes* 53; "Let us reveal another feature of his extraordinary social plasticity: a complete or practically complete lack [. . .] of racial pride. Or at least, [a lack] of the obstinate pride, the enemy of compromise, that characterizes the peoples of the North"). For Buarque's discussion of agriculture, see *Raízes* 49–52, and 66–70, as well as 79–85 for his analysis of Brazil's patriarchal as opposed to bureaucratic approach to public administration.

39. See Candido's mention of the "relative [level of] theoretical indecision" to be found in the chapter "Nossa Revolução" (Monteiro and Eugênio 35).

40. For Buarque's initial mention of *sobrancería*, see *Raízes* 32.

41. For Candido's argument on *saudosismo*, see Monteiro and Eugênio 33.

42. See Candido's "O Significado de *Raízes do Brasil*" (Buarque, *Raízes* 19).

43. Santiago notes an enduring "traditionalism" in Buarque's argument, regardless of his acknowledgement of modernity's challenges: "The traditionalism inherent to Sérgio Buarque and to Octavio Paz [. . .] is often silent, like a guardian angel." Indeed, Santiago also notes a nostalgia in Buarque for "traditional"—implicitly Iberian and rural—values, which he ties back to the concept of *sobrancería* (227–28).

44. What Santiago overlooks here, as do many of Rodó's critics, is that *arielismo* advocates for "eurocentrism" not as an end in itself, but as a means to promote national and continental well-being. To reduce

Buarque's argument in "Ariel" (or Rodó's in *Ariel*) to an alleged eurocentrism overlooks the importance granted in his early journalism to themes of Brazilian cultural identity and political autonomy.

45. See particularly the following statement from Paz's chapter on "La 'inteligencia' mexicana," which strongly recalls both Rodó and Alfonso Reyes: "[V]olver a la tradición española no tiene otro sentido que volver a la unidad de Hispanoamérica" (*Laberinto* 166).

Works Cited

Alencar, José de. *Obra Completa*. Rio de Janeiro: José Aguilar, 1960. 4 vols. Print.

Anderson, Benedict. *Imagined Communities*. 1983. London: Verso, 1991. Print.

Andrade, Mário de. Unpublished preface to *Macunaíma*. *Macunaíma: O Herói Sem Nenhúm Caráter*. Belo Horizonte and Rio de Janeiro: Garnier, 2001. 169. Print.

Antelo, Raúl. *Na Ilha de Marapatá: Mário de Andrade Lê os Hispano-Americanos*. São Paulo: Editoria HUCITEC; MinC/Pró-Memória; Instituto Nacional do Livro, 1986. Print.

Ardao, Arturo. *Génesis de la idea y el nombre de América Latina*. Caracas: Centro de Estudios Latinoamericanos Rómulo Gallegos, 1980. Print.

———. *Rodó: Su americanismo*. Montevideo: Biblioteca de Marcha, 1970. Print.

Assis, Machado de. *Esau and Jacob*. Trans. Helen Caldwell. Berkeley: U of California P, 1965. Print.

———. "Notícia da Atual Literatura Brasileira: Instinto de Nacionalidade." *Obra Completa*. Ed. Afrânio Coutinho. Rio de Janeiro: José Aguilar, 1962. 3: 801–09. Print.

Bachelet, Michelle. "The Latin American Dream." *The Economist: The World in 2007* (2006): 42. Print.

Bagehot, Walter. *The English Constitution*. Ithaca, NY: Cornell UP, 1966. Print.

Bandeira, Manuel. *Literatura Hispano-Americana*. Rio de Janeiro: Irmãos Pongetti, 1949. Print.

Bañados Espinosa, Julio. *Balmaceda: Su gobierno y la Revolucíon de 1891*. 2 Vols. Paris: Garnier Hermanos, 1894. Print.

Barbosa, Francisco de Assis, ed. *Raízes de Sérgio Buarque de Holanda*. Rio de Janeiro: Rocco, 1988. Print.

Barker, Nancy Nichols. *The French Experience in Mexico, 1821–1861*. Chapel Hill: U of North Carolina P, 1979. Print.

Baron, Hans. *In Search of Florentine Civic Humanism: Essays on the Transition from Medieval to Modern Thought*. Princeton, NJ: Princeton UP, 1988. Print.

Barreto, Lima. *Prosa Seleta*. Ed. Eliane Vasconcellos. Rio de Janeiro: Nova Aguilar, 2001. Print.

Benedetti, Mario. *Genio y figura de José Enrique Rodó*. Buenos Aires: Editorial Universitaria de Buenos Aires, 1966. Print.

Bethell, Leslie, ed. *Ideas and Ideologies in Twentieth Century Latin America*. Cambridge: Cambridge UP, 1996. Print.

Beverley, John. "¿Existe un giro neoconservador en Latinoamérica hoy?" *Latin American Studies Association Forum* 40.1 (Winter 2009), 33–36. Print.

Bilbao, Francisco. *El autor y la obra*. Ed. José Alberto Bravo de G. Santiago de Chile: Cuarto Propio, 2007. Print.

Blakemore, Harold. "The Chilean Revolution of 1891 and Its Historiography." *Hispanic Historical Review* 45.3 (Aug. 1965): 393–421. Print.

Bolívar, Simón. *Cartas del Libertador*. Ed. Vicente Lecuna. 12 vols. Caracas: Lit. y Tip. del Comercio, 1929–59. Print.

———. "Contestación de un americano meridional a un caballero de esta isla (Carta de Jamaica)." *Obras completas*. Ed. Vicente Lecuna. La Habana: Lex, 1950, 1: 159–75. Print.

———. *El Libertador: Writings of Simón Bolívar*. Trans. Frederick H. Fornoff. New York: Oxford U, 2003. Print.

———. *Proclamas y discursos*. Ed. Geraldo Rivas Moreno. Bogotá: FiCa, 2001. Print.

Bollo, Sarah. *Sobre José Enrique Rodó*. Montevideo: Impresora Uruguaya, 1951. Print.

Bomfim, Manoel. *O Brasil na América: Caracterização da Formação Brasileira*. Rio de Janeiro: Topbooks, 1997. Print.

Bonifácio de Andrada e Silva, José. *José Bonifácio (O velho e o moço)*. Ed. Afrânio Peixoto e Constâncio Alves. Lisboa: Aillaud e Bertrand, 1920. Print.

———. *Projetos Para o Brasil*. Ed. Miriam Dolhnikoff. Rio de Janeiro: Companhia das Letras, 1998. Print.

Bové, Paul A. *Intellectuals in Power: A Genealogy of Critical Humanism*. New York: Columbia UP, 1986. Print.

Brading, D. A. *Marmoreal Olympus: José Enrique Rodó and Spanish American Nationalism*. Working Papers 47. Cambridge: Centre of Latin American Studies, Cambridge U, 1998. Print.

Buarque de Holanda, Maria Amélia. "Apontamentos para a Cronologia de Sérgio." *Sérgio Buarque de Holanda 100 Anos*. UNICAMP. Web. 7 Feb. 2010.

Buarque de Holanda, Sérgio. *Cobra de Vidro*. São Paulo: Martins, 1944. Print.

———. *O Espírito e a Letra: Estudos de Crítica Literária*. Ed. Antonio Arnoni Prado. 2 vols. São Paulo: Companhia das Letras, 1996. Print.

————. *Livro de Prefácios*. São Paulo: Companhia das Letras, 1996. Print.

————. *Raízes do Brasil*. 1st ed. Rio de Janeiro: José Olympio, 1936. Print.

————. *Raízes do Brasil*. 26th ed. São Paulo: Companhia das Letras, 2003. Print.

————. *Tentativas de Mitologia*. São Paulo: Perspectiva, 1979. Print.

Buarque de Holanda, Sérgio, and Richard Graham. "An Interview with Sérgio Buarque de Holanda." *Hispanic American Historical Review* 62.1 (Feb. 1982): 3–17. Print.

Bueno, Clodoaldo. *A República e Sua Política Exterior (1889 a 1902)*. São Paulo: Editora UNESP; Brasília: Fundação Alexandre de Gusmão, 1995. Print.

Burns, E. Bradford. *Nationalism in Brazil: A Historical Survey*. New York: Frederick A. Praeger, 1968. Print.

Cain, William. "The Crisis of the Literary Left: Notes toward a Renewal of Humanism." *After Poststructuralism: Interdisciplinarity and Literary Theory*. Ed. Nancy Easterlin and Barbara Riebling. Evanston, IL: Northwestern UP, 1993. 127–40. Print.

Caldeira, João Ricardo de Castro. "Sérgio Buarque de Holanda: Intelectual do Brasil." *Perfis Buarqueanos: Ensaios sobre Sérgio Buarque de Holanda*. Ed. João Ricardo de Castro Caldeira. São Paulo: Fundação Memorial da América Latina; Imprensa Oficial do Estado de São Paulo, 2005. 59–67. Print.

Campos Matos, Sérgio. "Iberismo e identidade nacional (1851–1910)." *Clio* ns 14/15 (2006): 349–400. Print.

Candido, Antonio. "Dialética de Malandragem." *O Discurso e a Cidade*. São Paulo: Duas Cidades, 1993. 19–54. Print.

————. "Literature and the Rise of Brazilian National Self-Identity." *Luso-Brazilian Review* 5.1 (June 1968): 27–43. Print.

————. *Recortes*. São Paulo: Companhia das Letras, 1993. Print.

Carvalho, José Murilo de. *A Construção da Ordem: A Elite Política Imperial. Teatro de Sombras: A Política Imperial*. Rio de Janeiro: Civilização Brasileira, 2003. Print.

————. *A Formação das Almas: O Imaginário da República no Brasil*. São Paulo: Companhia das Letras, 1998. Print.

Carvalho, Ronald de. *Toda a America*. Rio de Janeiro: Pimenta de Mello, 1926. Print.

Cavalcante, Berenice. *José Bonifácio: Razão e Sensibilidade, Uma História em Três Tempos*. Rio de Janeiro: Editora FGV, 2001. Print.

Chevalier, Michel. *Mexico, before and after the Conquest.* Trans. Fay Robinson. Philadelphia, 1846. Print.

——. *Society, Manners, and Politics in the United States: Letters on North America.* Ed. John William Ward. Trans. after the T.G. Bradford ed. Garden City, NY: Anchor, 1961. Print.

Conn, Robert T. "Official Nationalism in Mexico: Alfonso Reyes and the Hispanization of High Culture at the Turn of the Century." *Anales de la Literatura Española* 23.1–2 (1998): 99–115. Print.

Costa, João Frank da. *Nabuco e a Política Exterior do Brasil.* Rio de Janeiro: Gráf. Record, 1968. Print.

Costigan, Lúcia Helena, and Leopoldo M. Bernucci. "Introdução." *Revista Iberoamericana* 64.182–83 (Jan.–July 1998): 11–14. Print.

Da Cunha, Euclides. *Contrastes e Confrontos.* São Paulo: Lello Brasileira, 1967. Print.

Darío, Rubén. *Escritos dispersos de Rubén Darío (Recogidos de Periódicos de Buenos Aires).* Ed. Pedro Luis Bercia. La Plata: Universidad Nacional de La Plata, Facultad de Humanidades y Ciencias de la Educación, 1977. Print.

——. *Obras completas.* 5 vols. Madrid: Afrodisio Aguado, 1950–55. Print.

——. *Los raros.* 2nd ed. rev. and expanded. Barcelona: Maucci; Buenos Aires: Maucci Hermanos, 1905. Print.

Dennison, Stephanie. *From Monarchism to Panamericanism: The Development of Joaquim Nabuco's Political Ideology in National and International Contexts 1888–1910.* Liverpool, UK: U of Liverpool, 1978. Print.

——. *Joaquim Nabuco: Monarchism, Panamericanism and Nation-Building in the Brazilian Belle Epoque.* New York: Oxford UP, 2006. Print.

Derrida, Jacques. *Specters of Marx.* Trans. Peggy Kamuf. New York: Routledge, 1994. Print.

Ellison, Fred P. *Alfonso Reyes e o Brasil: Um Mexicano Entre os Cariocas.* Rio de Janeiro: Topbooks, 2002. Print.

——. "Alfonso Reyes y Manuel Bandeira. Una amistad mexicano-brasileña." *Hispania* 70.3 (Sept. 1987): 487–93. Print.

Espinosa, Aurelio M. "The Term Latin America." *Hispania* 1.3 (Sept. 1918): 135–43. Print.

Etcheverry, José Enrique. *Rodó y el Brasil.* Montevideo: Instituto de Cultura Uruguayo-Brasileño, July 1950. Print.

Faoro, Raymundo. *Existe Um Pensamento Político Brasileiro?* São Paulo: Ática, 1994. Print.

Fernández Moreno, César, ed. *América Latina en su literatura.* México: Siglo XXI; Paris: UNESCO, 1972. Print.

Fitz, Earl. "Internationalizing the Literature of the Portuguese-Speaking World." *Hispania* 85.3 (2002): 439–48. Print.

Ford, Trowbridge H. "Bagehot and Mill as Theorists of Comparative Politics." *Comparative Politics* 2.2 (Jan. 1970): 309–24. Print.

Foster, David William. "Spanish American and Brazilian Literature: A History of Disconsonance." *Hispania* 75.4 (Oct. 1992): 966–78. Print.

Freyre, Gilberto. *A Americanidade e Latinidade da América Latina e Outros Textos Afins.* Ed. Edson Nery da Fonseca. Brasília: Editora UnB; São Paulo: Imprensa Oficial do Estado, 2003. Print.

———. *O Brasileiro entre os Outros Hispanos: Afinidades, Contrastes e Possíveis Futuros nas Suas Inter-relações.* Rio de Janeiro: José Olympio; Brasília: Ministério da Educação e Cultura, 1975. Print.

———. *O Luso e o Trópico.* Lisboa: Comissão Executiva das Comemorações do V Centenário da Morte do Infante D. Henrique, 1961. Print.

———. "A Propósito de José Bonifácio." Recife: MEC; Instituto Joaquim Nabuco de Pesquisas Sociais, 1972. Print.

Fuchs, Barbara. "An English *Pícaro* in New Spain: Miles Philips and the Framing of National Identity." *New Centennial Review* 2.1 (Spring 2002): 55–68. Print.

Fuentes, Carlos. Prologue. *Ariel.* By José Enrique Rodó. Trans. Margaret Sayers Peden. Austin: U of Texas P, 1988. 13–28. Print.

García Mérou, Martín. *El Brasil intelectual: Impresiones y notas literarias.* Buenos Aires: Félix Lajouane, Editor, 1900. Print.

García Morales, Alfonso. *El Ateneo de México 1906–1914. Orígenes de la cultura mexicana contemporánea.* Sevilla: Escuela de Estudios Hispano-Americanos, 1992. Print.

Garrett, Almeida. *Obras.* 2 vols. Porto: Lello & Irmão, 1966. Print.

Glissant, Edouard. *Caribbean Discourse: Selected Essays.* Trans. J. Michael Dash. Charlottesville: UP of Virginia, 1989. Print.

Gómez-Gil, Orlando. *Mensaje y vigencia de José Enrique Rodó.* Miami: Universal, 1992. Print.

Gonzaga, Tomás Antônio. *Cartas chilenas.* São Paulo: Companhia das Letras, 2006. Print.

245

Graham, Richard. "Joaquim Nabuco, Conservative Historian." *Luso-Brazilian Review* 17.1 (Summer 1980): 1–16. Print.

Guerra Vilaboy, Sergio, and Alejo Maldonado Gallardo. *Laberintos de la integración latinoamericana*. Morelia, Méx.: Facultad de Historia de la Universidad Michoacana de San Nicolás de Hidalgo, 2002. Print.

Heater, Derek. *A Brief History of Citizenship*. New York: New York UP, 2004. Print.

Hegel, Georg Wilhelm Friedrich. *The Philosophy of History*. Trans. J. Sibree. New York: Dover, 1956. Print.

Henríquez Ureña, Max. *Rodó y Rubén Darío*. La Habana: Sociedad Editorial Cuba Contemporánea, 1918. Print.

Henríquez Ureña, Pedro. *Obras completas*. Santo Domingo: Universal, 2003. Print.

———. *La utopía de América*. Caracas: Ayacucho, 1978. Print.

Herder, Johann Gottfried. *J. G. Herder on Social and Political Culture*. Trans. F. M. Barnard. Cambridge: Cambridge UP, 1969. Print.

Hobsbawm, Eric. "Introduction: Inventing Traditions." *The Invention of Tradition*. Ed. Eric Hobsbawm and Terence Ranger. Cambridge and New York: Cambridge UP, 1983. Print.

Iglésias, Francisco. Introduction to *O Abolicionismo*. *Intérpretes do Brasil*. Ed. Silviano Santiago. 3 vols. Rio de Janeiro: Nova Aguilar, 2002. 1: 5–17. Print.

Intérpretes do Brasil. Ed. Silviano Santiago. 3 vols. Rio de Janeiro: Nova Aguilar, 2002. Print.

Jocelyn-Holt Letelier, Alfredo. "La crisis de 1891: Civilización moderna versus modernidad desenfrenada." *La Guerra Civil de 1891: Cien años hoy*. Ed. Luis Ortega. Santiago: Departamento de Historia, Universidad de Santiago de Chile, 1991. 23–35. Print.

Juderías, Julian. *La leyenda negra: Estudios acerca del concepto de España en el extranjero*. 16th ed. Madrid: Nacional, 1974. Print.

Júlio, Sílvio. *José Enrique Rodó e o Cinqüentenário do Seu Livro "Ariel."* Rio de Janeiro: Ministério de Educação e Cultura; Serviço de Documentação, 1954. Print.

Kahan, Alan S. *Aristocratic Liberalism: The Social and Political Thought of Jacob Burckhardt, John Stuart Mill, and Alexis de Tocqueville*. New York: Oxford UP, 1992. Print.

Kristeva, Julia. "Thinking in Dark Times." *Profession 2006*. New York: Modern Language Association of America, 2006. 13–21. Print.

Larboud, Valery, and Alfonso Reyes. *Correspondance 1923–1942*. Ed. Paulette Patout. Paris: Marcel Didier, 1972. Print.

Larsen, Neil. *Determinations: Essays on Theory, Narrative and Nation in the Americas*. London: Verso, 2001. Print.

Licínio Cardoso, Vicente. *Pensamentos Americanos (Livro Póstumo)*. Rio de Janeiro: Estabelecimento Graphico, 1937. Print.

———. *Pensamentos Brasileiros (Golpes de Vista)*. Rio de Janeiro: Annuario do Brasil, 1923. Print.

Lima, Oliveira. *Impressões da América Espanhola (1904–1906)*. Rio de Janeiro: José Olympio, 1953. Print.

Madariaga, Salvador de. *Bolívar*. London: Hollis & Carter, 1952. Print.

Martí, José. "Nuestra América." *Política de Nuestra América*. México: Siglo XXI: 1982. 37–44. Print.

Martius, Karl F. P. von. *O Estado do Direito entre os Autóctones do Brasil*. Belo Horizonte: Editora Itatiaia; São Paulo: Editora da Universidade de São Paulo, 1982. Print.

Masur, Gerhard. *Simon Bolivar*. Albuquerque: U of New Mexico P, 1948. Print.

Meinecke, Friedrich. *Cosmopolitanism and the National State*. Trans. Robert B. Kimber. Princeton, NJ: Princeton UP, 1970. Print.

Menezes, Djacir, ed. *O Brasil no Pensamento Brasileiro*. Rio de Janeiro: Centro Brasileiro de Pesquisas Educacionais, 1957. Print.

Mignolo, Walter. *The Idea of Latin America*. Malden, MA: Blackwell, 2005. Print.

———. "The Movable Center: Geographical Discourses and Territoriality during the Expansion of the Spanish Empire." *The Latin American Cultural Studies Reader*. Ed. Ana Del Santo, Alicia Ríos, and Abril Trigo. Durham: Duke UP, 2004. 262–90. Print.

Mill, John Stuart. *On Liberty and Other Essays*. Oxford: Oxford UP, 1998. Print.

Miller, Nicola. *Reinventing Modernity in Latin America: Intellectuals Imagine the Future, 1900–1930*. New York: Palgrave Macmillan, 2008. Print.

Monteiro, Pedro Meira. *A Queda do Aventureiro*. Campinas, SP: Editora da UNICAMP, 1999. Print.

———. "As Raízes do Brasil no Espelho de Próspero." *Novos Estudos* 83 (Mar. 2009): 159–82. Print.

Monteiro, Pedro Meira, and João Kennedy Eugênio, eds. *Sérgio Buarque de Holanda: Perspectivas*. Campinas, SP: Editora da UNICAMP; Rio de Janeiro: edUERJ, 2008. Print.

Morse, Richard. *O Espelho de Próspero*. Trad. Paulo Neves. São Paulo: Companhia das Letras, 1988. Print.

Nabuco, Carolina. *The Life of Joaquim Nabuco.* Trans. and ed. Ronald Hilton. Stanford: Stanford UP, 1950. Print.

Nabuco, Joaquim. *O Abolicionismo. Intérpretes do Brasil.* Ed. Silviano Santiago. 3 vols. Rio de Janeiro: Nova Aguilar, 2002. 1: 19–167. Print.

———. *Diários.* 2 vols. Rio de Janeiro: Bem-Ti-Vi; Recife: Massangana, 2005. Print.

———. "Lincoln's Centenary: Speech of the Brazilian Ambassador Joaquim Nabuco at the Celebration in Washington of Lincoln's Centenary Organized by the Commissioners of the District of Columbia, February 12th, 1909." Washington, DC: n.p., 1909. Print.

———. *Minha Formação.* Brasília: Senado Federal, 1998. Print.

———. *Obras Completas.* 14 vols. São Paulo: Instituto Progresso, 1949. Print.

———. "The Share of America in Civilization." *American Historical Review* 15.1 (Oct. 1909): 54–65. Print.

Nabuco, Joaquim, et al. "The Pan-American Conferences and Their Significance." *Annals of the American Academy of Political and Social Science* Vol. 27, Supplement 17 (May 1906): 1, 3–22. Print.

Needell, Jeffrey D. "A Liberal Embraces Monarchy: Joaquim Nabuco and Conservative Historiography." *The Americas* 48.2 (Oct. 1991): 159–79. Print.

Niemeyer, Oscar. "No traço do arquiteto, o sonho de união e liberdade." *Nossa América* Número Zero (1989): 21. Print.

O'Gorman, Edmundo. *La invención de América: El universalismo de la cultura de occidente.* México: Fondo de Cultura Económica, 1958. Print.

Ortega, Luis, et al. *La Guerra Civil de 1891: Cien años hoy.* Santiago: Departamento de Historia, Universidad de Santiago de Chile, 1991. Print.

Paz, Octavio. "El jinete del aire: Alfonso Reyes." *Obras completas.* Barcelona: Círculo de Lectores, 2001. 3: 278–88. Print.

———. *El laberinto de la soledad/Postdata/Vuelta a El laberinto de la soledad.* México: Fondo de Cultura Económica, 2000. Print.

Pereda, Clemente. *Rodó's Main Sources.* San Juan, PR: Imprenta Venezuela, 1948. Print.

Pérez Petit, Victor. *Rodó: Su vida–su obra.* Montevideo: Claudio García, n.d. Print.

Pineda Franco, Adela, and Ignacio Sánchez Prado, eds. *Alfonso Reyes y los estudios latinoamericanos*. Pittsburgh: U of Pittsburgh, 2004. Print.

Prado, Eduardo. *A Ilusão Americana*. São Paulo: Brasiliense, 1961. Print.

Puente, Glicerio Albarrán. *El pensamiento de José Enrique Rodó*. Madrid: Cultura Hispánica, 1953. Print.

Rama, Ángel. *La ciudad letrada*. Hanover, NH: Ediciones del Norte, 1984. Print.

———. *Transculturación narrativa en América Latina*. México: Siglo XXI, 1982. Print.

Ramón, Armando de. *Breve historia de Chile*. Buenos Aires: Biblios, 2001. Print.

Ramos, Julio. *Divergent Modernities: Culture and Politics in Nineteenth-Century Latin America*. Trans. John D. Blanco. Durham and London: Duke UP, 2001. Print.

Ranke, Leopold von. *History of the Latin and Teutonic Nations (1494 to 1514)*. Rev. Trans. G. R. Dennis. London: George Bell & Sons, 1909. Print.

Revista nacional de literatura y ciencias sociales. 3 vols. Montevideo: Tipo-Litografía Oriental, 1895–97. Print.

Revistas literarias mexicanas modernas. Antena 1924. Monterrey 1930–1937. Examen 1932. Número 1933–1935. México: Fondo de Cultura Económica, 1980. Print.

Reyes, Alfonso. *Cartas a La Habana: Epistolario de Alfonso Reyes con Max Henríquez Ureña, José Antonio Ramos y Jorge Mañach*. Ed. Alejandro González Acosta. México: UNAM, 1989. Print.

———. *Diario. 1911–1930*. Guanajuato: Editorial de la Universidad de Guanajuato, 1969. Print.

———. *Obras completas*. 26 vols. México: Fondo de Cultura Económica, 1955–93. Print.

Reyes, Alicia. *Genio y figura de Alfonso Reyes*. México: Fondo de Cultura Económica, 2000. Print.

Robb, James Willis. "Alfonso Reyes y Cecília Meireles: Una amistad mexicano-brasileña." *Hispania* 66.2 (May 1983): 164–66. Print.

Rocamora, José Antonio. *El nacionalismo ibérico: 1782–1936*. Valladolid: Universidad de Valladolid, 1994. Print.

Rodó, José Enrique. *Ariel*. Trad. Denise Bottman. Campinas, SP: UNICAMP, 1991. Print.

Rodó, José Enrique. *Obras completas.* Ed. Emir Rodríguez Monegal. Madrid: Aguilar, 1967. Print.

Rodríguez Monegal, Emir. "The Metamorphoses of Caliban." *Diacritics* 7.3 (Fall 1977): 78–83. Print.

Said, Edward W. *Humanism and Democratic Criticism.* New York: Columbia UP, 2004. Print.

———. *Representations of the Intellectual.* New York: Vintage, 1996. Print.

Salinas, Jorge Pedraza. *Tesoros de la Capilla Alfonsina.* Monterrey: Universidad Autónima de Nuevo León, 2007. Print.

Salles, Ricardo. *Joaquim Nabuco: Um Pensador do Império.* Rio de Janeiro: Topbooks, 2002. Print.

Sánchez, Luís Alberto. *Balance y liquidación del novecientos.* 3rd corrected ed. Lima: Universidad Nacional de San Marcos, 1968. Print.

Santiago, Silviano. *As Raízes e o Labirinto da América Latina.* Rio de Janeiro: Rocco, 2006. Print.

Santos, Luís Cláudio Villafañe G. *O Brasil entre a América e a Europa. O Império e o interamericanismo (do Congresso do Panamá à Conferência de Washington).* São Paulo: Editora UNESP, 2003. Print.

Saraiva, António José. *A Tertúlia Ocidental: Estudos sobre Antero de Quental, Oliveira Martins, Eça de Queiroz e Outros.* Lisboa: Gradiva, 1995. Print.

Schopenhauer, Arthur. "On Jurisprudence and Politics." *Parerga and Paralipomena: Short Philosophical Essays.* Trans. E.F.J. Payne. Oxford: Clarendon, 1974. 2: 240–66. Print.

Schwartz, Jorge. "Abaixo Tordesilhas!" *Estudos Avançados* 7.17 (1993): 185–200. Print.

Schwarz, Roberto. "As Idéias fora de Lugar." *Ao Vencedor as Batatas.* São Paulo: Duas Cidades, 1981. 13–28. Print.

———. "Machado de Assis: A Biographical Sketch." *Misplaced Ideas: Essays on Brazilian Culture.* Ed. John Gledson. London: Verso, 1992. 78–83. Print.

———. "Nacional por Subtração." *Que Horas São? Ensaios.* São Paulo: Companhia das Letras, 1987. 29–48. Print.

Seckinger, Ron L. "The Chiquitos Affair: An Aborted Crisis in Brazilian-Bolivian relations." *Luso-Brazilian Review* 11.1 (1974): 19–40. Print.

Seneca, Lucius Annaeus. *Hercules furens. Troades. Phoenissae. Medea. Phaedra.* Torino: G.B. Paravia, 1965. Print.

Shakespeare, William. *The Tempest.* The Works of Shakespeare. Cambridge: Cambridge UP, 1921. Print.

Silveira, Helder Gordim da. *Joaquim Nabuco e Oliveira Lima: Faces de Um Paradigma Ideológico da Americanização nas Relações Internacionais do Brasil.* Porto Alegre: EDIPUCRS, 2003. Print.

Skorupski, John. "Introduction: The Fortunes of Liberal Naturalism." *The Cambridge Companion to Mill.* Ed. Skorupski. Cambridge: Cambridge UP, 1998. 1–34. Print.

———. "John Stuart Mill." *Routledge Encyclopedia of Philosophy.* Ed. Edward Craig. London and New York: Routledge, 1998. 6: 360–75. Print.

Smith, Anthony D. *The Ethnic Origins of Nations.* Oxford, UK and Cambridge, MA: Blackwell, 1986. Print.

———. *Nations and Nationalism in a Global Era.* Cambridge, UK: Polity, 1995. Print.

Sodré, Nelson Werneck. *História da Imprensa no Brasil.* Rio de Janeiro: Civilização Brasileira, 1966. Print.

Souza Andrade, Olímpio de. *Joaquim Nabuco e o Brasil na América.* São Paulo: Companhia Editora Nacional, 1978. Print.

———. *Joaquim Nabuco e o Pan-Americanismo.* São Paulo: Companhia Editora Nacional, 1950. Print.

Stavans, Ilan. Introduction. *The Oxford Book of Latin American Essays.* New York: Oxford UP, 2002. 3–17. Print.

"El Te-Deum." Originally published in the periodical *Zig-Zag* [Santiago de Chile], 24 Sept. 1910. *Memoria Chilena, Dirección de Bibliotecas, Archivos y Museos.* Web. 24 Sept. 2007.

Torres Caicedo, José María. *Unión Latino-Americana. Pensamiento de Bolívar para formar una liga Americana; su orígen y sus desarrollos.* Paris, 1865. Print.

Unamuno, Miguel de. *Escritos de Unamuno sobre Portugal.* Ed. Ángel Marcos de Dios. Lisboa: Fundação Calouste Gulbenkian; Paris: Centro Cultural Português, 1985. Print.

———. *Obras completas.* 9 vols. Ed. Manuel García Blanco. Madrid: Escelicer, 1966–71. Print.

Valera, Juan. "Sobre la idea de la Unión Ibérica." *Artículos de "El Contemporáneo."* Ed. Cyrus C. DeCoster. Madrid: Castalia, 1966. 231–33. Print.

Vaz Ferreira, Carlos. *Lógica viva. Moral para intelectuales.* Caracas: Ayacucho, 1979. Print.

Veloso, Caetano, and Gilberto Gil. "Haiti." *Tropicália 2.* 1993. Recording.

Ventura, Roberto. "Calibanismo de Americano Atrai Críticas." *Folha de São Paulo*, 7 Jan. 1989. Print.

Veríssimo, José. *Cultura, Literatura e Política na América Latina*. Ed. João Alexandre Barbosa. São Paulo: Brasiliense, 1986. Print.

———. "A Revolução Chilena e a Questão da América Latina." *Estudos de Literatura Brasileira*. 1st series. Belo Horizonte: Editora Itaiaia; São Paulo: Editora USP, 1976. 35–47. Print.

———. "O Sr. Joaquim Nabuco: A Propósito do Seu Livro 'Minha Formação.'" *Estudos de Literatura Brasileira*. 3rd series. Belo Horizonte: Editora Itaiaia; São Paulo: Editora USP, 1977. 89–97. Print.

Viana Filho, Luiz, ed. *Estudos Vários sobre José Bonifácio de Andrada e Silva*. Santos, Braz.: Grupo de Trabalho Executivo das Homenagens ao Patriarca, 1963. Print.

———. *A Vida de Joaquim Nabuco*. São Paulo: Companhia Editora Nacional, 1952. Print.

Vianna Moog, Clodomiro. *Bandeirantes e Pioneiros: Paralelo entre Duas Culturas*. Rio de Janeiro: Graphia, 2002. Print.

Viotti da Costa, Emília. *The Brazilian Empire: Myths and Histories*. Rev. ed. Chapel Hill: U of North Carolina P, 2000. Print.

Vitale, Luis. *Interpretación marxista de la historia de Chile*. Vol. 4. Santiago: LOM Ediciones, 1993. Print.

Williams, Raymond. *Culture and Materialism: Selected Essays*. London: Verso, 2005. Print.

———. *Marxism and Literature*. Oxford: Oxford UP, 1977. Print.

Zaïtzeff, Serge I. "Alfonso Reyes en el Brasil a través de su correspondencia con Genaro Estrada." *Essays in Honor of Frank Dauster.* Ed. Kirsten F. Nigro and Sandra M. Cypress. Newark, DE: Juan de la Cuesta, 1995. 155–68. Print.

Zamora, Andrés, "Alfonso Reyes: El intelectual o la efímera magia de la palabra." *Hispanic Review* 64.2 (Spring 1996): 217–36. Print.

Zum Felde, Alberto. *Processo intelectual del Uruguay y crítica de su literatura*. 2 vols. Montevideo: Imprenta Nacional Colorada, 1930. Print.

Index

About the Author

Robert Patrick Newcomb teaches Portuguese and Spanish at University of California–Davis. His articles, generally on comparative Luso-Hispanic topics, have been published in *Estudos Avançados, Chasqui, Hispania,* and *Luso-Brazilian Review,* among other journals. He is the translator of Alfredo Bosi's *Colony, Cult and Culture* (University of Massachussetts–Dartmouth, 2008).